The Pope and the pill

The Pope and the pill

Sex, Catholicism and women in post-war England

David Geiringer

Manchester University Press

Copyright © David Geiringer 2020

The right of David Geiringer to be identified as the author of this work has been asserted by them in accordance with the Copyright, Designs and Patents Act 1988.

Published by Manchester University Press
Altrincham Street, Manchester M1 7JA
www.manchesteruniversitypress.co.uk

British Library Cataloguing-in-Publication Data
A catalogue record for this book is available from the British Library

ISBN 978 1 5261 3838 5 hardback
ISBN 978 1 5261 5595 5 paperback

First published 2020

The publisher has no responsibility for the persistence or accuracy of URLs for any external or third- party internet websites referred to in this book, and does not guarantee that any content on such websites is, or will remain, accurate or appropriate.

Typeset by Newgen Publishing UK

For Mum.
For Nat.
For Gabby.

Contents

List of figures	*page* ix
Acknowledgements	xi
Introduction	1
1 Uncovering the sex lives of Catholic women	26
2 The Catholic Church's understanding of female sexuality	46
3 Sexuality in later marriage	66
4 Sexuality in early marriage	108
5 Early life and pre-marital sexuality	149
Conclusion	186
Appendices	198
Select bibliography	200
Index	209

Figures

1	John Ryan cartoon published in the *Catholic Herald*, 2 August 1968. Reproduced with permission from the *Catholic Herald* and Isabel Ryan	*page* 111
2	Extract and graph illustration from *Preparing Engaged Couples for Marriage*, CMAC training manual (London, 1969)	119
3	Graph detailing the different readings possible from rectal and oral use of a thermometer when practising NFP, from J. Marshall, *The Infertile Period: Principles and Practices* (Baltimore, MD, 1963)	128
4	Front cover of a sexual advice manual aimed at young Catholics, Q. de la Bedoyere and I. de la Bedoyere, *Choices in Sex* (Dartford, 1964)	159
5	Front cover of a Catholic marriage guidance manual, Q. de la Bedoyere, *My Wife and I Don't Agree* (Dartford, 1972)	160

Acknowledgements

There are many people who have provided invaluable help and support while I was completing this book. The participation of the twenty-seven interviewees has made this project what it is – this book is theirs more than mine. I am extremely grateful for their brave, insightful and candid reflections on Catholicism, sexuality, history and a myriad of other topics.

I would like to thank Claire Langhamer and Lucy Robinson for their guidance and encouragement throughout this project. Their insights have been vital to the development of the book, both in terms of direct comments and broader lessons about gender, emotions and memory. I only hope the final product goes some way to reflecting their influence on me as a historian and person.

I am very grateful to Matt Houlbrook and Chris Warne for their insightful suggestions and dutiful responses to a steady stream of reference requests. Often in acknowledgements there is an extensive list of academic colleagues who have read drafts. My list is Sian Edwards – this is testament to not only my own social laziness, but also her incisive and generous feedback.

A number of individuals have offered me their valuable time, encouragement and professional support. My thanks go to (in no particular order) Alana Harris, Neil Armstrong, Gemma Simmonds, Trevor Stammers, Stephen Bullivant, Chris Kemshall, Matt Cook, James Baker, Clive Webb, Helen McCarthy, Rob Saunders, Dan Todman, Julian Jackson, Mark Condos, Alastair Owens, Quentin and Irene de la Bedoyere, Fr Jerry O'Brien, Joanna Bogle, Teresa Kelly and Harry Cocks. Harry set me on my way in Nottingham nine years ago and his knowledge and lessons continue to provide a vital impetus behind my research.

I would also like to thank the staff at the *Catholic Herald*, *Edgeways* magazine, St Pius X parish, Norbiton, St Raphael parish, Surbiton, the University of Notre Dame Archives, Marriage Care (notably Terry

Prendergast) and *The Tablet* (notably Christopher Lamb). The editorial team at Manchester University Press have been great throughout the process – thank you to them, particularly Alun Richards, and the anonymous peer reviewers. Some of the ideas contained here have informed articles in *Twentieth Century British History* and *Cultural and Social History* – the editorial teams and reviewers at both of these publications provided valuable feedback.

I would like to thank all my friends who, as well as offering emotional support, have suffered countless lectures from me in pubs. The staff and students at the University of Sussex and Queen Mary University of London have also contributed to the development of the project in numerous ways.

My family – Mum, Dad, Bill and Emma. Their patience, proofreading and love have been immeasurably appreciated. My mum in particular has been amazing – I am grateful as much for her endless reading and rereading of drafts as I am for our affecting discussions after family dinners. This book is for her and people like her – open-minded, thoughtful and kind.

My new family – Nat and Gabby – have sustained me through the final stages of this project with their love, joy, patience and smiles. Nat has helped me see the world through new eyes – thank you for making me happy every day.

Finally, my grandparents, John and Eileen Marshall. My interest in this subject was prompted by Grandjohn's mischievous claim to have 'invented the rhythm method', and the later revelation that Granny disagreed with his 'liberal' stance on birth control and supported the Pope's teaching. They inspired and then enabled the project from its very inception. The book would not exist without them – it is a testament to and expression of the people they were.

Introduction

On 25 July 1968, Pope Paul VI shook the world. His encyclical letter *Humanae Vitae* rejected widespread calls to permit use of the contraceptive pill and deemed artificial birth control 'intrinsically evil'. The decision split, or perhaps exposed an existing split, within a Catholic community which represented almost one in five of the global population – some gave up on the Church, more gave up on the Pope specifically, priests contradicted the encyclical covertly from the privacy of the confessional and, in some cases, brazenly from the public platform of the pulpit, while other Catholics welcomed the reassertion of theological consistency at a moment of profound cultural agitation. For this latter group, the Pope was upholding the integrity of a transcendent, God-given law which he had no authority to meddle with. In the UK, the upheaval and outcry which greeted the encyclical extended well beyond the Catholic community, filling the columns, editorials and letters pages of leading secular publications. Vincent Broome was to ask in the *New Statesman* later that year:

> If a man can be shown to be responsible for wrecking thousands of marriages, sexually tormenting countless numbers of simple-minded people and starving millions of young children, would not any moral civilisation indict that man as the arch criminal of the day?[1]

Emmanuelle Arsan, the author of a collection of famed erotic novels which inspired a franchise of eponymous softcore pornographic films, felt moved to publish an open letter to Pope Paul VI pleading for a change of heart.[2] *Humanae Vitae* established the Catholic Church as the antagonist in a story of sixties sexual revolution – a stubborn stone resisting the stream of sexually liberal modernity.

Forty-five years later, Margaret, an eighty-one-year-old Catholic widow, was sitting at her dining-room table describing the intimate details of her sex life to a young, male researcher. After recalling the limited sexual education she received in her youth, she went on to speak of her marriage to fellow Catholic John in 1954. Her most abiding memory was of a 'life-changing' shift in her contraceptive behaviour. In the first ten years of her marriage, Margaret had dutifully obeyed the Church's prohibition on all forms of artificial contraception, grappling instead, somewhat unsuccessfully, with natural family planning (or the rhythm method) – the only form of birth regulation permitted by the Vatican. The introduction of the pill in 1961, widely heralded as the catalyst for a 'revolution' in sexual practice across English society, had not shaken her resolve. Like many 'liberal' Catholics, Margaret had been hopeful of a change in the Church's teachings during the spring of 1968, but found herself bitterly disappointed when she learned of *Humanae Vitae* over a radio news bulletin. In her mid-thirties, after six children and a decade of sexual frustration, she defied the Pope's dictate and chose to go on the pill. She explained that this decision had come through a process of agonising soul searching, but ultimately allowed her to enjoy sex in an entirely new way and 'achieve her first orgasm'. Margaret asserted that it was only at this point that she discovered her 'true self'.

As the interview drew to a close, the glow of passionate optimism which had coloured her emancipatory narrative seemed to flicker somewhat. After a long pause she looked up from her cup of tea, held the gaze of the researcher and reflected on what she had lost:

> All the things we were taught were absolutely logical; if this was so, then this must be so. It was all fitting together like a wonderful jigsaw, and in my teens I thought that was wonderful, you know. We Catholics have the answer for everything. But, when you get into adulthood and real life you find that it isn't as simple as all that, it's impossible really. Vatican II coincided with the sexual revolution; it sort of took the cork out of the bottle and you're never going to be able to put it back ... I really don't know from one day to the next what I do anymore. It really, in many ways it's a bereavement. Because all these beliefs that I've been brought up with, I now find it increasingly difficult to believe in them, towards the end of my life.[3]

This moment of raw emotional expression encapsulated not only the experiences of many Catholic women, but also, in ways that might not seem immediately apparent, the questions that faced many non-Catholics living in post-war England. The absolute authority of the Catholic Church was shaken in this period as Catholics began questioning its official teachings about sex, gender and the body. If the Pope was wrong about birth control, what else could he be wrong about? In a broader sense, growing affluence in wider society saw an increase in personal freedoms, but this licentiousness was attended with the dissolution of established codes and comforting certainties. It left men and women in a precarious state of moral and existential flux, caught in what certain scholars have described as a 'paradox of choice'.[4] Increased opportunities brought with them heightened expectations, and heightened expectations brought increased opportunities for both fulfilment and disillusionment.

Sex was at the heart of Margaret's story of religious change. She identified a 'sexual revolution' as the key historical development which let the 'cork out of the bottle' on her Catholic faith. In this sense, Margaret's personal life story chimed with a dominant narrative of collective post-war change. The idea that a process of 'sexual liberation' in the 1960s destroyed Britain's Christian culture has become a powerful trope in both popular commentary and historical analysis. Historians such as Callum Brown have argued that a sudden and abrupt sexual revolution saw women turn away from Christian beliefs and take up a new, sexually liberated version of femininity.[5] Proponents of this theory argue that 'discursive Christianity', that is, the language, ideals and moral constructs that women draw on to make sense of their worlds, was permanently replaced by a modern, sexualised understanding of female identity in the swinging sixties.[6] Beyond academic texts, there is today a prevailing belief that religion is somehow unsexy, and that sex, 'good' sex at least, cannot possibly be religious. In the pages that follow, we will both interrogate and historicise this tale of 'sex destroying religion'.

The main subject of this book is, therefore, not sex or Catholicism in isolation, but the relationship between the two.[7] It is about the way this relationship was experienced by 'ordinary' men and women on an everyday basis – how they negotiated spiritual and sexual demands at a moment when the two seemed to be at odds with each other. An original oral history project, in which Margaret was one of twenty-seven Catholics interviewed, is used to explore these intimate daily negotiations. This book is also about how the relationship between sex and Catholicism was discussed and constructed by various authorities – the Pope, parish priests, marriage guidance counsellors, physicians, cultural commentators, sociologists and historians. What emerges is a unique insight into the constellation of ideas and assumptions that underpinned personal understandings of sex and religion in an apparently secular age.

Above all else, Margaret's testimony offers an insight into what is at stake in this book. It became clear that through the interview, Margaret was confronting her own mortality. It was the spectre of her approaching death that brought into focus the full implications of her altered belief system. She was not simply reflecting on changing values and beliefs, but an entirely new way of making sense of her existence. And ultimately, her eventual non-existence. This book is about the stories that people tell themselves about meaning, morality and being, and the way these stories changed in the second half of the twentieth century. Moreover, it's about the everyday experiences that informed and were informed by these stories. Too often historians of religion have focused on the discourses, ideas and language of religious faith, while neglecting its material, embodied experience. As we shall see, this tendency amongst historians is itself a product of much larger trends at work in the twentieth century.

The book works *with* rather than *on* Catholic women and their life stories.[8] Since the emergence of socio-scientific and psychoanalytical disciplines at the start of the twentieth century, studies of religious belief, sexuality and, in many cases, women have shared a tendency to 'unpack' or 'deconstruct' their subjects. Meanings have been arrived at by critiquing or suggesting alternative explanations to those narrated by religious women, especially Catholic women. An effort has been taken here to treat Catholic women as reflexive authors of their own stories. This commitment to really listening to the interviewees' accounts of their lives is reflected not only in the book's methodology, but also in its structure. The organisation of the chapters has been calculated to challenge any temptation to simply ascribe Catholic women's life stories to their upbringing. When describing the project to others, I was invariably told that Catholic women's sex lives were all about childhood indoctrination – the daily decisions and experiences of a forty-year-old married woman in relation to contraception, foreplay, sexual pleasure, masturbation and monogamy were all determined by her upbringing, so the story went. The aim here is to eschew this Freudian way of thinking – to recognise the agency of the interviewees in their everyday lives, but also as analytical interpreters of these lives. Working with rather than on Catholic women animates a new set of questions about religion, sex and power.

Scholars have already moved beyond asking questions which assume that sex and religion were diametrically opposed in the post-war decades. Historians of religion have been roundly warned against falling back on the lingering assumptions of a once totemic 'secularisation' theory. Conversely, historians of sexuality have been encouraged to critique the notion of 'sexual liberation'. These two developments, although largely existing in isolation from one another, have encouraged an optimistic, complementary reading of the relationship between sex and religion. We can now point to examples of a dialogue between sex and religion – points of reciprocation between modern sexualities and traditional Christian ideals. Harry Cocks has shown that religious impetuses informed the early development of sexological theories at the turn of the twentieth century; Laura Ramsay has demonstrated that actors within the Church of England played a formative role in bringing about the 'permissive' legislation of the sixties; and Sam Brewitt-Taylor has emphasised the centrality of clergymen to the 'myth of the sexual revolution' in the same decade.[9] Catholicism however, remains defined by a sex-negative status in the historical imagination, cut adrift from the processes which produced the 'modern' sexual subject.

Grand narratives of religious decline and sexual liberation have fallen out of vogue: their propensity to flatten out the messy and textured nature of everyday life has left them open to condemnation. 'Post-secular' is the latest expression to trend in the vocabularies of contemporary historians: it neatly crystallises the death of the 'secularisation thesis' as an explanatory narrative, but the term also seems to imply a supplanted 'secular age'. While there is a greater complexity to post-secular thinking than this characterisation suggests, it serves to highlight the problematic nature of all-encompassing labels.[10] The material collected here on sex, women and Catholicism reaffirms the need to be cautious when drawing up any straightforward, linear narratives: the terms 'sexual liberation' and 'secularisation' tell only part of the story, or at least part of society's story.

The memories of Catholic women, as well as the documents of the central Catholic Church, do suggest that there was something of a *recategorisation* in the relationship between sex and religion in the middle of the twentieth century. Rather than being about an emancipation from the confines of religious subjugation, a deeper, conceptual separation between the religious and the sexual opened up in the decades after the war. Sex became understood to be a material, embodied instinct while religious belief was increasingly identified as its counterpoint – a matter of transcendent, abstract theory. This recategorisation of the religious and the sexual was about shifting regimes of *materiality* as opposed to morality; the categories of existence that objects and ideas are placed within. As we will discover, this system of classification was at the heart of 'liberal' Catholic women's often painstaking decisions to reject the Church's teaching on contraception, written into the Vatican's 'orthodox' writings on sex and the body, and continues to underscore the explanatory frameworks employed by historians of religious decline.[11] It was a trend which was both personal and institutional in its scope, discursive and experiential in its nature, historical and historiographical in its implications. We find it in Brown's narrative, Pope Paul VI's Encyclical and Margaret's rejection of this Encyclical. The causes and consequences of this recategorisation are elucidated through the course of the book, but let us first look at the position of Catholicism in post-war England.

Catholicism in post-war England

The Catholic community was steadily expanding in the middle of the century thanks to Irish and continental immigration, but remained a relatively small percentage of the English population throughout the period – 2.23 million Catholics were recorded as regular churchgoers in 1940 (4.6 per cent of the national population), 2.43 million in 1950 and 2.85 million by 1960 (5.4 per cent of the population).[12] Despite its diminutive demographic, Catholicism represents a particularly valuable case study when considering the way religion and sexuality were experienced in post-war England.[13] The significance of the Catholic example lies in its distinctive ecclesiastical identity within British society. The Church of England may have constituted the leading denomination in term of institutional affiliation and population size, but Catholicism had always occupied a very particular cultural space in relation to the politics of the body.[14] Moreover, the Catholic Church's response to questions of 'sexual permissiveness' in the 1960s received far more public attention than that of the Church of England. Gerard Parsons is of the opinion that 'the pivotal significance of the 1960s in Christian decline is stressed by placing more emphasis on the Catholic Church than Brown did'.[15] Parsons' view seems to be substantiated by Church attendance statistics, which indicate that, unlike the Protestant denominations, Catholic disaffiliation increased at the end of the decade rather than the beginning.[16]

The belief that Catholicism was damaged by a 'sexual revolution' to a greater extent than any other Christian faith tends to be based on the issue of birth control. The introduction of the pill in 1961 is often identified as a central component of a sexual revolution, if not its very catalyst. Hera Cook characterises this view, making a case for the revolutionary impact of the pill:

> It increased the control of fear and allowed a greater experience of pleasure and increased emotional aspirations ... [the pill brought about] substantial improvement, amounting to a transformation, in the lives of English women over the past two centuries.[17]

Although the Catholic Church had traditionally prohibited the use of artificial means of birth control, the creation of the pill prompted many in the Catholic community to call for this teaching to be revised, not least because to many observers it appeared less 'artificial' than existing forms of contraception. In the autumn of 1962, a secretive commission was set up by Pope John XXIII to investigate the matter, the final report of which, leaked to the press in 1966, recommended a change in the Church's teaching. The hitherto unpublished papers of this Papal Commission for Birth Control reveal the contested and mutating understandings of female sexuality that circulated within the boundaries of the 'Church'. Indeed, the boundaries of the 'Church' were themselves appearing to blur in the middle of the 1960s, as initiatives such as the papal commission brought in lay experts from secular disciplines such as biology, sociology, medicine, anthropology, economics and psychology. Change seemed to be in the air; Catholics were preparing themselves for a fundamental shift in not only the content of Catholic doctrine, but also the way this doctrine was constructed. As the revolutionary 'spirit of '68' trickled across Europe, Catholicism was being shaken to its core by questions of sex.

In its unexpected rejection of this clamour for change, *Humanae Vitae* became the object of heated public debate which played out as much in parish church halls as the pages of theological scholarship. The responses of the Catholic community to the Pope's pronouncement were certainly mixed but almost always impassioned. As a consequence, the years immediately preceding the encyclical's publication have been largely neglected by historians of both Catholicism and modern sexuality. Furthermore, intellectual assessments of Catholic sexuality in the post-war tend to focus solely on the circumscribed topic of birth control rather than considering the broader dimensions of marital sexuality. Catholic women who married in the decades after the war confronted a set of questions that had not existed for any previous generation. In a climate that increasingly encouraged personal expression and sexual independence, their beliefs on the morality of the body became the object of fierce personal and public scrutiny. These questions were not just theological abstractions to be pondered over, but immediate dilemmas that shaped marital relations, religious practice and daily family life. They were dilemmas which were peculiar to the Catholic experience – the belief systems, social communities and traditions that defined life as a 'Catholic' – but also part and product of wider societal developments in the post-war decades. Recognising the 'same but different' nature of post-war Catholicism is an important imperative for historians of Catholicism, sexuality and British society in general.

The interplay between change and continuity has been a central motif in the history of post-war Catholicism. Until recently, Michael Hornsby-Smith's extensive sociological research had been the main contribution to the field. Hornsby-Smith used large-sample surveys and opinion polls to argue that the years surrounding the Second Vatican Council (1962–1965) witnessed a number of vital changes in the character and composition of English Catholicism.[18] Announced by Pope John XXIII on 25 January 1959 and convened on 11 October 1962, Vatican II, as it is generally referred to, drew together over 2,500 bishops from around the world to carry out John XXIII's call for *aggiornamento* (translated as 'updating'). The Council eventually ratified sixteen documents that paved the way for reforms in many areas of Catholic life, including the introduction of vernacular language in the Mass, new and more sympathetic relations with other faiths and changes to the Catholic liturgy. While the decrees and declarations of the Council are easily described, and have been elsewhere, their impact and legacy continue to represent a point of contest for scholars of twentieth-century Catholicism.[19]

Hornsby-Smith emphasised the fundamental changes that the Council invoked and expressed. He optimistically described a movement from 'collective-expressive to individual-expressive religiosity', whereby Catholic lay people began 'creating their own' personal beliefs and devotional practices as opposed to 'passively receiving an official spirituality'.[20] Conversely, a recent book on Catholic disaffiliation in Britain and America, opening with the statistic that nearly half of all born-and-raised Catholics no longer consider themselves to be 'Catholic', is framed with the question of whether Vatican II caused this 'mass exodus' from the Church – 'Did the Council Fail?' its epilogue asks.[21] Catholic commentators of both a liberal and orthodox persuasion have interpreted the middle of the 1960s as something of a historical watershed for English Catholics, be that as a point of modernising progression or regression away from an apparent 'golden age'. Margaret's reflections epitomised this seismic and yet ambivalent rendering of Vatican II, she placed it alongside the 'sexual revolution' as the event which let the cork out of Pandora's Catholic bottle.

But not everyone has agreed with this story of Catholic revolution in the sixties. Alana Harris built on Hornsby-Smith's analysis in her timely addition to the field, *Faith in the Family* (2013), but also diverged from some of his central conclusions. Where Hornsby-Smith emphasised the changes that occurred in the lives of 'ordinary' Catholics, Harris stressed the 'little-appreciated elements of continuity' that existed throughout the post-war decades. Her main contention was that Hornsby-Smith drew too sharp a distinction between pre- and post-conciliar Catholicism:

> Rather than interpreting this period as a period of caesura or rupture, especially through an over-emphasis on the social dislocation of the 1960s, this book reinterprets these movements as modulations or gradual, non-linear modifications of Catholics' understandings of their identities, beliefs and practices.[22]

Harris situated her research in the emerging histories of gender and emotion which 'increasingly assert that change in twentieth-century Britain should be viewed as part of a longer-term continuum'. Her work demonstrated that there was no sudden movement away from a 'ghettoised', coercive form of Catholicism in the sixties as Hornsby-Smith suggested. Harris' emphasis on what she termed the 'longue durée of the second half of the twentieth century' chimes with the approach taken here.²³ *Humanae Vitae* was itself a reassertion of an earlier encyclical, *Casti Connubii* (1930), which had initially prohibited the use of artificial means of contraception for Catholics. *Casti Connubii* was a response to the Lambeth Conference of the Anglican Church in the same year which had approved the use of artificial birth control, including condoms, in certain circumstances. It seems that in the area of marital sexuality, a number of central continuities defined the Catholic Church's ecclesiastical identity throughout the twentieth century.

However, the build-up, backdrop and response to *Casti Connubii* and *Humanae Vitae*, in the 1930s and 1960s respectively, were very different. In fact, when we focus on the *relationship* between Catholic belief systems and the processes of the body, something which can be described as a rupture can be evinced in the post-war decades: a fundamental change that superseded many of the continuities that Harris dwelt on. The interviewees I spoke to were eager to stress a significant, historically unprecedented shift in the way they understood religion and its relationship to sex. Like many changes in social history, it was a shift that occurred at different speeds and at different times for different people. Nailing down a tight periodisation like the 'sixties', or even 1963 specifically, as Brown does, is therefore unhelpful and ultimately misleading.²⁴

As the title of a recent edited collection indicates, the heady summer of 1968 saw something of a schism emerge within European Catholicism (although contributors to the collection disagree as to whether the schism was caused by *Humanae Vitae*, or whether the encyclical simply revealed an existing divide).²⁵ Those who continued to identify as Catholic after *Humanae Vitae* tended to fall into one of two camps – liberal or orthodox. Put simply, liberals wanted the Church to change its stance on a number of issues, notably surrounding sex and body, orthodox Catholics did not. Within these tribes there were divergent views on certain aspects of liturgical and doctrinal reform, but contraception was almost always a litmus test – liberals campaigned vociferously for a relaxation of the Church's prohibition, orthodox Catholics were steadfast in their support of continuity. As the theologian Stephen Bullivant wrote in an article marking the fiftieth anniversary of *Humanae Vitae*, it was only after 1968 that tribal divisions between 'liberal' and 'conservative', or 'progressive' and 'traditional' Catholics began to carry serious meaning. In the past, Catholics were typically divided into 'good' and 'bad', or 'practising' and 'lapsed'. But these were, in a sense, degrees on a single scale of being Catholic. They were not two different modes, different camps, of being Catholic … On the face of it, a person's views on *Humanae Vitae* need not correlate in any predetermined way with their positions on various doctrinal points (women priests, say) or on their liturgical preferences. In practice, however, they very often do.[26]

The interviewees all identified as either orthodox or liberal – the next chapter provides a fuller account of the weighting of the sample and how this related to the size of two factions in the English Catholic population. The entrenched polarity running through the Catholic community today is a major legacy of the battle lines over sexual morality which formed in the post-war decades.

But the frays and disruptions of this period were not only about politicised theological positions, played out in public arenas and invariably articulated by men, but also the fabric of everyday married life. For the generation of women getting married in the years immediately following the war, new technologies and opportunities refashioned the emotional and physical experience of intimacy. At an address to Italian midwives in 1951, Pope Pius XII officially endorsed the practice of natural family planning (NFP, also known as 'rhythm' or the 'safe method').[27] This method of birth regulation involved calculating the fertility of the wife, generally by charting their temperature, and then abstaining from sex in the periods of ovulation. The simplicity of this description belies the great complexity of feeling and outcome which accompanied the method. Many Catholics found that NFP did not facilitate effective 'family planning': unexpected pregnancies, or at least the perennial fear of them, caused anxiety and marital tensions. Frustration in the periods of abstinence, and then a heightened pressure in the 'safe period', created difficulties in the bedroom that seeped out into other parts of marital relations. As the author David Lodge said of his own experience of the method in his early marriage, ' "Rhythm" or the "Safe Method" was in practice neither rhythmical nor safe, and therefore a cause of considerable stress.'[28] For a significant minority of couples, the method worked and became an integral part of a 'holistic' Catholic union, just as it was advertised to do.

The inconsistency of experience led to the method being dubbed Vatican Roulette by certain commentators and indeed doctors – this formulation was adopted as the title for the American version of Lodge's comedic novel of 1965, *The British Museum Is Falling Down*. Written twenty years earlier than his most famous fictionalisation of Catholic marriage *How Far Can You Go?*, and three years before the publication of *Humanae Vitae*, the book depicted the trials and tribulations of a young Catholic couple's unsuccessful attempts to practise NFP. The book's protagonist Adam Appleby whimsically reflects on the centrality of sex and NFP to Catholic life in the 1960s, mentally composing an entry, 'Catholicism, Roman', for a Martian encyclopaedia compiled after life on earth had been destroyed by atomic warfare:

> Roman Catholicism was, according to archaeological evidence, distributed fairly widely over the planet Earth in the twentieth century. As far as the Western Hemisphere is concerned, it appears to have been characterized by a complex system of sexual taboos and rituals. Intercourse between married partners was restricted to certain limited periods determined by the calendar and the body-temperature of the female. Martian archaeologists have learned to identify the domiciles of Roman Catholics by the presence of large numbers of complicated graphs, calendars, small booklets full of figures, and quantities of broken thermometers, evidence of the great importance attached to this code. Some scholars have argued that it was merely a method of limiting the number of offspring; but as it has been conclusively proved that the Roman Catholics produced more children on average than any other section of the community, this seems untenable. Other doctrines of the Roman Catholics included a belief in a Divine Redeemer and in a life after death.[29]

Appleby's sardonic summary of Catholicism captured a number of aspects of his historical setting – a rising consciousness of a decline in the Christian faith (sociologists such as Peter Berger were predicting the 'death of religion' by the end of the century), a wider cold-war concern over the destruction of Western civilisation and the almost farcical idiosyncrasy of Catholic contraceptive behaviour.[30] Sex, above and beyond any other belief or practice, defined Catholicism in the 1960s.

The shortcomings of NFP appeared all the more acute with the arrival of the contraceptive pill. Catholic men and women looked around them to see, or more likely overhear, English couples enamoured with the efficacy, ease of use and inconspicuousness of the pill. At different times, for different reasons, and with different consequences, Catholic couples started contravening the Church's teachings and taking up artificial means of contraception. Some made the decision before *Humanae Vitae* was published, others after, some agonised over the decision for years, others did not. As we shall see in Chapter 3 and Chapter 4, common to virtually every transition was the experience of NFP as a driving motivational force. It was these changes, these breaks in everyday religious and sexual behaviour, that characterised Catholic life in the years between the mid-1950s and the 1980s. The oral history interviews presented here offer the closest depiction to date of the pain, frustration and sorrow experienced with Vatican Roulette, the profoundly transformative decisions on contraceptive morality which took place in Catholic bedrooms and the new forms of sexual and spiritual sensation which these decisions introduced. It is my belief that these memories, personal spotlights on the very intersection of sex and religion, tell us something vital about the history of modern England. They help us understand why religious belief does not structure the lives of most English men and women today in the way it did seventy years ago, why sex holds a place of such significance in our modern culture and, crucially, how these two developments relate to one another.

Catholic women and a history of power

The historical relationship between sex and religion has invariably been understood as a question of shifting power relations. Historians who advocate both a 'sexual revolution' and a 'religious crisis' in the 1960s invoke tropes of 'liberation', 'authority' and 'autonomy'. Brown's model of Christian decline works at a level of straightforward, top-down power dynamics. It was about women freeing themselves from the oppression of the Church – individuals taking the power into their own hands. In a number of ways, this was an important aspect of the Catholic experience in the post-war years. The moral authority of the central Church in matters of sex was fundamentally undermined by the events of the 1960s. The Catholic commentator Quentin de la Bedoyere describes *Humanae Vitae* as a 'historical watershed' for the consciences of Catholic men and women:

> [F]or the first time the general Catholic community was faced by the solemn reiteration of a formal moral teaching which many had come to doubt – and acting on that doubt did not exclude them from the Church.[31]

It is important to remember that *Humanae Vitae* was not an infallible teaching (when the Pope is deemed to be incapable of error in pronouncing dogma), but for many Catholics, it called into question the absolute authority of the Church as a source of moral guidance. After the 1960s, the classical, coercive form of power that the clerical hierarchy had exercised over the laity for centuries ceased to function in the same way for large swathes of England's Catholic community.

The reason Brown's theories are given a position of such prominence here is not simply because of the academic acclaim his model has achieved, but because many of his ideas resonated with the interviewees' testimony. 'Liberation', 'revolution', 'repression' and above all the character of the 'self' were all formative terms of understanding in the way the interviewees constructed their life stories, terms which form the backbone of Brown's narrative. However, this shared vocabulary alone does not vindicate Brown's conclusions or indeed the intellectual framework he constructed around the subject. My intention is to scratch below the surface of terms like 'liberation' and 'autonomy' to get at the subjective, highly personalised meanings that individuals attach to them.

Historians of religion are increasingly turning their attentions to the material cultures which forge and are forged by religious belief. As the philosopher of religion Grace Janzen points out, this is a necessary response to the tendency amongst Western modernity's key thinkers, including Durkheim, Marx and Weber, to push God into a metaphysical heaven, away from the material realities of earth.[32] We can see this tradition at play in Brown's construction of 'discursive Christianity', with its attendant emphasis on language, ideas and words.[33] For Brown, 'discursive Christianity' constitutes a corrective to the statistical methodologies employed by 'traditional' sociologists.[34] He claims his 'modern cultural theory' approach to oral history allows him to get beyond dry church attendance figures and access the 'personal':

> This failure [of 'traditional' social scientists] is caused by a focus on 'structures' (such as churches and social classes) to the neglect of 'the

personal' in piety. The 'personal' is intrinsically wrapped up with language, discourses on personal moral worth, the narrative structures within which these are located, and the timing of change to these.[35]

Like Brown, I also use oral testimony to get at the complex and highly subjective meanings that are attached to personal religiosities. Unlike Brown, my rendering of the personal pays particular attention to the experiential – spatial and temporal – moments of material existence. The formulation 'discursive Christianity' needs to be thought about historically (as does my own approach to religion – the following chapter offers some thoughts on this). Intellectual investigators of religion in the twentieth century have continually attributed changes in religious belief systems to the operation of liberating ideas and languages opening up an individual's consciousness.[35] This approach, like that of the quantitative sociologists Brown chastises, is liable to obscure the ways in which discourse and experience are intertwined. It is therefore, equally at risk of overlooking aspects of 'personal' Catholic religiosity.

'Discursive Christianity' also has a distinctly post-war flavour to it. Brown points out that his focus on discourse has been produced by his engagement with the 'linguistic turn', an intellectual movement which is generally seen to be located in the deconstructionism of the 1960s.[36] The 'postmodern-inspired discourse analysis' that Brown employs to evaluate personal religiosity is not idiosyncratic, but indicative of a much larger recategorisation of the religious that has taken hold in the post-war era. Religion has been rendered ethereal, immaterial, abstract; removed from the earthly domain of daily living. This approach to religion is itself historically specific, based on a particular, ideological understanding of religion and power relations. As Lucie Matthews-Jones and Timothy Willem Jones point out in the introduction to their timely collection *Material Religion in Modern Britain* (2015):

> The intellectual tradition that has privileged religion-as-thought over religion-as-material is part of that highly problematic modernist condition in which all sorts of binaries – mind/body, male/female, modern/pre-modern, civilized/uncivilized, and so on – have taken on the appearance of universal truth rather than ideological construct.[37]

Traditional narratives of religious decline may no longer hold the sway they once did, but their intellectual infrastructure, and the resulting definitions of religion and power, continue to be reproduced in a transposed form.

Despite widespread efforts to resist the hegemonic authority of the secularisation paradigm, elements of it continue to shape the intellectual apparatus which historians construct around religious subjects. The idea that 'modernity' went hand in hand with a process of linear religious decline has been rightly dismantled in the last twenty years. The sociologist Peter Berger, a particularly combative proponent of the secularisation theory during the 1960s, predicted the death of religion in Britain within the space of twenty years. By the 1980s, Berger was to speak candidly about how his prediction and approach to religion had been misguided: 'I think what I and most of the other sociologists wrote about secularisation in the 1960s was wrong.'[38] Notwithstanding these concessions, religious change continues to be assessed within a win/lose framework that is premised on static, absolute ideas of liberation, authority and autonomy. These ideals map out a secularist portrait of power relations, one in which the 'transcendent', the 'mysterious', the 'spiritual' have no place. The symbols, values and meanings of everyday life are analysed in what Catholic philosopher Charles Taylor would call an 'immanent frame', denying integral aspects of religious sensibility.[39] The memories of Catholic women encourage us to problematise these concepts and place them in an alternative, metaphysical framework: regimes of materiality undercut the changes they lived through as much as regimes of power. With this, a different story of not only religious but also sexual change emerges.

Much like the historiography of the 'religious crisis', historians of sexuality have tended to see their primary task as explicating the changing nature of authority. Hera Cook's account of a 'long sexual revolution' was a story of contraceptive technology enabling women to throw of the shackles of societal, religions and patriarchal repression.[40] In short, women became free to enjoy a more autonomous form of sexuality because of the pill. Matt Houlbrook attributes the history of sexuality's focus on 'questions of regulation, power and subjectivity' to the 'over-determining influence of Foucault'.[41] With his story of pathological discourses usurping Catholic regimes of regulation, Michel Foucault claimed to reconceptualise the way power worked in relation to the sexual subject. Whether through confessional or therapeutic techniques, discipline and governance have been exercised as much from within the individual as from without according to Foucault.[42] His model of historical change was therefore primarily concerned with how power worked, even if the nature of this power differed from previous definitions. As a result, Houlbrook argues, 'ironically, we seem to have a history of sexuality with the sex written out'.[43] Regardless of the culpability of Foucault's legacy, intellectual assessments of sex have been more preoccupied with theorising over the meanings that have been attached to certain actions rather than the actions themselves.

This book marks an explicit attempt to challenge this tendency and 'write the sex back into the history of sex'.[44] It follows the line of a more recent offering from Hera Cook, an analysis of Edwardian sex education, which argues that 'a focus on corporeal experience and emotion enables a deeper understanding of cultural mores and of transmission to the next generation, which is fundamental to the process of change'.[45] Embedding Catholic women's sexual experiences in a material frame of reference enables us to recognise the body as a 'thing', as Susan Bordo would have it, as opposed to a symbolic on which meaning and power are inscribed.[46] Just as the lens of Catholicism can prompt historians of sexuality to rethink the nature and purpose of their discipline, so it can equally prompt historians in general to reappraise the position of power in their stories of the past.

This is not to deny the operation of a traditional form of coercive power in the Catholic experience. We will see how questions of autonomy and authority were very real dimensions of the changes in Catholic women's sexual behaviour, contraceptive choices and religious identities. What I am attempting to do with this traditional story of power dynamics will hopefully be a little more subtle – digging beneath its apparently self-evident values to show how categories of materiality intersected with a narrative of liberation, while simultaneously suggesting that history, particularly the history of sexuality, should not always be treated as a thought experiment in 'how power works'. Even when subverted by a Foucauldian twist, historical attentions continue to be preoccupied with unpicking the way individual experience has been governed and disciplined by external structures. The sexual and religious experiences of Catholic women in the post-war period have hitherto been understood in this context, an exemplar of shifting modes of authority between the institution and the individual, structure and agency, science and religion. The interviewees' memories prompt us to engage with an alternative, 'vertical' dimension, looking beyond but also resituating the question of power in a deeper framework.[47] Their testimony ultimately encourages us to broaden the horizons of historical practice.

Book structure: Catholic women's life cycles

This book is ordered in a way that illustrates the implications of its findings for public debates within both Catholicism and secular society. The first chapter introduces the sources and methods of the project, discussing the specific methodological issues which surround the sex lives of Catholic women. It begins by outlining the processes involved in carrying out the oral history research, before discussing the nature and function of individual memory in the Catholic birth-control debates of both the immediate post-war decades and the present day. The chapter then moves on to consider the relationship between the historical and the personal, both for the interviewees and the interviewer. I reflect on the constitutive role of my own identity, my religious beliefs, sexuality, academic status, family background (notably the place of my grandfather, a self-proclaimed 'Catholic sexpert'), in generating and analysing the memories of Catholic women. The chapter demonstrates that intellectual approaches to both sexuality and religion in the twentieth century have tended to be based on abstract theory as opposed to experience. It then puts forward the dual aims of the book – first, to historicise this privileging of the theoretical at the expense of the experiential when making sense of sex and religion, and second, to provide an antidote through oral history material.

Chapter 2 explores the Church's relationship with 'sexual liberation' in the post-war decades. It analyses public pronouncements and papal encyclicals such as *Humanae Vitae*, as well as private, secretive discussions within the Vatican, to provide a fresh insight into how the Catholic Church understood human sexuality. The chapter argues that the Catholic Church's attempts to investigate sexual experience in the 1960s was contingent on the conception of the 'personal' its representatives employed. Within the discussions of the Papal Commission for Birth Control, the individual testimony of Catholic lay people, notably Catholic women, was overlooked. While the Church engaged with secular expertise drawn from psychology, sociology and biology in its deliberations over the morality of birth control, at no point were the individuals at the centre of these debates offered a space in which to interpret their own experiences. In the central three chapters that follow, human memory is used to redress this omission and reconstruct the sexual experiences of Catholic women.

The clearest theme that emerged from the interviews was the centrality of life-cycle stage to Catholic women's sexual and religious development. Accordingly, the book is structured in a way that reflects this trend. Oral historians addressing love, sex and the body have tended to split women's life cycles into three compartments – youth, courtship and adult life.[48] As such, marriage is broadly treated as a single, unified life-cycle stage. This is a prevalent and, in many ways, intuitive way of conceptualising women's personal development, but the testimony of Catholic women does not fit neatly within this model. Almost all the interviewees spoke of a clear break in their personal sexual development *during* marriage. This break was often but not always aligned with a change in contraceptive practice – most interviewees tied it in with the uptake of artificial means of contraception and the resulting removal of a fear of pregnancy. A handful remembered this break as being less linked to contraceptive behaviour and more a 'natural progression' that came through the passing of time. In both cases, what was emphasised was a 'liberation' from the confines of doctrinal obedience and a resulting resolution of the conflicts that had dogged their early married lives. In keeping with this marital partition, the book's oral history material is organised into three life-cycle stages with chapters devoted to 'later marriage', 'early marriage' and 'early life'.

Of course, these life-cycle stages fell at different times for different people at different historical moments. For example, 'early marriage' tended to start and finish at an earlier age for those married at the start of the sixties than those married at the end of the decade. For the vast majority of the interviewees, the transition from early to later marriage occurred in the 1970s, but there were notable exceptions.[49] A more detailed picture of how these stages related to age, time and place is given at the start of each chapter, but it should be remembered that these were fluid formulations that were contingent on a range of factors.

These life-cycle stages were both identifiable periods in a person's life that were lived through in a concrete, quotidian sense, and also discursive formulations – topics of discussion that were underpinned by shifting cultural norms and mores. They are treated as such in this book. For example, the last chapter on 'pre-marital sexuality' does not work chronologically through childhood, youth and then courtship, but is organised around the key themes and questions that emerged from the interviewees' memories of the period. One section of this chapter deals with 'infantilism' as a social construction, exploring the way popular psychoanalytical understandings of religiosity and its relationship with childhood have affected Catholic women's experiences in the post-war. In this sense, the book merges a thematic approach with a life-cycle-stage approach.

The interviewees' emphasis on 'later marriage' as the pivotal moment of change could be explained by their proximity to this period at the point of interview. However, rather than seeing this emphasis as a product of a failing or 'inaccurate' memory, I will be following my conviction to take the decisions made by the interviewees seriously – paying close attention to the choices inherent in remembering and unremembering.

When human memory is interpreted as nothing more than a random filter, individual women's capacity to serve as the authors of their own life stories is irrevocably undermined. This constraint will be particularly familiar to religious individuals in a post-war setting. A pathological diagnosis of religion, reinforced by the growing authority of psychoanalytical modes of understanding, took hold in the second half of the twentieth century. In academic texts and the wider imagination, childhood has been placed at the centre of 'rationalist' explanations of religious belief.[50] Religiosity, to a greater degree than any other belief system, ideology or source of identity, has become understood to be the product of psychological programming in a person's early life. This link between religion and infantilism was a conspicuous presence in the interviews; the interviewees adopted elements of it while also actively resisting the association. The final chapter examines the historical development of this 'infantile hypothesis' in more depth.

The problem with an overemphasis on the role of childhood in the formation of religious belief systems is that it denies the agency of religious women acting at a later stage of their lives. Their life stories, and through this their identities, are thought to be entirely determined by the intricate details of a period that is distant or unrecognisable to them. As stated earlier, this form of determinism is both methodologically and ethically problematic for my research – not least because we are dealing with interview subjects for whom the concept of free will is so important. To counter this tendency, Chapters 3 to 5 move through life-cycle stages, but do so in reverse. We start with later marriage, move back through early marriage and finish with youth. As such, the order mirrors the life of F. Scott Fitzgerald's eponymous character Benjamin Button.[51] Henry Alexander argues that Fitzgerald's story, about a man born with the mental and bodily features of an old man who gradually becomes younger as his chronological age advances, should be interpreted as a lesson in how the 'levels of importance' we attribute to memory can overlap into moral concerns:

> Benjamin Button's life evokes awareness of the breakdown of such levels of importance and of their various claims to a place in memory. His life stresses the disruption and havoc that can emerge when the threads of memory are severed from salient features of a life. It brings out how such severance is an obstacle to change. And by contrast it brings out equally and vividly – what we may have failed to notice because so evident – namely, the importance of the threads of memory to the significance that a person can find in life. By highlighting how forgetfulness damages and dissipates Benjamin Button's topsy-turvy existence, we can grasp how forgetfulness may overlap into moral concerns.[52]

The levels of importance that the interviewees attached to their different life-cycle stages were shaped by moral concerns, but also borne out of lived experience. Reversing the chronology of their lives allows us to recognise the choices that are being made in the retelling of a life, while also respecting the way this life was made up of lived, transient moments.

This ordering replicates human memory rather than historical narrative. Starting from the point of interview, it works back through the interviewees' lives in a manner not unlike Foucault's genealogies.[53] In this way, we are encouraged not to attribute the behaviour and decisions of married Catholic women to an infantile event or environment, but to treat them as lived moments shaped by individual agency and external structures. Kierkegaard wrote that 'life must be lived forwards, but it can only be understood backwards'.[54] This musing on the temporality of existence illuminates the problems of oral history research but also its inherent virtues. The act of remembering allows us to think on the paradoxes and constraints of linear time. Working backwards through a life demonstrates how understanding and experience are not distinct from one another for a religious believer, but intimately intertwined. Perversely, working backwards enables a clearer picture of how Catholic women lived forwards.

Notes

1. Referenced in L. Pyle (ed.), *Pope and Pill* (London, 1968), p. 116.
2. Referenced in T. P. Marquez, 'The Politics of Catholic Medicine: "The Pill" and *Humanae Vitae* in Portugal', in A. Harris (ed.), *The Schism of '68: Catholicism, Contraception and Humanae Vitae in Europe, 1945–1975* (Oxford, 2018), pp. 161–186.
3. Margaret, interviewed 29/09/2013. Pseudonyms are used for all interviewees to protect anonymity (in line with the University of Sussex research ethics procedure).
4. A. Offer, *The Challenge of Affluence: Self-Control and Wellbeing in the United States and Britain since 1950* (Oxford, 2006), p. 1.
5. C. Brown, *The Death of Christian Britain: Understanding Secularisation, 1800–2000* (Cambridge, 2000), pp. 9–17.
6. Ibid., p. 202.
7. This book focuses on *marital* sexuality as opposed to single, pre-marital or lesbian experiences (all of which would make for valuable areas of future research). Amongst the extensive debates that existed within the Christian community over sex in the 1960s, the prohibition of pre-marital sex was never really questioned within any of the major Christian denominations. This doctrinal principle remains an integral aspect of the Catholic creed. Marital sexuality therefore provides an apposite and strangely underexplored terrain for assessing the Church's relationship with sexual change.
8. I am indebted to Lucy Robinson for this formulation. L. Robinson, 'Collaboration In, Collaboration Out: The Eighties in the Age of Digital Representation', *Social and Cultural History*, 13 (2016), pp. 403–423.
9. L. Ramsay, 'The Ambiguities of Christian Sexual Discourse in Post-War Britain: The British Council of Churches and Its Early Moral Welfare Work', *Journal of Religious History*, 40:1, pp. 82–103; H. Cocks, 'Religion and Spirituality', in M. Houlbrook and H. G. Cocks (eds), *Palgrave Advances in the Modern History of Sexuality* (London, 2006), p. 157; S. Brewitt-Taylor, 'Christianity and the Invention of the Sexual Revolution in Britain, 1963–1967', *Historical Journal*, 60 (2017), pp. 519–546.
10. For a discussion, and nuanced example, of post-secular histories of modern Britain, see S. Brewitt-Taylor, *Christian Radicalism in the*

Church of England and the Invention of the British Sixties, 1957–1970 (Oxford, 2018).

11 P. Heelas and L. Woodhead, *The Spiritual Revolution: Why Religion is Giving Way to Spirituality* (Oxford, 2005).

12 C. Brown, *Religion and the Demographic Revolution: Women and Secularisation in Canada, Ireland, UK and USA since, the 1960s* (Woodbridge, 2012), p. 79.

13 The main focus of this book is on England, as this is where the vast majority of the interview respondents lived during their marriages. There are a few notable exceptions – included in the sample is one interviewee from Scotland, one from Northern Ireland, one who spent most of her married life in Wales and another who grew up in France. There is then some potential for extending the analysis to include a consideration of national variations within Britain, but only in a cautious manner. Particularly in the cases of Ireland and Scotland, the Catholic experience had a very distinctive character shaped by social, political and sectarian contexts which make comparisons over a national plane problematic.

14 Cocks, 'Religion and Spirituality'.

15 G. Parsons, 'How the Times They Are A-Changing: Exploring the Context of Religious Transformation in Britain in the 1960s', in J. Wolffe (ed.), *Religion in History: Conflict, Conversion and Coexistence* (Manchester, 2004), p. 164.

16 McLeod shows that 52.4 per cent of Catholics attended church regularly in 1960 and 47 per cent still did so in 1970, but by 1980 this figure had fallen to 38.6 per cent. Mary Eaton's study of Catholic women's organisations in the 1960s indicates that the biggest drop in membership occurred in the last two years of the decade. These statistics suggest that the events of the 1960s had a more direct impact on disaffiliation within the Catholic Church than in the Protestant denominations. H. McLeod, *The Religious Crisis of the 1960s* (Oxford, 2007), p. 65; M. Eaton, 'What Became of the Children of Mary?', in M. Hornsby-Smith (ed.), *Catholics in England 1950–2000: Historical and Sociological Perspectives* (London, 1999), p. 220.

17 H. Cook, *The Long Sexual Revolution: English Women, Sex and Contraception 1800–1975* (Oxford, 2004), p. 8.

18 Ibid.

19 A. Harris, *Faith in the Family: A Lived Religious History of English Catholicism, 1945–1982* (Manchester, 2013), p. 5.

20 M. Hornsby-Smith, *Roman Catholic Beliefs in England: Customary Catholicism and Transformations of Religious Authority* (Cambridge, 2009), p. 60.

21 S. Bullivant, *Mass Exodus: Catholic Disaffiliation in Britain and America since Vatican II* (Oxford, 2019), p. 2.
22 Harris, *Faith in the Family*, p. 3
23 Ibid.
24 C. Brown, 'Sex, Religion, and the Single Woman *c.* 1950–75: The Importance of a "Short" Sexual Revolution to the English Religious Crisis of the Sixties', *Journal of Social History*, 22 (2011), pp. 189–215.
25 Harris, *The Schism of '68*.
26 S. Bullivant, 'How *Humanae Vitae* Changed the Church', *Catholic Herald*, 20 July 2018.
27 The Pope's endorsement of NFP was given at addresses of 29 October 1951 to the Italian Catholic Union of Midwives and 26 November to the National Congress of the Family Front and the Association of Large Families, National Catholic Welfare Conference, Washington, DC.
28 'Afterword', in D. Lodge, *The British Museum Is Falling Down* (London, 2011, first pub. 1965), p. 168.
29 Ibid., pp. 8–9.
30 P. Berger, *The Sacred Canopy: Elements of a Sociological Theory of Religion* (New York, 1967).
31 Q. de la Bedoyere, *Autonomy and Obedience in the Catholic Church* (London, 2002), p. 2.
32 G. Janzen, referenced in T. W. Jones and L. Matthews-Jones, 'Introduction: Materiality and Religious History', in T. W. Jones and L. Matthews-Jones (eds), *Material Religion in Modern Britain: The Spirit of Things* (London, 2015), pp. 1–16.
33 Brown, *Death of Christian Britain*, pp. 9–17.
34 Ibid., pp. 195, 203.
35 É. Durkheim, *The Elementary Forms of the Religious Life*, trans. Carol Cosman (Oxford, 2001); Berger, *The Sacred Canopy*.
36 Brown, *Death of Christian Britain*, p. 202.
37 Jones and Matthews-Jones, 'Introduction'.
38 'Epistemological Modesty: An Interview with Peter Berger', *Christian Century*, 114 (1997), p. 974.
39 C. Taylor, *A Secular Age* (Cambridge, MA, 2007), p. 548.
40 Cook, *Long Sexual Revolution*.
41 M. Houlbrook, 'Sexing the History of Sexuality', *History Workshop Journal*, 60 (2005), p. 217.
42 M. Foucault, *The History of Sexuality*, vol. 1 (London, 1976).
43 Houlbrook, 'Sexing the History of Sexuality', p. 221.
44 Ibid.
45 Ibid.; H. Cook, 'Emotions, Bodies, Sexuality and Sex Education in Edwardian England', *Historical Journal*, 55 (2012), p. 475.

46 S. Bordo, *Unbearable Weight: Feminism, Western Culture and the Body* (Berkeley, CA, 2003), p. 3.
47 Taylor, *A Secular Age*, pp. 706–708.
48 C. Langhamer, *Women's Leisure in England* (Manchester, 2000).
49 Anne represented a notable exception, an interviewee who will be discussed in greater depth in Chapter 3.
50 The start of Chapter 5 has more details on this indictment, see for example E. Erikson, *Childhood and Society* (New York, 1950); C. Hitchens, *God Is Not Great* (New York, 2007), pp. 217–228.
51 F. Scott Fitzgerald, *The Curious Case of Benjamin Button and Other Stories of the Jazz Age* (Claremont, CA, 2008).
52 H. Alexander, 'Reflections on Benjamin Button', *Philosophy and Literature*, 33 (2009), pp. 1–17.
53 C. Koopman, *Genealogy as Critique: Foucault and the Problems of Modernity* (Bloomington, IN, 2013).
54 M. Strawser, *Both/And: Reading Kierkegaard: From Irony to Edification* (New York, 1997), p. 17.

• 1 •

Uncovering the sex lives of Catholic women

Gender, belief and memory

If accessing personal experiences in the past is a difficult task in general, then getting at the sexual and religious experiences of Catholic women is a particularly perilous pursuit. Both religious belief and sexual behaviour are widely considered to be private, intimate aspects of personhood. This may have been the case for matters of sex for centuries before the Second World War, but religion has only recently been treated in such a way. According to a number of scholars of popular religion, the twentieth century saw religious belief pushed out of the public realm, back into the private arenas of the home, the family, the personal. In fact, there has been something of a reversal in the fate of sex and religion when it comes to public disclosure. Sex is now on everyone's lips, whereas questions of religion have become strangely closeted. To ask and articulate about religious belief can be viewed as more of an intrusion than to probe about sexual preferences. As one interviewee explained:

> People don't seem to ask much about my religion ... my beliefs these days. It's too personal, maybe they think it's too sensitive. There was a time when the same could be said of sex, but I think that's changed![1]

Gaining an insight into sex and religion may have been made all the more difficult by the stigmas and silences which have emerged in the decades after the war, but changing codes of intimacy, the shifting lines between the public and the private, offer the historian opportunities as well as challenges. This is where individual memory comes into its own as a historical resource.

This book is based on the interview testimony of twenty-seven Catholic laypeople, twenty-two women and five men. Following in the line of recent scholarship on post-war religion, the focus will be on the way religious devotion worked along gendered lines. While there is a growing body of work on Christian masculinities in the twentieth century, the notion of 'pious femininity' remains a central building block in dominant models of religious decline.[2] Callum Brown's oral-history research has demonstrated that expectations and experiences surrounding religiosity differed greatly for men and women in post-war England. Regardless of whether we accept the conclusions that Brown drew from this life-history material, the relationship between femininity and religious belief has been established as a vital explanatory terrain for competing narratives of Christian change. The decision to focus on femininity was a response to the popularity of Brown's thesis, as well as the centrality of gender to discussions about and within contemporary Catholicism.[3]

Unlike Brown's 'secularising' sample, the interview participants for this project all identified as Catholic believers in one way or another. Of course, this 'Catholic' identity meant different things to different interviewees. There will be no attempt to judge the 'legitimacy' of the interviewees' claims to Catholicism; their personal understandings of this identity are a major point of interest. Interviews were carried out over a three-year period and aimed at exploring the everyday experiences of negotiating spiritual and sexual demands. How did Catholic women's religious beliefs shape their contraceptive behaviour, marital relationships and wider sexual experiences?[4] Efforts were made to speak to individuals from a range of backgrounds, with the sample including representatives from different class and educational bases, Catholic upbringings and geographical settings. The clearest consistency was the racial composition of the sample - the interviewees were all white. This was an unintended consequence of the project's advertising strategy, the social networks it tapped into and the prevalent demographics of the post-war Catholic population. The experiences of black and Asian Catholics will be the subject of my next project. The interviewees hailed from a range of locations up and down the country. There was a slight weighting in favour of the south-east as this was where the researcher was based, but towns in the north of England with traditionally large Irish immigrant communities such as Bolton, Liverpool and Manchester were also represented. The distinctness of the Anglo-Irish Catholic experience was touched on by a number of the interviewees, but interestingly, more so by those not from this heritage themselves. It was a distinction that was more readily observed in others than claimed personally.

Inevitably there were some slight imbalances in the composition of the sample. When researching a sensitive subject like sex, the fear would be that only a self-selecting minority with special characteristics would be comfortable discussing such topics. The interviewees were, of course, representative only of individuals who were willing to talk about such matters to a researcher. It was, though, possible to limit any 'distortions' that might be seen to be produced by the sample.[5] This included thinking about the audiences to which the project was exposed and how this exposure was achieved. The respondents were elicited in a number of ways – through advertising in national and local Catholic newspapers and magazines, notices on local parish notice-boards, newsletters and group emails within Catholic organisations and societies, personal contacts, notably from family members and then from existing networks branching out from these contacts. The same project description was used every time and is detailed in Appendix A.

It was likely that many of these spaces and networks would have been more frequented by middle-class Catholics. As a result, the sample is slightly weighted in favour of individuals from middle- to upper-middle-class backgrounds. This should not necessarily be viewed as a limitation of the research – the history of sexuality as a discipline has been somewhat preoccupied with attempts to penetrate 'the working-class experience' to date.[6] Nevertheless, ten of the twenty-seven interviewees described themselves as 'working class'. A range of socio-economic backgrounds were represented within the material which allowed for some examination of the way class intersected with sexual behaviour and beliefs. However, the intention of the project was never to classify the beliefs of individual women along class or any other lines in a manner akin to that of Hornsby-Smith. A comprehensive commentary on the variations between groupings such as 'cradle Catholics' and converts, Irish immigrants and English Catholics has been attempted before.[7] The way these variants shaped Catholic experiences in the post-war is touched on at various points in the body of book, but does not constitute a major priority here.

The only clear disparity that existed in the composition of the sample related to the interviewees' politicised identity within Catholicism. Almost all the interviewees chose to describe themselves as either 'liberal' or 'orthodox' Catholics, unprompted by a direct question from the interviewer. There was overlap between members of the two groups on issues such as abortion, female priests and liturgical reform, but birth control represented a clear point of delineation. Interviewees who identified as 'orthodox' believed the central Church was right about the intrinsic immorality of birth control, those who identified as 'liberal' did not. Crucially, every 'liberal' interviewee believed in and practised the Church's teaching in the early stages of their marriages – it was through a process of questioning, often driven by great physical and emotional frustrations, that they eventually changed their minds. The relationship between the development of politicised Catholic identities and the question of contraceptive morality represents a central line of enquiry in Chapters 3 and 4 on marital sexuality. The Catholic press has made much of the differences between 'liberal' and 'orthodox' Catholics, and this book certainly pays close attention to these differences, but it also reveals the little-appreciated similarities between the two groups. While there was a clear discrepancy over the question of papal authority, there were underlying consistencies in the way sex and religion were conceptualised and experienced.

The number of 'liberals' outnumbered the 'orthodox' interviewees twenty-one to six. There is more than one potential explanation for this trend. It could be suggested that the liberal interviewees would have been more naturally predisposed to speak about sexual matters, be that because of a comfort with the subject or the motivation to voice dissent. It is dangerous to start artificially profiling 'liberal' and 'orthodox' Catholics in this way, though. What was apparent from the interviews was that motivation for participation and a willingness to talk about sex did not correlate neatly with 'liberal' or 'orthodox' categories. It could also be suggested that the project was advertised in spaces that were more exposed to the 'liberal' community. This would be true of the initial four respondents, who were sourced through personal association with my grandfather (a figure who will be discussed further in the next section). However, as it became apparent that 'orthodox' women could be under-represented in the sample, active efforts were taken to engage with this community. This included placing advertisements in more 'traditionally minded' publications like the *Catholic Herald*, contacting women's organisations of a similar persuasion and asking existing interviewees if they knew of any potential 'orthodox' participants.

The final explanation for why there were more liberal than orthodox interviewees is that this discrepancy simply reflected the composition of the contemporary Catholic community. In fact, the special efforts that were taken to reach out to orthodox individuals suggest that they could have been over-represented in the sample. Recent survey data seems to support this idea.[8] However, it should be stated again that this book makes no claims to be quantifiably representative of English Catholicism. While there remains room for further research into the 'orthodox' Catholic experience, the focus on women who identify as 'liberal' Catholics is not a limitation of the book but the very thrust of its intervention. Putting aside for a moment the 'liberal' and 'orthodox' dichotomy of the birth-control debate, my overarching aim is to interrogate what 'liberation' meant to Catholic individuals and institutions in a post-war context.

The issue of representativeness has consistently been viewed as a stumbling-block for oral historians. How can the subjective testimony of twenty-seven individuals be seen to represent a Catholic population numbering over 2 million, one might ask. These subjectivities are, though, the very subject of the book. A taxonomy of different Catholic beliefs on hell has been produced before; Michael Hornsby-Smith has provided a detailed anthropological survey of how variants such as class, geography, ethnicity and religious upbringing shaped Catholic belief systems in this time period.[9] It is not claimed that the memories presented here are 'representative' of the entire Catholic experience. Instead, qualitative testimony is used to reconstruct a spectrum of the intimate, personal understandings of Catholic female sexuality at work in the post-war decades.

Individual memory offers an admittedly problematic and yet uniquely suggestive insight into religious beliefs, sexual behaviour and gendered identities.[10] The respondents' memories are used in a way which encompasses *both* 'social' and 'cultural' approaches to oral testimony.[11] Leading theorists of oral history research have identified two contrasting methodologies in the field. First, that of the social historian, where personal testimony is valued for the insight it can offer into the lived experiences of a particular neglected group. Second, that of the cultural historian, which focuses on the discourses, cultural constructs and ideologies that shape or even construct human memory.[12] But to what extent are these two approaches mutually exclusive? According to Anna Green, this dichotomy does not offer any answers to the questions of how and why individuals adopt specific perspectives.[13] Surely it is possible to look at the 'stories', 'myths' and 'cultural scripts' that individuals draw on in the way they compose their memories while simultaneously treating their testimony as providing an insight into an actual lived experience.[14] Sexuality and religiosity were both discursive formulations shaped by the changing historical contexts in which they were understood, and also drivers of everyday actions and material existence. As we shall see, a rigid dichotomy between the 'discursive' and the 'experiential' is itself a historically specific problematic when tracing the relationship between sex and religion in the post-war years.

I intend to build on the insights of Green and focus on the decisions that are made by the interviewees when narrating their life stories.[15] Much like the study of religious belief, certain exponents of oral history have favoured a 'discursive' approach.[16] Inspired by the theories of postmodern deconstructionism, this approach tends to be based on the premise that the 'present-centred' and linguistic context of production means that memory can only be used to study the discursive regimes that circulate at the point of interview.[17] In this book, I argue that oral history participants select and choose different discourses when recalling their life stories, and that these selections offer a valuable insight into an actual lived experience. The way Catholic women remember their sexual experiences does tell us something about the moment of recollection, but the decisions they make when remembering should not be treated as random or devoid of meaning. The interviewees' *decisions* also offer us an insight into the moment being remembered. Moreover, these decisions reveal a layer of emotional and personal meaning which traditional 'objective' sources are blind to.

By attending to the specific details that the respondents choose to emphasise when elucidating their decisions, the agency of individual Catholic women, who are commonly taken to be passive victims of indoctrination or psychological programming, will be placed at the centre of my analysis. As such, there is an ethical dimension to the methodology used here. Catholics believe that individuals have the capacity to interpret their own experiences and personal history. Under the heading 'The Judgement of Conscience', the *Catechism of the Catholic Church* outlines its teaching on the rational and moral faculties which men and woman possess for making sense of the world.[18] Equally, feminist theorists have pointed out that women are continually denied the right to act as authors of their own life stories. Speaking about oral history specifically, Sherna Berger Gluck and Daphne Patai argue that female subjects are rarely afforded the same capacity as men to interpret their own experiences.[19] In employing a methodology which responds to these contexts, it could be argued that my approach to oral history theory is ambitious, even optimistic. It is, in fact, intellectually and ethically appropriate for the subjects at hand: Catholic women. In placing the world-view of the interviewees at the heart of our methodology, we can move towards an understanding of oral-history methods which brings 'post-secular' and feminist ideas into dialogue.

Taking Catholic women's accounts of their own experiences seriously has direct consequences for the wider impact of the book, notably for debates about contraceptive morality. The interviewees' testimonies offer an intimate insight into the emotional, physical and spiritual dimensions of everyday, and every night, Catholic life – from the excitement of discovering new pleasures and passions to the pain and suffering of grappling with NFP. Many of the interviewees recalled stories of great anguish, frustration and loss when describing their attempts to keep to the Church's teaching on contraception in particular. Feelings, sensations and sensibilities were closely intertwined with their changing religious belief systems.

In shining a light on these feelings, sensations and sensibilities, oral history can help reframe the somewhat exhausted debates surrounding sexual morality within the Catholic community. For all the optimism Pope Francis' rhetoric has instilled in the 'liberal' Catholic community, he has kept the door to doctrinal change firmly shut. His recent comments on the need for the Church to move on from its 'obsession with the issues of abortion, gay marriage and contraception' have been welcomed by many 'progressives', but in lumping these issues together, their theological and ethical specificities have been muddled and dissolved.[20] Moreover, the drive to transcend such matters has also served to marginalise and silence meaningful dialogue about doctrinal scrutiny. In a climate in which the Catholic birth-control debate appears to be closed off, I want to ask whether historicising its emergence in decades after the war could provide an alternative point of entry. Did Pope Paul VI's rejection of a highly intellectualised, theological case for change in the 1960s close the door to doctrinal change altogether, or did it close only this route to change? Oral history can provide a new way of approaching these debates in the twenty-first century, placing the emotional and embodied experiences of Catholic women at the heart of a discussion which has hitherto been dominated by men (indeed, often celibate men). Crucially, this is possible only when Catholic women are accredited with the intellectual capacity to represent and interpret their own experiences. A methodology which dismisses the experiential risks silencing their voices once again.

Religious history and the personal

Academic investigators of religion tend to follow a rule: do not talk about yourself. There is a widespread reluctance to offer the reader any hint of the author's own religious beliefs or identity. Despite a growing zeal to uncover the intimate, personal religiosities of their 'subjects', researchers prefer to stick to Alastair Campbell's infamous edict: 'we don't do God'. This is true of both neo-secularisationalists such as Brown, and of practitioners of 'lived religious history' – a new methodology based on critiquing the 'constraining academic paradigms surrounding secularisation and modernity'.[21] Writers in both camps leave little or no trace of their own theological convictions, even in forewords, acknowledgements or references. Presumably such details are seen as irrelevant to the form, rendering intellectual analysis mere theo-journalism and thereby diluting the credentials of the study.

This approach to religion came of age, or at least found a grown-up name, in the period this book focuses on. 'Methodological agnosticism' was a term coined by Ninian Smart in the late 1960s and quickly became established as the equitable approach for students of religion. Smart posited that the social scientist should study religious beliefs and their effects in society without passing any judgement on the truth or falsity of those beliefs.[22] By extension, he maintained that the investigator's theological identity should be imperceptible to the reader. Methodological agnosticism served as the dominant practice through the 1970s and 1980s and still holds sway today, as John Cox asserts:

> The idea that academics must adopt a neutral, value-free position with respect to the study of religions and restrict themselves to the tasks of describing, classifying and comparing religious phenomena has come to define even up to today mainstream thinking among scholars of religions within departments of religious studies in Western academic institutions.[23]

The popularity of such a principle should be understood in the context of its wider historical setting. A Freudian diagnosis of religious commitment continues to have currency, and with this, religious modes of understanding are considered to corrupt the legitimacy of dispassionate, intellectual practice.

The virtues of methodological agnosticism have been questioned in recent years, with Michael Bourdillon arguing that academic neutrality on religious matters is based on the flawed premise that the scholar of religion can or should exclude personal judgements from academic discourse. Bourdillon contends that 'our personal judgements are relevant to academic debate, and academic debate can affect our personal judgements'.[24] In popular culture, the veracity of agnosticism in a broader sense has become a target. Yann Martel's hugely popular novel *Life of Pi* and the resulting film include a compelling deconstruction of the rhetorical rationale behind agnosticism.[25] If the God question is inescapably one of belief rather than knowledge, and if there either is or is not a God, then surely everyone, and by extension no one, is agnostic?

Rather than pursuing 'methodological agnosticism', this study borrows from a recent trend amongst historians known as the 'reflexive turn'. Social and cultural historians are increasingly eager to reflect on the way their own identity shapes their historical analysis, and how, in turn, their historical analysis shapes their personal identity. Indeed, as Michael Lynch points out, reflexivity, whether in the form of 'interpretive reflexivity', 'substantive reflexivity' or 'mechanical reflexivity', has become fetishised somewhat within the academy.[26] The impetus behind this reflexive revolution resonates with my will to uncover Catholic subjectivities. But the language of reflexivity, applied as it is to the researcher rather than the researched, seems to form a distinction between the academic and the 'ordinary' subject. The term has a distinctly socio-scientific flavour to it, with something pseudo-empirical about its intentions. I would place this concept in the more encompassing and yet simpler descriptive of 'the personal'. With this, the subjectivities of researcher and subject are not distinguished from each other through a hierarchical language but held together.

When it comes to matters of religion, and indeed sexuality, the personal cannot be entirely separated from the historical. This is not simply a question of acknowledging the author's subjectivity in an introductory passage, but also recognising the peculiarities of religion and sexuality as subjects of enquiry. Practitioners of religious studies have long grappled with the extent to which their subject is exceptional to other pursuits. In recent years, much energy has been spent by historians on the valuable task of trying to resituate religion alongside other social, intellectual and material topics. Sue Morgan and Jacqueline de Vries celebrate the fact that within the field of gender history, religion is re-emerging from decades of neglect to find a space in conference panels and edited collections.[27] While it is right to emphasise that religion can be studied and understood as a legitimate and immanent historical phenomenon, the tendency to stress its 'normalness' has lead certain authors to overcompensate and neglect its essential 'strangeness'. This book seeks to develop a methodology that creates and maintains a space within which religion's 'strangeness' can be articulated.

Timothy Fitzgerald asks what makes religion somehow 'distinct, sui generis, and unique?'. The only available answer, according to Fitzgerald, must be its transcendental referent, variously called God, the sacred or the ultimate.[28] There may be something beyond this metaphysical dimension that sets religion apart in a specifically post-war context, though. Charles Taylor argues that in the period after the cultural revolution of the 1960s, described by Taylor as the 'Age of Authenticity', religion has not only moved from an unconscious backdrop to an active choice, but has become something that must satisfy a sense of individualistic spirituality. Finding a place in a Church no longer matters, religious or non-religious identity serves as the ultimate expression of authentic individualism.[29] The link between religious identity and a sense of self that Taylor forges has found much concurrence amongst sociologists of contemporary religion.[30] This being the case, efforts from the investigator to completely remove any sense of the personal denies a central component of the modern religious subject they are attempting to explore.

This particular conception of the personal can be seen to have distinctly Catholic colourings. In merging it with authorial reflexivity, a Foucauldian scholar would detect something of the confessional in the call to divulge intimate details of the writer's identity. There is certainly a quasi-spiritual quality to the way this responds to a modern incitement to 'tell everything'.[31] But rather than identifying the confessional as a point of reference, my understanding of the personal draws more on the theoretical contributions of Ken Plummer and his notion of 'storytelling'. Plummer maintains that Foucault's model of a modern confessional culture is 'couched at a level of generality – of the deployment of discursive strategies and power/knowledge spirals – which is too opaque'. For Plummer, Foucault provides little space for the generation of particular kinds of stories at particular moments; his strangely undifferentiated model chiefly neglects the rise of mass media in late modernity.[32] Accordingly, the methodology of this study is informed by a process of 'storying' rather than 'confessing'. The stories we tell do not simply give meaning to our interactions with the social world, but also constitute what we consider to be the personal. In the contemporary historical setting, stories do not just make us; they are us.

Many of the interviewees asked about my own story. They were interested in my Catholicism, sexuality, marital status, family history, political affiliations, beliefs on the morality of contraception, abortion, papal infallibility, gender theory. And I told them everything they wanted to know. Certain oral history theorists have urged the interviewer to keep silent about themselves to avoid inflecting the interviewees responses. But as Lorraine Sitzia points out, the presence of the interviewer will always shape the context of production.[33] Rather than leaving the interviewee to postulate over my religious or indeed sexual proclivities (one interviewee had assumed I was gay simply because I lived in Brighton, many assumed I was a militant atheist because of my academic status), an honest and reciprocal exchange ensured we both discovered what we wanted to about the other. Moreover, a non-dialogic interview technique can serve to sever natural conversation – if I am probing into the interviewees' intimate lives, then it is surely unfair not to answer their questions. In discussing my own identity, the interviews were typified by a mutual knowledge of the other that broke down reservations and status hierarchies.

If aspects of my own 'story' were present at the point of interview, then it only seems appropriate to share them here. So what was the relationship between Catholic women's stories and my own tale? A debate in religious studies known as the 'Insider/Outsider problem' can help us think on this question. George Chrysillius discusses it thus:

> Does one have to be a member of a community for your testimony about that community to be valid? Or does your membership of the community invalidate your objectivity? It is certainly the opinion of a large minority within the academic study of religion that, in the words of Andrew Walls, 'religion can best understand religion' … However, from another perspective a personal religious

commitment, whether to the group being studied or another group, can be seen as a hindrance to seeing the social reality of the matter at hand.[34]

I could be classed as both an insider and an outsider, or perhaps as neither. I do not believe in a Catholic God or creed at the time of writing, but am inspired by a conviction that Catholicism has been unfairly dismissed as irrational and pathologically unmodern. I did, though, grow up believing in a Catholic God and theology, albeit a theology that might be described as 'liberal'. I was encouraged from an early age to question the Church's absolute authority on a range of matters. For some commentators, the fact that I was brought up a Catholic would go a long way to determining the course of my analysis. For others, the 'liberal' nature of my Catholicism would equally be seen to determine my conclusions. As stated earlier, though, this study moves away from such a reading of religiosity as being rooted in childhood indoctrination. The evolution and undulation of my beliefs have continued to shape the form and content of this project from its inception to its completion. Equally, the research process has recalibrated my own faith, sexuality and the relationship between the two. Reflecting on this circuit places the reader in a privileged position when forming his or her own personal responses to the material.

My own story, and its relationship with this project, was shaped by one individual above and beyond any other. My grandfather, Professor John Marshall, the self-proclaimed Catholic sexpert, was a counsellor and chairman of the Catholic Marriage Advisory Council (CMAC) between 1952 and 1996, a medical representative on the Papal Commission for Birth Control and author of a corpus of advice literature on sex for Catholics. In his early career as a neurologist and medical researcher, he developed and published the first guide to the basal temperature method of natural family planning. This method, endorsed by the Pope in 1951 ('Grandjohn' as he was known to his family, was to mischievously claim he had 'invented the rhythm method'), was widely used by Catholic couples in the following years – every one of the interviewees tried the method at one point in their marriages. Marshall was brought into the papal commission by Pope John XXIII in 1962 as a medical representative and defender of the Church's line on artificial contraception, but changed his mind in the course of the deliberations. For the remaining years of his life, he was a leading advocate of a change in the Church's teaching on contraception. There can be no doubt that his legacy, and politicised Catholic identity, not only inspired but also enabled the completion of the research.

As a prominent figure in the Catholic community, Marshall was familiar to some of the respondents. Five of the interviewees were in fact contacted through personal affiliation with my grandfather. This could be seen to have had a number of effects on the course of the interview. The familial tie gave the interviewer a sense of legitimacy and encouraged an atmosphere of trust which was conducive to candid dialogue. The social connection between interviewer and interviewee could equally be seen to distort the testimony. The interviewee could feel reluctant to divulge certain details, particularly in regard to sexual behaviour, to a source that was in some way linked to them outside of the research context. Listening back on the interview recordings, it is difficult to detect what, if any, effect this association might have had. What is important is that this dynamic was acknowledged prior to the interviews and steps were taken to negate its impact. The interviewees were briefed on the rigorous ethical review process that had been carried out. It was also stressed that their anonymity would be preserved throughout the process, and that the interviewer was bound by institutional and legal codes of practice.

When talking about the project at academic conferences or over unenviable pub conversations with friends, it was not my religious or familial backgrounds that were identified as the main issues with my 'story'. Two, more visually discernible, aspects of my identity were picked up on: age and gender. The most common question tended to boil down to:

> Why do you think these elderly Catholic women will speak to you, a young male, about these sensitive sexual topics?

The gender and age of the interviewer were identified as the key barriers to the completion of the research. It is important to acknowledge that these factors would have undoubtedly shaped the interviewees' testimony in some way. There are a set of questions relating to my own identity as a young, unmarried, actively heterosexual male that I have to be conscious of both in the interview, and also in analysing the material afterwards. For example, the gender and age discrepancy might be seen to contribute to or even account for what some oral historians have described as 'silences' in the interviewees' narrative. Certainly, my own characteristics would have affected what the interviewees were and were not happy to talk about. However, any interviewer would have to confront a certain set of questions based on his or her own identity. An elderly woman, for example, would have to think about the way their own proximity to the experiences being discussed might introduce an element of comparison. A female interviewer would equally have to think about how gendered codes of respectability might shape the details that a respondent was willing to disclose, or at least the manner in which these details were divulged. Alessandro Portelli has found that similarity between interviewer and interviewee can serve to 'paralyze dialogue'.[35] It is possible to view the gender and age of the interviewer as features of the interview dynamic without seeing them as determining. This, after all, would be making assumptions about the interviewee's own disposition.

When discussing the effect of the interviewer's identity, the word 'questions' rather than 'problems' is used advisedly. A distance between the researcher and subject can also serve as a palpable benefit. Kate Fisher's extensive oral history project *Birth Control, Sex and Marriage in Britain, 1918–1960* represents something of a blueprint for this research.[36] Fisher outlined the way that her own identity as a young, unmarried woman could encourage elderly male interviewees to 'educate her naivety' and this perception of ignorance sometimes even served as the initial motivation for participation. The justification given by one of Fisher's male respondents for speaking to her – 'I don't think you, you really understand how we lived' – is one that was replicated in various forms by a number of my interviewees. There were instances where my own unfamiliarity with the experiences being discussed also served as a comfort for the interviewee:

> I have not really talked about this with my friends or anyone really because I'd be worried they would say 'It wasn't like that for me!' … That's probably why I'm happy to talk to you, you wouldn't know about things like this.[37]

The shared knowledge of the interviewer's essential difference often created an atmosphere conducive to open and frank discussion where the interviewee felt a sense of control and ownership over the subject matter.

There was another element of the interviewer's identity that was not picked up on by conference audiences or even myself initially, that of the academic investigator, specifically the academic investigator of religion. As I introduced the main themes of the research to Lynn at the start of our interview, she asked why I was interested in such a project. After explaining the issues I had with the existing literature and my own personal and familial affiliation with the topic, Lynn pointed out 'and you want a PhD'. Although I had not seen my research as an acquisitive endeavour, I realised that it might seem self-serving and in some sense it was. There is a particular tradition of academic interrogation of Catholic 'subjects' that might unsettle a potential interviewee. Patricia for example wanted reassurance that the project would not be like the BBC4 documentary *Catholics* which had recently aired. There were some within the Catholic community who regarded the series as exploitative, framing interviews with Catholic women in particular in a manner that was misleading to both viewer and participant.[38] It was important that I attempted to distance myself from such a tradition, while also acknowledging that my identity as an 'intellectual investigator of religion' was an inescapable feature of the interview dynamic. The 'academic gaze' has been a perennial presence in the story of postwar Catholicism – from sociologists in the 1960s to Brown at the start of the twenty-first century, Christian women's sexuality has become a major point of interest for intellectual authorities. The approaches to the subject taken by these academics, much like my own, has been coloured by historically specific definitions of both sex and religion.

The interviews were conducted between 2012 and 2015, and in this period, both the academic and non-academic 'gaze' on Catholicism was defined by one issue above any other: clerical child abuse. The public scandal surrounding the revelation of these crimes and their coordinated cover-up was an important part of the context in which the interviews took place, and yet it featured relatively fleetingly in the interview exchanges. As we shall see, a small number of the liberal interviewees referred to clerical child abuse when criticising the clergy's lack of sexual experience – celibacy was identified as the root cause of the Catholic Church's destructive approach to human sexuality. But this connection between child abuse and contraceptive prohibitions was made only very briefly, and by a small minority of interviewees. In the Conclusion I offer some further reflections on the significance of clerical child abuse to the research, but it cannot be said to have represented a major topic in the interviews. The design of the project would have accounted for this in part – the intention was to place an attentive focus on the sexual experiences of Catholic women, and my questions reflected this. But it also seemed that the interviewees wanted to mark out the distinctiveness of the issues that they faced, to not have them subsumed into contemporary public discourses about sex and Catholicism. In recent years, scholars in the USA have made important steps towards historicising the abuse in their country.[39] There remains little research on child abuse and its suppression within the English Catholic Church – the limited insight that this project can offer will hopefully prompt others to address the subject directly.

In this book I will be rejecting agnosticism as both a personal theology and methodological virtue. The project was inspired by the realisation that my personal story could be mapped on to a collective, historical story. My sexual 'awakening' in teenage years coincided with moving away from and eventually renouncing Catholicism. While being conscious of this parallel, I did not see any causal connection between the two. I was, though, interested to learn that the dominant, historical way of thinking about religious decline at a national level adhered to this very story. James Hinton describes his work *Nine Wartime Lives* as a 'sounding board for his own puzzles about the meaning of life', and admits that the way in which the stories have been framed reflects the 'unresolved muddles of my own selfhood'.[40] As is the case with Hinton, my intention is not merely therapeutic expression, but to lay bare the personalised dialogue between researcher and subject so as to augment the reader's place in this tripartite relationship.

Conclusion

This chapter has outlined an approach to Catholic women's sex lives which emphasises the need to hear, not just listen to, Catholic women themselves. Debates and discussion about sex within Catholicism during the post-war years have been dominated not only by men, but also by abstract, theological discourse. The approach taken here is informed by a movement within the humanities and social sciences that attempts to prioritise experiential knowledge. The reconception of the 'personal' that underscores the book's methodology is one which borrows from and reworks notions of reflexivity, subjectivity and agency which have been circulating in the last ten years. In this sense, my approach to Catholic women's sexuality is very much a product of its wider intellectual environment, just as was the case for Catholic authorities ruminating on the subject in the 1960s. The next chapter moves on to address the Catholic Church's understanding of female sexuality during this decade of supposed sexual revolution. It embeds the Church's image of sex in its wider intellectual context, showing it to be not only an anomaly within a 'liberalising' culture, but premised on dominant secular constructions of the 'personal'. What we think of as the 'personal' has a history – it has meant different things, at different times. By extension, the personal has a future, a fact which could have radical implications for the Catholic birth-control debate.

Notes

1 Georgina, interviewed 22/11/2012.
2 Research into Catholic masculinities in the post-war period has begun to emerge. See A. Harris, '"The People of God Dressed for Dinner and Dancing"? English Catholic Masculinity, Religious Sociability and the Catenian Association', in L. Delap and S. Morgan (eds), *Men, Masculinities and Religious Change in Twentieth-Century Britain* (Basingstoke, 2013), pp. 54–89.
3 A project that apportioned equal attention to husbands and wives or one that looked at Catholic masculinities would make a valuable source of future research, but it would be an essentially different undertaking from the one presented here.
4 It should be acknowledged that the composition of the sample would have inevitably encouraged more of a focus on some issues, and less on others. For example, the lack of consideration of homosexuality, or the significance of race, is a consequence of the design and sample of the oral history research.
5 In reference to the Mass Observation Project (MOP), Annebella Pollen has argued that the self-selective nature of qualitative samples need not be viewed as a 'distortion' at all: 'Rather than seeing self-selection as a weakness, and despite continuing positivist pressures, some users of the MOP, have argued that the 'volunteered' nature of the material is, in fact, one of its unique strengths … The desire to write for MO has been described as "an autobiographical impulse", but the archival nature of the project clearly also attracts those with a historical consciousness. Correspondents give generously of their thoughts,

feelings, experiences and opinions in part because they enjoy the process as self-developmental or even therapeutic, but also, at times, as a kind of social altruism, as an oppositional "ordinary" voice against "official" culture.' This was also true of many of the participants in my research: Catholics who were highly informed and keenly aware of their own position in wider ecclesiastical politics. A. Pollen, 'Research Methodology in Mass Observation Past and Present: "Scientifically, About as Valuable as a Chimpanzee's Tea Party at the Zoo"?', *History Workshop Journal*, 75 (2013), pp. 213–235.
6 Kate Fisher's oral history project looked directly at the intersection of class and sexual experience and this work focused on working-class respondents. There has been limited oral history research on the sexual experiences of middle- or upper-class communities. K. Fisher, *Birth Control, Sex and Marriage in Britain, 1918–1960* (Oxford, 2006).
7 M. Hornsby-Smith, *Roman Catholic Beliefs in England: Customary Catholicism and Transformations of Religious Authority* (Cambridge, 2009).
8 A recent YouGov poll found that nine out of ten Catholics support the wide availability of artificial contraception. Referenced in 'Most Catholics Support Abortion and Use of Contraception', *The Independent*, 19 September 2010, accessed at www.independent.co.uk/news/uk/home-news/most-uk-catholics-support-abortion-and-use-ofcontraception-2083291.html.
9 Hornsby-Smith, *Roman Catholic Beliefs in England*.
10 For an illuminating discussion of how oral history can be used to offer an insight into popular religion, see S. Williams, 'The Problem of Belief: The Place of Oral History in the Study of Popular Religion', *Oral History*, 24 (1996), pp. 27–34.
11 The oral history material comes out of my PhD research. This thesis includes more details about the methodological approach taken and is available from the University of Sussex library. 'The Pope and the Pill: Exploring the Sexual Experiences of Catholic Women in Post-War England' (University of Sussex, 2016).
12 P. Summerfield, 'Culture and Composure: Creating Narratives of the Gendered Self in Oral History Interviews', *Cultural and Social History*, 1 (2004), pp. 65–93.
13 A. Green, 'Individual and "Collective" Memory: Theoretical Presuppositions and the Contemporary Debates', *Oral History*, 32 (2004), pp. 35–44.
14 My use of the term 'experience' borrows from Selina Todd's discussion of this highly contested concept. Todd argues that social historians have disregarded the experiential and calls for a 'renewed analysis of

experience' that takes into account feminist and post-structuralist challenges. S. Todd, 'Class, Experience and Britain's Twentieth Century', *Social History*, 39 (2014), pp. 489–508.

15 Green, 'Individual and "Collective" Memory'.
16 C. Brown, *The Death of Christian Britain: Understanding Secularisation, 1800–2000* (Cambridge, 2000), pp. 9–17.
17 For a discussion of this approach to oral history theory see L. Abrams, *Oral History Theory* (Oxford, 2016).
18 'The Judgment of Conscience', *The Catechism of the Catholic Church*, nos. 1777–1782.
19 S. B. Gluck and D. Patai (eds), *Women's Words: The Feminist Practice of Oral History* (London, 1991).
20 Reported in *The Independent*, 19 September 2013.
21 R. Orsi, 'Everyday Religion and the Contemporary World: The Un-Modern, or What was Supposed to Have Disappeared but Did Not', in S. Schielke and L. Debevec (eds), *Ordinary Lives and Grand Schemes: An Anthropology of Everyday Religion* (Oxford, 2012), pp. 145–161.
22 N. Smart. *The Science of Religion and the Sociology of Knowledge* (Princeton, NJ, 1973). See, for example, R. A. Segal, 'Contributions from the Social Sciences', in P. Clayton and Z. Simpson (eds), *The Oxford Handbook of Religion and Science* (Oxford, 2006), p. 314.
23 J. Cox, 'Religion without God: Methodological Agnosticism and the Future of Religious Studies', the Hibbert Lecture, 13 April 2003, Herriot-Watt University, Edinburgh.
24 M. Bourdillon, 'Anthropological Approaches to the Study of African Religion', in J. Platvoet, J. Cox and J. Olupona (eds), *The Study of Religions in Africa: Past, Present and Prospects* (Cambridge, 1996), pp. 139–154.
25 In short, Martel holds that since the existence of God is essentially unknowable and therefore a matter of belief, agnosticism cannot represent a meaningful philosophy or identity. Everyone and no one is agnostic by definition. Y. Martel, *Life of Pi* (Edinburgh, 2001).
26 In his article 'Against Reflexivity as an Academic Virtue and Source of Privileged Knowledge', Lynch documents the competing versions of reflexivity that have been proffered by different writers, stating: 'According to this version [of reflexivity], investigations of reflexive organizations of practical actions can lead to deep sociological insight, but "reflexivity" is not an epistemological, moral or political virtue. It is an unavoidable feature of the way actions (including actions performed, and expressions written, by academic researchers) are performed, made sense of and incorporated into social settings.

In this sense of the word, it is impossible to be unreflexive.' M. Lynch, 'Against Reflexivity as an Academic Virtue and Source of Privileged Knowledge', *Theory, Culture & Society*, 17 (2000), pp. 26–54.

27 S. Morgan and J. de Vries, 'Introduction', in S. Morgan and J. de Vries (eds), *Women, Gender and Religious Cultures in Britain, 1800–1940* (Abingdon, 2010), p. 1.

28 T. Fitzgerald, *The Ideology of Religious Studies* (New York, 2000), p. 27.

29 C. Taylor, *A Secular Age* (Cambridge, MA, 2007), p. 108.

30 For example see L. Woodhead and P. Heelas, *Religion in Modern Times: An Interpretive Anthology* (Oxford, 2000).

31 M. Foucault, *The History of Sexuality*, vol. 1 (London, 1976), pp. 17–36.

32 K. Plummer, *Telling Sexual Stories: Power, Change and Social Worlds* (London, 1995), pp. 121–123.

33 L. Sitzia, 'A Shared Authority: An Impossible Goal?', *Oral History Review*, 30 (2003), pp. 87–101.

34 George Chrysillius, 'George Chrysillius on the Insider/Outsider Problem', Podcast for the Religious Studies Project, 20 February 2012, accessed at www.religiousstudiesproject.com/podcast/podcast-george-chryssides-on-the-insideroutsider-problem/.

35 A. Portelli, 'A Dialogical Relationship. An Approach to Oral History', online article, accessed at www.swaraj.org/shikshantar/expressions_portelli.pdf.

36 Fisher, *Birth Control, Sex and Marriage*, p. xi.

37 Mary, interviewed 25/09/2012.

38 The point should be made that many in the Catholic community welcomed the series. The *Catholic Herald*'s review ran under the title 'Thank you, BBC, for a sympathetic portrayal of our faith'. It stated: 'Given the validity of the regular criticisms against the BBC – that it invariably shows a Left-wing, secularist bias and so on – I was agreeably surprised to find none of this displayed in BBC4's hour-long programme last night.' *Catholic Herald*, 24 February 2012.

39 For example, the American Catholic History Association Convention 2019 included a panel on 'A Church in Crisis: Catholic Sex Abuse in Historical Context' in which leading scholars shared their ongoing research into Catholic sex abuse.

40 J. Hinton, *Nine Wartime Lives* (Oxford, 2012), p. 199.

• 2 •

The Catholic Church's understanding of female sexuality

On 8 February 1964, eleven clergymen, six physicians and one economist gathered in an unheated conference room overlooking Rome. It had been almost a year since Pope John XXIII had tasked the group with preparing a response to the UN's involvement in programmes of active population control – it seemed the commission was moving further away from achieving its brief.[1] When a little-known Belgian canon named Pierre de Locht suggested that the primary ends of marriage could entail something beyond procreative purposes, papal theologian Fr Bernhard Häring retorted, 'But you are talking about questions of fundamental theology!' A pensive de Locht replied, 'I suppose I am.' After a hushed pause, the group's secretariat suggested they should break for coffee – the commission members separated into groups to discuss the implications of what had been said, and de Locht paced the balcony clutching his rosary.[2]

Häring had, in fact, understated the significance of de Locht's challenge; it called in to question not only the content of Catholic sexual theology, but also the processes through which this theology was constructed. The exchange between the two therefore signified a broader dispute that had emerged within Catholicism during the post-war years – what, or more pointedly who, constituted the 'Church'? This question continues to represent a point of dispute amongst members of the Catholic community, but is only beginning to be engaged with by historians of religious change. As such, this chapter will adopt a broader, historically accurate, definition of the term 'Church'. It will look beyond and beneath the official pronouncements of the Pope to uncover how these teachings came to be.

At its inception, the Papal Commission for Birth Control (1962–1965) had been expected to provide the Holy See with a response that accorded with the Church's existing teachings: the primary purpose of sex was procreation and the use of any artificial means to prevent conception was deemed 'intrinsically evil'. In response to de Locht's entreaty in that marbled conference room, Pope Paul VI extended the commission in terms of its brief and membership. It was now afforded full licence to scrutinise the Church's doctrine on birth control and, if necessary, reformulate the Catholic understanding of human sexuality. To this end, the commission expanded to sixty-four members, calling in leading experts from the new intellectual disciplines that had come to redefine the sexual in the preceding decades. Specialists were drawn from established fields like biology, medicine and theology, but a particular emphasis was placed on engaging with the 'new sciences of man' such as sociology, anthropology, psychology and psychoanalysis. The process of 'taking in' the expertise of these secular fields implicitly repositioned the Church in relation to its own epistemology and moral authority. The commission's very existence was based on the principle that sex represented a subject to be understood rather than an object to be known, a fundamental departure from the Church's traditional stance.

If the Catholic hierarchy decided that elements of sexual experience fell beyond the bounds of its existing knowledge, how did Catholic authorities attempt to measure, interrogate and understand this experience in the 1960s? What intellectual tools and apparatus were used to construct the Church's image of sexuality, particularly female sexuality, and what can these tools tell us about both Catholic and secular notions of the personal at this historical moment? This chapter addresses these questions through an analysis of the workings of the Papal Commission for Birth Control. The story of the commission has hitherto received little historical attention, no doubt a consequence of the Pope's eventual rebuttal of its suggestion for a change in doctrine. Of its sixty-four members, sixty agreed that artificial means of contraception should no longer be prohibited by Catholic teaching and signed a final report saying so. The dearth of source material on the commission also accounts for its historical neglect. Because of the secrecy of the commission's workings, the only sources available to historians have been the official reports produced by the commission's secretariat Fr Henri de Riedmatten and leaks to the press. The unpublished papers of commission member John Marshall allow us access to these covert debates and discussions. Despite Pope Paul VI's public and now infamous rejection of the commission's final report in *Humanae*

Vitae, the encyclical was predicated on a number of significant aspects of the commission's understanding of marital sexuality. As Tom Burns, the contemporary editor of the Catholic newspaper *The Tablet*, pointed out, the workings of the commission offer an unparalleled insight into 'the mind of the Church in the process of change'.[3] They also reveal the oversights and assumptions that left this process ultimately unrealised.

The interviewees repeatedly identified *Humanae Vitae* as the principal example of the Church's inability to grasp the experiential realities of marital sexuality. Sorcha explained that 'it just showed the world how the Church did not know what it was dealing with. It was a symbol of how out of touch they were.'[4] While Catholic women's immediate responses to the publication of *Humanae Vitae* are addressed more fully in Chapter 4 on early marriage, this chapter focuses on how this 'symbol' of the Church's detachment from the laity came about. Two related arguments are advanced; first, that the commission did indeed neglect certain aspects of women's sexual experience. However, contrary to popular belief, this was not simply the failing of 'conservative' opponents of change, but was also written into the way 'liberal' commission members approached female sexuality.[5] At no point in the commission's discussions were 'ordinary' Catholic women asked to speak about their sexual experiences. Sex was treated as a biological, instinctive entity that could be measured exclusively through empirical, quantitative methods. It was analysed within a material framework that was juxtaposed to the transcendent realm of theological thought. Indeed, this conceptual divide appeared in a transposed form in the rationale behind *Humanae Vitae*. Second, the chapter demonstrates that this way of thinking was not limited to Catholic authorities, but reflected broader intellectual definitions of sex and religion in the 1960s. In this sense, the papers of the commission destabilise the rigid 'internal' (within the Church) and 'external' (outside of the Church) categories that Brown and McLeod identify as causes of a 'religious crisis'. The understanding of female sexuality that the Church employed was not simply an exception to its historical setting, but a composite part of a 'liberationist' climate.

Investigating Catholic women's sexual experience

Throughout the history of the Catholic Church, the meaning and function of sex had been considered to be trans-historical, prescribed by the strictures of natural law. That the Church's definition of sexuality could be shaped by human intervention represented a significant shift in itself. Critically, it was recognised within the commission that the meaning of sexuality was determined by cultural change rather than being a condition of nature: 'Sexuality cannot be understood as an isolated function or separate problem … It has a dynamic evolution, in other words a history.'[6]

English theologian the Rev. Charles Davis presented a paper to the commission that argued that natural law was to be interpreted by man through his rationality rather than being a known entity. Davis advanced the idea that the meaning of the natural evolves, and in this sense drew from the same constructionist impetuses that were directing intellectual thinking in linguistics and the social sciences at the time.[7] The very first point in the conclusion of Fr de Riedmatten's final report stated:

> Nature is not something ready-made, it is 'making itself'. Nature is constantly revealing herself in such a way that the mind never has to adapt itself to a ready-made nature, but to see it as something constantly on the move. Essence and historicity condition each other.[8]

The commission recognised sexuality to be a protean term that could be shaped by the changing currents of history – a noteworthy concession to the post-modern milieu of the contemporary intellectual community. Brown attributes the breakdown of Christianity's 'discursive power' to the maturing of a 'post-modernity'; an intellectual epoch defined by the deconstruction of language, signification and discourse.[9] We can see that the Church was hardly impervious to this development. Hera Cook argues that feminist writers in the 1960s were primarily responding to Masters and Johnson's de-contextualised understanding of sexuality that treated the human body as a fixed entity with its own empirical laws and processes.[10] In rejecting this form of essentialism, the Catholic Church moved in lockstep with the secular expositors of a 'sexual revolution' and paved the way for a potential change in its understanding of married love.

The British media interpreted the prohibitions of *Humanae Vitae* as being a consequence of the Church's long-held disregard for, perhaps even opposition to, the healthy expression of female sexual pleasure. The *Economist* captured the prevailing opinion of the Church when it described the 'male body of the Curia' as being 'sorely out of touch with Catholic womanhood'.[11] The source of this reputation was addressed directly by a female medical representative on the commission:

> [U]ntil recently 'nice' people believed women not to have a spontaneous sexual arousal ... it is separate from falling in love, but is a physiological state of arousal which arises spontaneously and has no relation to any specific man.[12]

The commission discussed female sexuality as something that did not simply represent a composite part of marital relations, but as an important consideration in itself. Women's sexual desire was understood as a psychological reflex, a spontaneous and essentially physical response that was distinguishable from the emotion of love. Consequently, the commission involved single women in its considerations, as well as commenting on previously uncharted topics such as female masturbation.[13] Hornsby-Smith described Catholic institutions as 'lagging behind the rest of society' in their stances towards women's changing sexual status in the 1960s.[14] It seems this disjuncture was acknowledged at the time by Catholic representatives and provided a salient imperative for the commission's workings.

Female sexuality was measured in a way that was in keeping with the new disciplines that had come to define 'the sexual' in the twentieth century, not only adhering to a psychological model of sexual health, but examining sexual behaviour through the methods and techniques of the social sciences. Hugh McLeod maintains that 'scientific' attacks on the Catholic Church were more likely to be inspired by the social sciences than the natural sciences in the 1960s.[15] Cardinal Heenan's expression of disapproval at the growing number of sociology students and their 'inevitable demands for fresh surveys' in 1967 seems to substantiate this portrayal of Christian versus sociological conflict.[16] Sections of the Catholic community still baulked at the very idea of sex being studied for intellectual purposes. Hera Cook draws attention to the Catholic academic Leslie Paul, who had this to say in 1969 about the growing spate of scientific sex surveys:

> The goal may be the lofty one of human knowledge but there does remain the question of the entitlement of any one individual to so deep an invasion of the privacy of another as the Kinsey – or the

Masters and Johnson investigation demanded. [The latter had] an insolence of which only the most humble scientists are truly capable … as though their own motives could never be suspect even to themselves… and the value … of their knowledge is beyond question.[17]

A mistrust of academic interest in sex had defined Catholic thinking for centuries and remained a presence within certain conservative parties throughout the decade. The decision to expand the papal commission represented a direct break with such a tradition for the central hierarchy. The techniques and apparatus of sociological methodology were heavily integrated into its discussion of female sexuality. The research that was undertaken for the commission even made notable contributions to secular socio-scientific scholarship. Professor Marshall's survey into the responses of Catholic couples to NFP attempted to provide an empirical analysis of the psychological and libidinal implications of the method on the husband and the wife separately, an undertaking that had no precedent in sociological research at the time:

> Some of the trials of oral contraceptives have included questions about the 'libido' defined as sexual desire … but studies in depth of the psychological effects upon individuals and their relationship with their spouses do not appear to have been made.[18]

In this sense, Catholic initiatives were not only harnessing the methodological techniques of the social sciences, but introducing a different set of 'interpersonal concerns' to anthropological analysis in the 1960s. At a moment when socio-scientific research and Catholic thought appeared to be heading in different directions, the papers of the commission indicate that a dialogue between the two also existed.

Contrary to popular perception, the debate within the commission over the suitability of NFP centred on the question of women's sexual fulfilment. The way this fulfilment was measured tells us much about the way human sexuality was understood by both Catholic and socio-scientific authorities during the 1960s. The method had been criticised for being incompatible with natural sexual desires and therefore at odds with a healthy marital union.[19] It required the wife to take her own temperature and then refer to a graph so as to calculate her period of fertility. The couple was then expected to abstain from sex during these fertile periods if they wished to avoid conception. Professor

John Cavanagh presented a paper to the commission that argued NFP was psychologically damaging to women in particular as it denied them copulation at their most fertile. He cited an extensive anthropological study of individual responses to different birth-control methods in support of his contention.[20] Marshall rebutted this critique of the method, deploying his own statistical survey in riposte.

Marshall's data indicated a broad consistency in the responses of husbands and wives to the method, with 74 per cent and 75 per cent respectively finding NFP 'helped their marriage'. Where there were discrepancies, it was men who seemed to be struggling with the periods of abstinence to a greater extent than women. NFP was judged almost entirely on its capacity to facilitate women's sexual pleasure, but this pleasure was measured through a set of prescribed questions devised by academic researchers. Responses often had to fit within a binary agree/disagree framework that provided limited scope for additional comments or deeper reflections on the affectionate aspects of married love. The accredited methods of the social sciences were harnessed by the commission in its examination of women's sexual fulfilment – the rigidly empirical criteria that were employed were more a reflection of the prevailing sociological climate than a prudishness from the Church.

The commission's adherence to the ideas and apparatus of contemporary secular intellectual disciplines had the effect of framing human sexuality as an intellectual 'problem' to be rationally solved. Pope Paul VI's private address to the expanded commission repeatedly identified sex as a 'problem' for Catholicism, explaining that the Church was 'anxious to give a solution adapted to the great problems which men face'.[21] Pope Paul optimistically asked the expanded commission:

> If certain very difficult problems have arisen, those very problems which we ask you to examine in complete objectivity and liberty of spirit – is there not the begging of solutions to the problems which today seem so difficult?[22]

This sentence alone included three 'problems' and two 'difficults' in its call for 'objectivity and liberty of spirit'. The commission's unequivocal adherence to the idea of sexual education represented the only real point of convergence between the liberal and conservative factions within the group. The purpose of this educating initiative was detailed as 'confronting the challenge of modern sexuality'.[23] The words 'problem', 'difficulty' and 'challenge' are ubiquitous in the papers of the commission.[24] Attempts by the Church to engage with sexuality as an emerging body of expert knowledge were continually articulated in a language that defined sex as an intellectual challenge, obstacle or even battle.[25]

The Church's efforts to engage with psychoanalytical thought in the 1960s epitomised its shifting relationship with secular intellectual disciplines. The Catholic hierarchy was initially hostile to the publication of Sigmund Freud's theories and continued to warn against the dangers of psychoanalysis up until the mid-1950s. In 1952, Pope Pius XII vigorously cautioned against 'psychotherapeutic treatments that seek to unleash the sexual instinct for seemingly therapeutic reasons'.[26] In the same year, *Time* magazine ran an article under the heading 'Is Freud Sinful?' which included a number of comments from Vatican officials, notably that of Monsignor Pericle Felici, an official of the Sacred Congregation of the Sacrament, who attacked the 'absurdity' of psychoanalysis and claimed that 'anyone who adopts the Freudian method is risking mortal sin'.[27] Nevertheless, the psychoanalytical language of the 'self' provided the principal resource for the commission's revised definition of human sexuality ten years later. The commission was presented with a paper drawn up by British psychologist Professor D. Barrett at the request of Fr de Riedmatten that outlined the Church's new conception of the relationship between sexual identity and selfhood:

> The acceptance of sexuality is the acceptance of reality. It is to accept oneself with one's qualities and deficiencies. Love of self, of another and of God is one and the same thing. Refusal of self brings in its train perversion and ultimately destruction of the self and the other. This acceptance of sexuality which is acceptance of self requires unceasing effort.[28]

Catholic discourses mirrored the developments of the secular world in forging a connection between sexuality and the introspection of the self. For Professor Barratt, it was only through alerting oneself to one's instincts and desires that an individual could realise the true nature of sexuality. Human subjectivity was thereby understood to be the product of a hermeneutic process through which men and women were required to interpret a hidden and autonomous self. This definition of the human psyche was one that was in vogue within the contemporary scientific community, but posed a number of questions when considered in relation to a Catholic understanding of moral agency. Matthew Thomson points out that since the start of the century a collection of writers had grappled with the apparent tensions between a Christian notion of free will and psychology's emphasis on the subconscious.[29] The commission's adherence to a psychoanalytical model of selfhood was the culmination of its ardent quest to reconcile Catholicism with an emergent body of sexual expertise.

The word 'self' peppered de Riedmatten final report to Pope Paul and was even present in *Humanae Vitae*: 'Whoever truly loves his marriage partner loves not only for what he receives, but for the partner's self.'[30] In both *Humanae Vitae* and the papers of the commission, there was a sense of the Church attempting to confront the subject of the self, a self that was defined as being concealed, instinctive and sexual. Under the heading 'Mastery of Self', *Humanae Vitae* reads:

> The honest practice of regulation of birth demands first of all that husband and wife ... tend towards securing perfect self-mastery.[31]

The emphasis on mastering rather than accepting the self is an important distinction. Self-mastery was described in *Humanae Vitae* as 'dominating instinct by means of one's reason and free will'.[32] The self that was constructed within the commission was one that the Pope identified as an object to be governed and overcome rather than accepted. The psychoanalytical terms of reference that were used to articulate the commission's case for change were simultaneously harnessed and rejected in *Humanae Vitae*. Perhaps this should come as no surprise; in his opening address to the enlarged commission, Pope Paul explained that 'the substance of the faith is one thing, the way in which it is presented is quite another.'[33] I am not interested in speculating over the basis of the Pope's final decision. Countless other Catholic commentators have done so; the inevitably sparse source material surrounding the Pope's mind-set make this largely a matter of conjecture, and with this something of a diversion.[34] However, the language of self-realisation that was deployed by the commission does tell us something important about the historical setting the birth-control debate existed within. The dominance of psychotherapeutic models of normality and pathology shaped the discourses that were available to both liberal Catholic authorities and the Pope in the 1960s. The intellectual parameters of the birth-control debate were circumscribed by a historically specific, liberationist model of the 'personal'.

What was notable by its absence from the papers of the commission was a qualitative account of Catholic women's everyday experience of sex. As we have seen, the female libido was addressed directly within the commission, but it was measured by quantitative survey data that was then interpreted by intellectual experts who were themselves often male. At no point were the women at the centre of this debate asked to talk about their own sexual experiences and contraceptive choices. In this way, a distance was maintained between the formulations of the commission and the lived experience of Catholic individuals. The lack of female involvement was, in part, a straightforward consequence of the Church's particular conception of womanhood. As has been shown by Karen Trimble Alliaume among others, the Catholic Church has resisted changes in gender roles more than any other feature of modernity.[35] The fact that women's ordination did not really feature as a mainstream topic of discussion in the 1960s was an indication of the Church's entrenched attitude on the subject. Catholic women were expected to be sexually active, but continued to be prescribed a subordinate role in terms of authority. This extended beyond the intimate realms of conjugal rights and bodily autonomy, both of which have been discussed widely elsewhere, to the public sphere of theological debate.[36]

Alongside the perennial question of gender, the lack of female testimony in the commission's reckonings also reflected a particular understanding of sex that was specific to its historical setting. Writing in the middle of the 1970s, Foucault was to observe that sex had become defined by scientific values, constructed as a matter of truth which was removed from its human, corporeal sensitivities:

> The essential point is that sex was not only a matter of sensation and pleasure, of law and taboo, but also of truth and falsehood, that the truth of sex became something fundamental, useful, or dangerous, precious or formidable: in short, that sex was constituted as a problem of truth.[37]

Catholic authorities repeatedly defined female sexuality as an intellectual problem to be rationally understood and scientifically remedied.

Rather than being entirely anomalous, this understanding of sex tells us as much about the intellectual infrastructure of a 'sexual revolution' ethos as it does the Church's perceived relationship with such a phenomenon. Alana Harris has shown how the politics of the family and associated constructions of gender were becoming increasingly contested within the Catholic community in the years 1945–1965.[38] As the idea of a 'sexual revolution' became an explicit and conspicuous presence by the end of this period, these contests began to centre on the question of what constituted a 'healthy', 'liberated' and above all 'natural' understanding of sex. Catholic authorities struggled to break away from a script that increasingly cast religious sensibilities as the antagonist.

Humanae Vitae *and the conceptual separation between sex and religion*

Humanae Vitae has often been interpreted as Pope Paul's personal take on the question of birth control, bearing little or no relation to the work of the commission or the wider Catholic community. Robert Nowell, for example, described the encyclical as 'no more than the private views of the Bishop of Rome'.[39] Despite its obvious rejection of the commission's suggestion for doctrinal change, there were in fact a number of underlying consistencies shared by the encyclical and the workings of the commission. The commission's construction of sexuality as an intellectual 'problem' was mirrored in the language of *Humanae Vitae*: 'The problem of birth, like every other problem concerning human life, is to be considered beyond partial perspectives.'[40] The word 'problem' was an integral feature of the way *Humanae Vitae*'s argument was set up; it's very first section was titled 'New Aspects of the Problem'. The idea that questions of birth and sexual love represented a problem for the Church was one that had not existed in papal pronouncements before the post-war period.[41] In defining sex as a problem, the Pope was encouraged to provide an absolute and emphatic 'solution'. As certain commentators have pointed out, *Humanae Vitae* did include a noteworthy change in the Church's marital theology. In what is otherwise a highly critical appraisal of *Humanae Vitae,* Lionel Keane wrote in 1968:

> To put marital union or conjugal love first as the Pope does is in fact to accept the new theology which evaluates the marital act in terms of human sexuality, and this is to depart from the constant teaching of the Church that the primary purpose of human intercourse is procreation.[42]

The concerns raised by Fr Häring in a marbled conference room had been justified; it was a change in fundamental theology that was being discussed. The circumscribed nature of this change, limited as it was to abstract, theological semantics, should not be dissociated from the intellectual processes through which it was achieved. *Humanae Vitae* was not simply the product of a predetermined 'conservative' victory over the 'liberal' case for change as is commonly thought; it reflected the ideas and assumptions that underscored both conservative and liberal understandings of sex, Catholic theology and the relationship between the two. Moreover, it reflected wider intellectual definitions of the sexual and the religious that had emerged in the post-war years. As this section demonstrates, *Humanae Vitae* was part and product of a conceptual divide between sex and religion that extended well beyond the boundaries of the central Catholic Church.

A number of commentators have pointed out that there were not one but two Catholic birth control debates running concurrently in the late 1960s – one over the question of papal authority in doctrinal reform and a second about the intrinsic morality of artificial means of contraception.[43] The papers of what has come to be known as a second, 'minority report' have recently been released to the public and appear to confirm this notion of two separate strands of argumentation.[44] Just half an hour after the commission's secretariat Fr de Riedmatten had delivered the 'majority report' to the Pope, Cardinal Alfredo Ottaviani, a powerful conservative cleric and the then head of the Congregation for the Doctrine of Faith, asked two similarly minded commission members to stay in Rome an extra week and draft a counter report.[45] This 'minority report' was almost solely based on the question of authority – it argued the Church could not go back on its existing teaching as this would corrupt the 'value and dignity of the Church's teaching authority':

> The Church cannot change her answer because this answer is true ... It is true because the Catholic Church, instituted by Christ to show

men a secure way to eternal life, could not have so wrongly erred during all those centuries of its history ... If the Church could err in such a way, the authority of the ordinary magisterium in moral matters would be thrown into question. The faithful could not put their trust in the magisterium's presentation of moral teaching, especially in sexual matters.[46]

The authors of the minority report, a moral philosopher called Dr Germaine Grisez and a clergyman, Fr John Ford, attempted to trump the question of contraceptive morality by appealing to a higher, transcendent set of epistemological questions about doctrinal authority.

The phrase 'especially in sexual matters' is of particular significance – Vatican II had already enacted a number of liturgical, constitutive and doctrinal reforms in areas such as the language of the Mass, the teachings on eating meat on Fridays and interdenominational dialogue. The establishment of the commission in the first place, removed as it was from the public forum of the Council, was based on the belief that sex and matters of the body were somehow special and needed to be separated out from other aspects of theology. The question of authority seemed to take on its heightened, numinous significance only when dealing with matters of sex.

If there were then two points of debate – one about the theological right of a Pope to change doctrine and a second about sexual morality – let us look a little deeper into how these two debates were framed and what the divide between the two signified. The question of authority was discussed within an abstract, transcendental framework – the last line of the minority report reads:

> For the Church to have erred so gravely in its grave responsibility of leading souls would be tantamount to seriously suggesting that the assistance of the Holy Spirit was lacking to her.[47]

In drawing on the image of the Holy Spirit, the architects of the minority report encapsulated the unearthly, celestial language through which the debate about religious authority was articulated. The co-author of the minority report, Fr Ford, chose to write key aspects of his case in Latin, as opposed to the vernacular French used by de Riedmatten in the majority report. The tone, language and rationale of the minority report were all calculated to transcend the profanity of the liberal case for change. The conceptual divide that was constructed within the minority report, between matters of earthly materiality and celestial transcendence, was replicated in *Humanae Vitae*:

> The question of human procreation, like every other question which touches human life, involves more than the limited aspects specific to such disciplines as biology, psychology, demography or sociology. It is the whole man and the whole mission to which he is called that must be considered: both its natural, earthly aspects and its supernatural, eternal aspects.[48]

While the Pope stressed his intention to provide a holistic view of man's 'whole mission', he simultaneously set up an explicit divide between 'natural, earthly aspects', and 'supernatural, eternal aspects' of the 'grave questions' at hand.[49] This conceptual separation was at the heart of *Humanae Vitae*'s internal logic. It provided the grounds for the eventual prioritisation of the question of 'theological authority' over and above that of 'intrinsic sexual morality'. Aside from the gendered language through which the encyclical was articulated (a feature of papal communications throughout the twentieth century), it was the particular regime of materiality within which 'the question of human procreation' was embedded that made *Humanae Vitae* distinctly of its time.

Conversely, we have seen how the debate about sexual morality worked within a material framework. The commission members treated sex as a biological phenomenon that could be measured and understood through empirical, scientific investigation. In this way, its members co-opted the Freudian behaviourist understanding of sexuality that was ascendant in the social and natural sciences at the time. As Michael Kimmel has argued, it was not until the start of the 1970s that intellectual approaches to sex underwent a paradigmatic shift, as social constructionists such as John Gagnon and William Simon began to show that sex was not simply driven by biological urges but shaped by a complex set of social and cultural meanings.[50] In failing to speak to Catholic women to garner a qualitative insight into their emotional and sensual subjectivities, the 'liberal' case for change neglected vital aspects of personal sexual experience. Catholic authorities positioned sex and religion in two diametrically opposing categories – the religious as unembodied transcendence and the sexual as fleshly carnality. In this sense, *Humanae Vitae*, the workings of the commission and the polarity of the wider Catholic birth-control debate were all expressions of a much deeper conceptual chasm that had opened up in the decades after the war.

Conclusion

Callum Brown maintains that in the midst of a religious crisis in the 1960s, the Christian Churches were in a 'constant state of panic over sex'.[51] The term 'panic' does not suitably describe the Catholic Church's approach to marital sexuality. Panic suggests a rushed and ill-conceived quality; we have seen that Catholic authorities constructed their sexual knowledge through a process of meticulous discussion that incorporated the views of both lay and clerical representatives. Panic also suggests a fear or distrust; we have seen that Church representatives engaged with sexual topics in a frank manner that drew on the 'modern' disciples that had come to redefine marital sexuality. Brown's depiction of the Church is not substantiated with much supporting evidence and this is understandable considering his enthusiasm for the 'external' causes of the religious crisis. However, his dispute with McLeod over the internal or external causes of the religious crisis does perpetuate the misconception that the Church was unilaterally at odds with contemporaneous medico-scientific understandings of sex.

The material evidenced here has suggested that something of a dialogue existed between Catholic and secular discourses, showing them to be a part and product of the same historical processes. Harry Cocks has called for the history of modernity as a simple story of secularisation to be reshaped in light of such examples, with his own work showing how early scientific efforts to understand the psychology of sex were informed by religious impetuses.[52] By the 1960s, this dialogue often saw the Church positioned as the counterpoint to secular sexual expertise, but there were also points of reciprocation between the two. Just as the marriage-guidance initiative had been driven by Protestant actors in the first half of the twentieth century, Catholic forays into socio-scientific research were making significant contributions to the field in their recognition of 'interpersonal concerns'.[53] It is often forgotten that one of the principal architects of the pill was a Catholic doctor who was motivated by his religious convictions; John Rock set out in 1952 to develop a form of birth regulation that replicated the 'natural' process of a women's ovulation and would therefore be endorsed by the Vatican.[54] The miscarriage of this ambition tells us something important about the 1960s as a whole.

The Pope's decision, as well as the commission's case for change, should not be simply understood as exceptions to the historical setting they existed within. They were instead reciprocal and yet composite facets of a 'liberationist' culture. Ostensibly, this culture was defined by an overturn of established authorities and orthodoxies; changes in both sex and Catholicism were presented as emancipatory movements away from authoritarian coercion towards individual autonomy. The traditional historiography of the 'sixties', epitomised by the work of Arthur Marwick and Christie Davies, would later reinforce this story of shifting power dynamics. Indeed, Marwick was to identify the Catholic Church as the archetypal antagonist in his account of sixties liberation, describing it as being 'in opposition to all the great movements aiming towards greater freedom for ordinary human beings in the 1960s'.[55] Digging beneath this narrative, we can see that a liberationist culture was underpinned by a break in the way sex and religion were conceptualised. In the climate of 'sixties' permissiveness, Catholic authorities considered the liberation of sexuality to be a distinctly secular phenomenon, ushered in by the technological advances of medical science, articulated through a psychotherapeutic language of self-realisation and verified by socio-scientific criteria. Paradoxically, the efforts that avowedly progressive Church representatives took to reconcile Catholic thought with a modern body of sexual knowledge were underpinned by an assumption about the foreign and strangely irreligious nature of the topic they were addressing.

This chapter has demonstrated how the Catholic Church's attempt to investigate sexual experience in the 1960s was impaired by the conception of the 'personal' it employed. This conception was specific to the historical moment the commission members were working within. The following chapters advance an alternative vision of the personal through which to consider Catholic women's marital sexuality. This model is equally an expression of the environment it has been constructed within, as academics increasingly look to resources that 'undermine the traditional division between objective study and personal experience'.[56] Recognising the contingent nature of the personal is itself the first step in moving beyond the sterile dichotomies of the Catholic birth control debate.

Notes

1. The commission was not initially established for the purpose of doctrinal scrutiny. It was set up by the 'Office of the Secretary of State' in the Vatican, the department that dealt with the Vatican's administrative and political relationships with other international bodies, rather than the 'Holy Office' (later renamed 'The Congregation for the Doctrine of Faith') that dealt with doctrinal matters.
2. Interview with commission member Professor J. Marshall, 12/05/2011. This exchange is also alluded to in Robert Kaiser's informative but avowedly journalistic account of the commission. R. Kaiser, *The Encyclical that Never Was* (London, 1987), p. 74.
3. Cited in Kaiser, *The Encyclical That Never Was*, p. 29.
4. Sorcha, interviewed 09/01/2014.
5. The idea that 'conservative' members of the commission neglected aspects of women's sexual experience was a recurrent feature of the British media's interpretations of the commission's workings and of *Humanae Vitae*. See G. Armstrong, 'Papal Dilemma on the Pill', *Guardian*, 11 April 1968, p. 11 and 'Pope Paul on Contraception', *Guardian*, 30 July 1968.
6. 'Medical Section Thursday 25th March 1965', John Marshall Papers (University of Notre Dame Archives, Illinois, hereafter UNDA), CBCC 1/06, p. 1.
7. C. Davis, 'The Morality of Contraception', John Marshall Papers (UNDA), CBCC 2/02 T-28, p. 2.
8. Henri de Riedmatten, 'Report of the 4th Session of the Commission', John Marshall Papers (UNDA),CBCC 1/05, p. 45.
9. C. Brown, *The Death of Christian Britain: Understanding Secularisation, 1800–2000* (Cambridge, 2000), p. 244.
10. H. Cook, *The Long Sexual Revolution: English Women, Sex and Contraception 1800–1975* (Oxford, 2004), p. 255.
11. Referenced in L. Pyle (ed.), *Pope and Pill* (London, 1968), p. 133.
12. 'Medical section Saturday 28th March', John Marshall Papers (UNDA), N CBCC 1/06, p. 2
13. Professor Lopez-Ibor introduced the topic of masturbation to the commission, explaining that 'Not only the difficulties of the married couples should be discussed, but also problems of the individual e.g masturbation', in 'Medical section', John Marshall Papers (UNDA) N CBCC 1/06, p. 4.
14. M. Hornsby-Smith (ed.), *Catholics in England 1950–2000: Historical and Sociological Perspectives* (London, 1999), p. 12.

15 H. McLeod, *The Religious Crisis of the 1960s* (Oxford, 2007), p. 166.
16 Quoted in Hornsby-Smith, *Catholics in England*, p. 7.
17 Quoted in Cook, *Long Sexual Revolution*, p. 253.
18 J. Marshall and B. Rowe, 'Psychological Aspects of the Basal Body Temperature Method of Regulating Births', *Fertility and Sterility*, 21 (1970), p. 18.
19 For an overview of the criticisms of NFP that were produced in the 1960s see C. Curran, *Critical Concerns in Moral Theology* (Notre Dame, IN, 1984), pp. 216–224.
20 J. Cavanagh, 'Psychological Response of Individuals to Specific Methods of Birth Control', John Marshall Papers (UNDA), CBCC 1/06, p. 33.
21 Pope Paul VI, 'Address of the Holy Father to the Commission', 26 March 1965, John Marshall Papers (UNDA), CBCC 1/02, p. 3.
22 Ibid., pp. 2–3.
23 De Riedmatten, 'Report of the 4th Session of the Commission', John Marshall Papers (UNDA), CBCC 1/05, p. 10.
24 The controversy of population restriction became associated with the 'challenge' of sexual liberation in the British media as well; the *Guardian* quoted progressive cleric Cardinal Suenens of Mechlin-Brussels as saying 'this is all a major problem for the Church', the exact nature of this 'problem' being left ambiguous.
25 The idea of the Church being in a 'battle' with medical science is reflected in the title of John Rock's book: J. Rock, *The Time Has Come: A Catholic Doctor's Proposals to End the Battle over Birth Control* (New York, 1963).
26 A. Elia, 'Vatican', in D. Leeming, K. Madden and S. Marlan (eds), *Encyclopedia of Psychology and Religion: L–Z* (New York, 2009), p. 940.
27 'Is Freud Sinful?', *Time*, 21 April 1952.
28 D. Barrett, 'Intervention in the Sexual Process According to the Culture and Mentality of Different People', John Marshall Papers (UNDA), CBCC 1/06, p. 6.
29 M. Thomson, *Psychological Subjects: Identity, Health and Culture in Twentieth-Century Britain* (Oxford, 2006), p. 179.
30 Pope Paul VI, *Humanae Vitae: Encyclical Letter of His Holiness Pope Paul VI on the Regulation of Births* (London, 1968), p. 13.
31 Ibid., p. 27.
32 Ibid.
33 Pope Paul VI, 'Address of the Holy Father'.
34 For example, see R. Nowell, 'Sex and Marriage', in P. Harris (ed.), *On Human Life* (London, 1968), p. 71, and E. Stourton, *Absolute Truth: The Struggle for Meaning in Today's Catholic Church* (London, 1999), p. 50.

Stourton argues that Pope Paul did not believe himself to be endowed with the authority to enact a change in the Church's teaching, despite sympathising with the commission's findings.

35 K. Trimble Alliaume, 'Disturbingly Catholic: Thinking the Inordinate Body', in S. St. Ville and E. Armour (eds), *Bodily Citations: Religion and Judith Butler* (New York, 2006), pp. 93–119.
36 G. Burns, *The Frontiers of Catholicism: The Politics of Ideology in a Liberal World* (Berkeley, CA, 1994).
37 M. Foucault, *The History of Sexuality*, vol. 1 (London, 1976), p. 56.
38 A. Harris, *Faith in the Family: A Lived Religious History of English Catholicism, 1945–1982* (Manchester, 2013).
39 Nowell, 'Sex and Marriage', p. 71.
40 Pope Paul VI, *Humanae Vitae*, p. 11.
41 Indeed, defining sex as a problem did not continue very far beyond this period, either – the latest translation of *Humanae Vitae* published on the Vatican's website has replaced the word 'problems' with the word 'questions'. Pope Paul VI, *Humanae Vitae: On the Regulation of Births*, accessed at http://w2.vatican.va/content/paulvi/en/encyclicals/documents/hf_p-vi_enc_25071968_humanae-vitae.html.
42 L. Keane, 'Natural Law and Birth Control', in Harris *On Human Life*, p. 37.
43 Pyle, *Pope and Pill*, pp. 1–4.
44 J. Ford and G. Grisez, *Minority Papal Commission Report*, accessed at www.twotlj.org/BCCommission.html.
45 C. Norris, 'The Papal Commission on Birth Control – Revisited', *Linacre Quarterly*, 80 (2013), pp. 8–16.
46 Ford and Grisez, *Minority Papal Commission Report*.
47 Ibid.
48 Pope Paul VI, *Humanae Vitae: On the Regulation of Births*.
49 Ibid.
50 M. Kimmel, 'John Gagnon and the Sexual Self', in M. Kimmel (ed.) *The Sexual Self: The Construction of Sexual Scripts* (Nashville, TN, 2007), p. vii.
51 This comment first appeared in a lecture by Callum Brown at the Anglo-American Historical Conference, London, 6 July 2006.
52 H. Cocks, 'Religion and Spirituality', in M. Houlbrook and H. G. Cocks (eds), *Palgrave Advances in the Modern History of Sexuality* (London, 2006), p. 157.
53 Marshall and Rowe, 'Psychological aspects of the basal', pp. 15–22. These findings were published in a leading, secular medical journal.
54 Certain commentators have seen the wording of *Humanae Vitae* as a direct response to Rock's book, *The Time Has Come*; see L. Marks,

Sexual Chemistry: A History of the Contraceptive Pill (London, 2001), p. 222.
55 A. Marwick, *The Sixties: Cultural Revolution in Britain, France, Italy, and the United States, c. 1958–c. 1974* (Oxford, 1998), p. 36.
56 L. Robinson, 'Gay Men and the Revolutionary Left since 1957', PhD thesis (University of Sussex, 2003), p. 7, published as *Gay Men and the Left in Postwar Britain: How the Personal Got Political* (Manchester, 2007).

• 3 •

Sexuality in later marriage

Later marriage was a life-cycle stage peculiar to both Catholic women and a particular historical moment. A distinctly 'modern' life cycle emerged in the decades after the Second World War – demographic statistics suggest that by the 1970s, British women were ending their period of childrearing at a considerably earlier stage than ever before. In the mid-nineteenth century the median age of women at the birth of their last child was about thirty-nine and many went on having children into their early forties. Even in the 1930s, women reaching the end of their childbearing were doing so on average at around the age of thirty-two. Those marrying after the Second World War, however, aided by a fall in the age of marriage, completed their childbearing significantly earlier, on average by about age twenty-eight. This left them with another expected fifty-two years of life. Michael Anderson linked this trend to the rise in women's economic status, as married women were afforded new opportunities to take up paid labour after full-time motherhood had ended.[1] It was also a trend which represented an extension of time and space for 'personal' considerations as opposed to familial duties. As the following chapter demonstrates, this modern life-cycle stage was of particular significance for the sexual and religious development of married Catholic women in post-war England.

Later marriage broadly denotes the years of sexual activity that came after the daily demands of childrearing had diminished.[2] The parameters of this life-cycle stage varied from person to person, but in general seem to have run from the interviewees' mid-thirties to sixties for those married in the immediate post-war years, beginning a little later for those married after the 1960s. Scholarly accounts of women and ageing tend to focus on the menopause.[3] However, the menopause did not represent a major topic of discussion in the interviews. This absence may have been a consequence of my own line of questioning and the social stigma that surrounds the subject, but, as this chapter suggests, it also reflected the way the interviewees chose to make sense of their lives. Rather than appealing to constructions of biology or fertility to delineate this life-cycle stage, later marriage is treated here as a category of the everyday – defined by familial routines, religious beliefs and, above all else, sexual experiences. As such, the chapter serves as a corrective to academic studies of female sexuality that devote more attention to younger than to older women.[4]

The divide between early and later marriage may be artificial, but it was one that came out of the interviews:

> Things didn't start coming together for me until my later marriage, my mid-forties. It was crucial that things changed at that stage because I was at breaking point. And they did.[5]

Although not always expressly using the terms 'early' and 'later' marriage as Doreen did, almost all the 'liberal' interviewees identified a clear break in their sexual development. This break was often but not always aligned with a change in contraceptive practice – most interviewees tied it in with the uptake of artificial means of contraception and the resulting removal of a fear of pregnancy. A handful remembered this break as being linked less to contraceptive behaviour and more a 'natural progression' that came through the passing of time. In both cases, what was emphasised was a 'liberation' from the confines of doctrinal obedience and a resulting resolution of the conflicts that had dogged their early married lives. This chapter interrogates what 'liberation' really meant for Catholic individuals, teasing out the complexities and contingencies that lay beneath this distinctly late-modern discourse.

The differing ways later marriage was remembered marked the key division between the 'liberal' and 'orthodox' interviewees. It was often at this stage that a 'liberal' Catholic identity was adopted whereas 'orthodox' interviewees tended to emphasise the continuities that ran throughout their married life. The discrepancies between the two groups have naturally received much attention, but I want to reflect on some of the commonalities that underpinned the way sex and religion were thought of by representatives of both. If we deconstruct the concept of Catholic 'sexual liberation', looking beyond the straightforward story of shifting power dynamics through which it is ordinarily understood, we find a process of active categorisation at its core. 'Liberals'' spoke of finally being able to separate their religious beliefs from their sexual morality in their later marriage, a distinction which was identified as the sole reason for the survival of their faith. Orthodox women, whilst taking an opposing view of 'categorisation', equally harnessed this discourse and saw it as an essential facet of 'liberal' Catholicism. Scratching below the surface of a liberation narrative, the notion of categorisation helps us rethink the way we understand the relationship between religious and sexual change in the post-war era. It raises the questions of what and who these categories were defined by, questions that this chapter moves towards answering.

The chapter begins by unpacking the interviewees' liberation stories at a discursive level, assessing the language and ideas that were used to construct this narrative. This is not done to construct what Penny Summerfield would label a 'false dichotomy' between discourse and experience, but to start from the moment of recollection which is inescapably linguistic, and then move to consider which elements of experience these memories can elucidate.[6] The overriding story of the interviews was one of sex replacing religion as the primary constituent of personal subjectivity, a narrative which fits neatly with Brown's and Taylor's models of post-war 'cultural revolution'.[7] The interviewees harnessed psychotherapeutic and popular 'liberationist' discourses to describe the 'discovery', 'realisation' or 'emancipation' of their sexual selves. The character of the 'self' was almost always constructed as an essentially sexual entity, an autonomous, instinctive operator for whom religious beliefs needed to fall in to line. Crucially, though, Catholic women remembered this reconceptualisation of individual identity as occurring in later marriage, rather than as a youthful 'coming of age'. It was a change that came out of gradual, often arduous physical experience rather than the liberating forces of a permissive ideology. Correspondingly, the change was often located in the 1970s rather than the 1960s. The 1970s, a somewhat forgotten decade in histories of post-war Britain, often overshadowed by its noisy neighbours the 1960s and 1980s, has enjoyed renewed attention in recent years.[8] The words and ideas of cultural elites at the vanguard of the swinging sixties did not speak for everyone, neither were they heard by everyone – many Catholics and non-Catholics had to wait a little longer for changes in their everyday lives to occur.

The second section of the chapter reconstructs the moments within which these changes in personal identity occurred. The interviewees' testimony placed a particular emphasis on the experiential when recalling changes in contraceptive practice and sexual behaviour. They were often eager to downplay the role of the new ideologies and texts they came across in the sixties, and stressed instead the operation of embodied physical and emotional sensibilities. These sensibilities were themselves inexorably linked to the material environment within which they existed – night-times, the bedroom, even the bed itself. The physical spaces that housed changes in contraceptive morality warrant as much historical attention as abstract, theological philosophies. Drawing on 'spatial' and 'materialist' methods recently developed in the histories of sexuality and religion respectively, we can see that these environments themselves have a history in the twentieth century. Recognising this contingency allows for a fuller picture of how Catholic beliefs on contraception were made up of an interaction between the theological and the material.

At the heart of Catholic women's disaffection with the clergy was the perception that priests could not understand or relate to the physical, embodied dimensions of marital sexuality. For many of the interviewees, this misgiving only fully formed in later marriage. As the final section demonstrates, the question of sexual experience was critical to the declining authority of the Catholic clergy in the post-war decades. The chapter therefore encourages us to rethink the way changing power dynamics within Catholicism are understood, emphasising the role of personal, embodied experiences rather than inanimate discursive ideologies in driving this process.

Stories of the self: narrating a Catholic liberation

The belief that the last sixty years have witnessed nothing short of a revolution in sexual behaviour and attitudes has become enshrined in popular and academic interpretations of post-1960s change. 'Sexual liberation' has developed into an axiomatic presence in the postulations of various historical, sociological and philosophical authorities, but is also a widely favoured rhetoric for 'ordinary' men and women. It is a story which the symbolic interactionist Ken Plummer treats as just that; a story, the story, in fact, of the late-modern individual. Plummer argues that within a web of competing and interacting narratives, 'libertarianism' has emerged as the dominant tale of our times: 'sex is now viewed as a joyous phenomenon, connected to personal health, happiness and self-fulfilment and social progress, [we have moved] towards a feminisation of sex, ultimately towards a democratisation of intimacy'.[9] Brown would agree with Plummer when he says that this narrative was produced in the transformatory social and cultural setting of the 1960s, but would contend that it was inescapably bound up with the rejection of religious commitment – it is a life story reserved for secularising, 'modern' individuals.

The interviewees' testimonies represented a clear and often-expressed refutation of Brown's indictment.[10] At the heart of all but five interviews was a story of emancipatory personal change. The 'liberal' interviewees readily constructed their own Catholic liberation narratives, describing a change from authoritarianism to conscience, from sensual repression to expression. Indeed, the zeal with which the interviewees pursued this optimistic life story offers an indication of how pervasive an exclusively secular reading of it has become. Phrases like 'I bet you didn't expect me to say that' and 'you may be shocked to know that I …' were common – the interviewees' candour was a conscious challenge to dominant readings of Catholic women's sexual oppression.[11] They wanted to shock me, a desire which tells us something important about how they felt Catholic women were perceived.

Questions about the use, production and validity of a 'liberation narrative' have abounded. Marxist and 'post-Marxist' scholars alike have sought to denude it of its Whiggish implications and show it to be an illusionary fiction – post-structuralists have asked whether 'liberation' can ever have a unified meaning, while Foucauldian scholars have argued that this emancipation has created new and more insidious forms of regulation and control.[12] I am not interested in assessing the authenticity of this story, but intend to treat it as a historical artefact in itself. Focusing on the language that the interviewees drew on when composing these narratives, we can situate ideas about human sexuality and religious authority within their wider historical context. Amidst the array of questions that have been levelled at a liberation narrative, I address a simple and yet underexplored question here: what exactly was it that was liberated? This line of enquiry allows us to get at the changing relationship between sex and identity for Catholic women in the post-war years.

When describing the changes in both religious and sexual development that occurred in later marriage, many of the interviewees started using a particular word for the first time in the interview: 'self'. It should be stressed that I did not use this word in my questions or project description – it was a discourse that the interviewees selected of their own volition. The term 'self' has become a staple feature of socio-scientific, historical and wider intellectual vocabularies in the last sixty years. Grace Janzen calls it the 'thinly veiled usurper of the "soul". In this way, the "self" has often been considered a symbol of secularism's triumph over religion'.[13] For scholars such as Nicolas Rose, the discourse of the self was symptomatic of an emergent psychotherapeutic culture which replaced Christianity as the dominant moral resource for individuals in the first half of the twentieth century.[14] As Michael Kimmel notes, however, it was not until the late 1960s that this discourse began to infiltrate popular consciousness and, with this, take on a revised meaning.[15] The sociologists Walter Gagnon and John Simon published their seminal work *Sexual Conduct* in 1970, which, similarly to Freud fifty years earlier, observed that sex had become a central building block in people's identities.[16] But Gagnon and Simon were to turn Freud on his head, arguing that it was less biological urges that drove sexual experience and more a complex set of cultural scripts which gave meaning to these urges.[17] The constructionism that underpinned their research, as well as the umbrage taken with Freudian behaviourism, was indicative of the wider social climate they were working within. It is between these two readings of a 'sexual self', a term used by both Freud and Gagnon and Simon, that we find the best description of the form of subjectivity that the interviewees constructed. They represented a generation who were conscious that their identity was a 'storied' construction that had been shaped by a mass-mediated, post-1960s sexual culture. The 'story' that Catholic women subscribed to above and beyond any other was one of sexuality being an essential, biological force that drove their identity and consciousness, with religion being defined as a 'side', 'aspect' or 'object' of this autonomous operator.

The Catholic sexual self

A liberation narrative was not unanimously subscribed to by the interviewees, with the five 'orthodox' Catholics all expressly resisting it to varying degrees. Elizabeth had this to say:

> I have always felt 'female emancipation' was a misplaced concept. I have always felt free – trained and practised as an Architect without any barriers, chose my boyfriends, husband, lived independently from age eighteen, treasured my virginity until marriage, never used contraception.[18]

Elizabeth's sense of individual autonomy may have been indicative of a specifically middle-class Catholic experience. Nevertheless, the 'orthodox' interviewees were all eager to stress how their sexual behaviour had not been produced by blind, doctrinal obedience but represented a set of choices that they were free to make. Many displayed a real sense of anger at the paternalistic suppositions that were bound up with a discourse of necessary 'liberation'.

Questioning the virtues of 'liberal' Catholicism was not limited to the orthodox interviewees. We saw in the opening passages of this book how Margaret, a proudly 'liberal' Catholic, expressed uncertainties and ambivalences about her chosen religious belief system. She described the pre-conciliar years as 'dark ages' where Catholics blindly followed laws and rules with no sense of 'ownership' over their faith.[19] However, the process of remembering seemed to undermine the optimism with which she spoke of her apparent emancipation. There was a clear sense of nostalgia to her recollections when she explained that:

> I suppose I have become a sort of pick and mix Catholic, I don't feel guilty anymore if I miss Mass on Sunday, I don't agree with a lot of the things the Church says, I think there should be women priests, I think there should be married priests. And, you know, I find it very difficult to … you see I … I didn't use to question things like, whether the resurrection actually took place, or think Adam and Eve is a mess so why do we need to be redeemed, I never thought of those, I probably never would have thought of them had it not been for the Council [Vatican II].[20]

Margaret's questioning of her 'pick and mix' Catholicism chimed with a recent trend in the wider historiography of the post-war period. Avner Offer, among others, has challenged the apparent virtues of increased 'choice' in the middle decades of the twentieth century. He argued that the 'affluence' of 1940s and 1950s Britain did not amount to an improvement in 'well-being'. In fact, the capacity for personal and social commitment was undermined by the 'flow of novelty' according to Offer, as expanded options brought new challenges to interpersonal relations, psychological health and heterosexual love:

> Affluence breeds impatience, and impatience undermines well-being … the paradox of affluence and its challenge is that the flow of new rewards can undermine the capacity to enjoy them.[21]

Just as Margaret reframed the way she interpreted her 'pick and mix' Catholicism in her later years, so Offer encouraged us to reassess the way material 'freedom of choice' is gauged and evaluated. The values that underpin a narrative of 'liberation', a narrative which dominates the historiographies of both post-war Catholicism and English society, are destabilised by these accounts of personal change.

Nevertheless, Margaret and the 'orthodox' interviewees represented a select minority within the sample in the way they interpreted post-war cultural change. 'Liberal' interviewees used a range of phrases to describe a change in their sex lives, the most popularly referenced, although not necessarily unreservedly subscribed to, being 'sexual liberation': 'I was not sexually liberated until, well almost my forties. It took that long!'[22] This interviewee was typical of many in that she was aware that her own 'liberation' occurred at a later stage than that of 'normal', non-Catholic women. There was also a sense of inevitability about the way she remembered her transition which accorded with popular teleological narratives of sexual emancipation.[23] Other 'liberals' were less comfortable with this descriptor. Lynn explained that she did not begin to enjoy sex until the later stages of her marriage when she suddenly uncovered her 'potential', but described 'sexual liberation' as 'your [the interviewer's] phrase'. She preferred instead the word 'maturing': 'I matured, I grew up. Simple as that.' Although I did use the phrase 'sexual liberation' in the interview, it was always in the context of describing other historians' views and was appended with physical quotation marks. I even made it clear at the start of the interview that it was a phrase I wanted to interrogate through the interviews. Lynn's 'your' grouped me together with other academic appraisals of women's sexuality, of which, she explained, she was often sceptical. Lynn was later to accede that the term liberation fairly described her experience after all, and went on to reflect on her reluctance to use the term – she did not want to render herself and other Catholic women passive objects 'in need of freeing'. She stressed that 'It was something I did, I decided and it took me a long time to work round.'[24] This will to take ownership of her liberation rather than attributing it to external cultural, political or technological forces represented a common theme within the interviews.

Aside from 'liberation', phrases such as 'freeing up', 'release' and 'emancipation' were used to describe a momentous shift in the interviewees' sex lives during later marriage. Although these linguistic divergences reflected the heterodox and varying nature of the changes that were described, there were also significant commonalities in the interviewees' liberation narratives. It should be noted that it was an ostensibly positive change that was remembered. This assessment may seem a little obtuse, but what was described was a transition from being 'unhappy', 'unsatisfied' and 'frustrated' to 'happy', 'free' and 'fulfilled'. It was a story of discovering, uncovering or increasing physical and emotional pleasure. Sarah explained that she had never had an orgasm before she reached her late thirties:

> Sarah I never, never, never, never had an orgasm, can you believe that! And my sister hasn't either still, I mean I have since, with a vengeance!
> DG Really, did you know what it was, then?
> Sarah I didn't until it began to click, I remember on holiday we discovered something that made me feel really nice, and then I recalled then when I was a little girl in the war, dying to go to the loo, and then this wonderful feeling, when I was eight or nine this was, I dare say school children now go through the same thing, and little boys, and I hadn't connected that little feeling with what was happening when you made love.
> DG When did you make that connection, then?
> Sarah Erm … I suppose after we'd been married and had all the children, it had never dawned on me before.[25]

A 'sexual awakening' was even framed in a positive light by an interviewee for whom this process resulted in the annulment of her marriage. June explained that her marriage had 'worked fine' when she and her husband had 'things to do' in their thirties, but that they both 'went off the rails' in their forties: 'I wasn't really awakened sexually until I had my children, and then you begin to realise "what am I missing".'[26] Both she and her husband had affairs at this stage – it was only with this second partner that June 'achieved an orgasm' (mirroring the language of Margaret). June spoke of the pain that the breakup of her marriage caused her and her family, but again emphasised how she thanked God every day that she had been through the process: 'the real shame is that we didn't ... recognise, didn't recognise ourselves earlier'.[27]

The expression 'recognise ourselves' was symptomatic of a second commonality that ran through many of the interviewees' liberation narratives. Both Sarah and June remembered their sexual awakenings as acts of self-discovery. Indeed, the word 'self' was startlingly prevalent in many of the interviewees' recollections. Anne decided to go on the pill after having eight children: 'I don't think I had fully discovered my full self until this happened.'[28] We will be delving deeper into Anne's change later in the chapter, but at this point I want to examine what exactly this 'self' was that was being discovered. It was a process of 'discovering', 'uncovering' and 'recognising' that tended to be described, as opposed to 'becoming' or 'creating' a new identity. What was implied through this choice of words was a sense of a single, fixed self that had previously been hidden or oppressed but could be illuminated through sexual experience.

Sexual fulfilment was not merely positioned as the vehicle of self-realisation but also the core constituent of this identity. Mary described what she termed her 'sexual enlightenment' in this way:

> I look back on those early years of marriage and can hardly recognise myself! I was a different person. It was not until those years after the children left that I discovered who I really was, who I really am![29]

Although not always set out as directly as this, many of the interviewees echoed Mary in remembering a change in their sex lives as the defining point in the formation of their person they thought themselves to be.

Even amongst the orthodox interviewees, sexuality was understood to be inherently 'personal', a facet of experience that held a particular relationship with individual identity. Elizabeth had converted from Anglicanism, leaving the Church of England at the age of eighteen, having spent two years researching and eventually adopting Catholic interpretations of biblical instruction on matters such as transubstantiation. Despite this theological adherence to what she considered the 'literal truth of the Gospel', she believed that sexual morality, notably contraceptive practice, was a matter for individual conscience rather than doctrinal law:

> DG Do you feel that people who don't 'practise the faith' [use artificial means] should be refused communion?
> Elizabeth No I don't feel that. On this matter, I don't really feel it's a sin unless one feels personally it's a sin, which I just do.³⁰

Elizabeth accorded with 'liberal' Catholics in the way she separated out sexual morality from other matters of faith and endowed it with a distinctively personal, subjective significance.

How then do these personal accounts of Catholic 'self-discovery' relate to wider, historical narratives of sexual change? The link that the interviewees forged between sexuality and individual identity is one that has been considered a peculiarly 'modern' phenomenon by a host of sexual theorists. For the likes of Foucault and Thomas Laqueur, this form of subjectivity was born at the turn of the century with the emergence of new regimes of expertise and inspection such as psychology, sociology and criminology.³¹ The interviewees' testimony seems to substantiate this hypothesis in some ways – the discourse of the 'self' that proved so popular among the interviewees had an undeniably Freudian flavour to it. Indeed, 'orthodox' interviewees adhered to this psychoanalytical discourse to a greater degree than the liberals. Returning to Elizabeth, she explained that the pill and its 'sexual liberation' had ushered in an era of unbridled hedonism with little regard for morals and meaning:

> As far as sex is concerned, I don't think one should sleep around. It's a precious commodity and once a girl sleeps around it devalues it for her as well as everything else it then becomes nothing, it's like will you have a cigarette or a sweet, which I think is terrible and very sad, because they no longer have any other meaning to it, it's animal.³²

Elizabeth repeatedly returned to the word 'animal' to describe the state of women's 'liberated' sexuality, juxtaposing this with the 'self-restraint' that Catholicism encouraged. Both 'orthodox' and 'liberal' Catholics positioned sexuality as the mainspring of an animalistic, instinctive self. For 'orthodox' women this self was to be resisted and mastered through Catholic commitment, just as the Pope had encouraged in *Humanae Vitae*. For 'liberals', this self was to be discovered and expressed as a means of augmenting Catholic commitment. Either way, sex lay at the core of the human self.

In variance with Foucault and Laqueur's models, many of the interviewees made a claim for this modern, sexualised self emerging in the course of their own lifetimes rather than sixty years earlier. As one interviewee said:

> Things are never going to be like they were for my mother's generation. Sex has changed so much in the last fifty years, it's so important now, it's everything to you and your marriage. I just don't think it was the same, being a Catholic, in my parents' time.[33]

If both liberal and orthodox interviewees constructed their selfhood as essentially sexual, they also agreed that this was a connection which had really only solidified in the post-war years for Catholics. The idea that Catholics 'lagged behind the rest of society' in terms of their personal sexual identities is one that has been advanced by the likes of Hera Cook and Michael Hornsby-Smith.[34] However, we should be cautious when defining this as an exclusively Catholic anomaly. Various historians of modern Britain have argued that new modes of 'self-fashioning' emerged in the course of the twentieth century.[35] Stevi Jackson speaks of a truly 'sexual self' only emerging in the decades after the 1960s, when a proliferation of 'sexual scripts' were thrust into peoples' consciousness by various cultural agencies.[36] The operation of the mass media was not lost on the interviewees – Doreen pointed to the 'modern obsession with sex in films and the media' making it (sex) an 'inescapable part of everyone'.[37] Ken Plummer maintains that Foucault's account 'neglects the rise of mass media in all its diverse forms [which Plummer argues 'took off' in the 1960s] and it provides little space for the generation of particular kinds of stories at different times'.[38] While the 'sexual self' that the interviewees composed in the course of the interviews demonstrated the continuing currency of a Freudian-behaviourist notion of human nature for a particular Catholic generation, it should also be viewed as a 'storied' construct that reflected the way Catholic subjectivities had been reshaped by a burgeoning post-war sexual culture. Whether traced back to the start of the century or considered a specifically sixties phenomenon, sex had assumed an unprecedented position in Catholic self-identities by the start of the 1980s.

Religious belief in later marriage

The emergence of this sexual self held profound implications for the religious belief systems of Catholic women. Charles Taylor has argued that since the 1960s an era of 'expressive individualism' has taken hold in the West, in which religious practice is not only viewed as a personal choice but also must make sense in terms of one's 'spiritual development'.[39] According to Taylor, religiosity must now enable the 'pursuit of happiness', happiness which is increasingly defined by sensual and sexual fulfilment.[40] Catholic women experienced profound changes in the way they lived out their faith in this era. These changes often coincided with the 'sexual awakenings' of later marriage and were recalled in a similar language of enlightenment and emancipation. However, housed within these stories of spiritual transformation was a reconceptualisation of the religious. 'Liberal' interviewees described a process of 'compartmentalisation' that saw their Catholic religiosity, in terms of a set of beliefs, experiences and sentiments, positioned in a new, extrinsic category. While this process of compartmentalisation was identified as something of a life-vessel for their Catholic identity, it also formed a lasting divide between matters of faith and the body.

Teresa, who had spoken about later marriage as the point at which she began to realise what she was 'missing' sexually, explained that her religiosity hardly changed at all from her youth until she was in her mid-forties:

> At that time it was crucial, at that time if I had not developed some sort of spiritual life, sort of personal relationship with God ...[41]

Teresa trailed off here, but it was clear that she attributed the survival of her faith to the changes that occurred in her later marriage. A key manifestation of this 'spiritual life' was a change in her 'prayer life' – a phrase which mirrored the more colloquially used 'sex life'. She described a shift from 'box ticking' to a 'personalised' form of prayer which related to her everyday life:

> So I would be saying, in those early years of marriage I would be saying my prayers but it was the box mentality, you know, saying my prayers to God were all about adoration and confession, not necessarily linked to my day-to-day living.

Prayer shifted from a routine of doctrinal reassertion to something that informed and was informed by Teresa's 'day-to-day' living. Although personal petitions had always been a part of their worship, many of the interviewees were praying about everyday events more than ever before by the later stages of their marriage, addressing topics such as 'family health', 'the kids' sport results' and 'things at work'.[42] This movement towards an active prayer life where prayers were constructed by the individual represented a common feature of many of the interviewees' later marriages. Teresa pin-pointed the moment when this personalised form of faith emerged:

> I went to confession at this Walsingham conference, I must have been approaching fifty at the time, and this lovely priest and he said, instead of these two 'Hail Marys' and one 'Our Father' sort of thing, for your penance, I want you to just go out and look at the crucifix and say, you did this for me. Well ... you know, I use that such a lot you know, but everyone can say that, you did this for me so that was when I started to develop a spiritual life, but the formal vehicles of the Church, actually no help at all (chuckles) I've actually never thought of it like that before, but no help at all.[43]

Teresa, like so many other interviewees, remembered later marriage as a period when her faith started to work for her rather than her for it. She became the agent within her beliefs, with her the 'doer' and her beliefs the 'done to'. This shift was remembered positively, just as her 'sexual liberation' had been, and allowed her to maintain her Catholic identity at a time when it was losing its meaning.

The declining devotion to a formalised version of prayer was exemplified by changing attitudes towards the rosary. Katherine said the rosary on a regular basis in her early marriage – she recalled attending the Rosary Crusade at West Ham's football ground Upton Park with her family as a teenage girl.[44] The Rosary Crusade was initiated in 1952 – as many as 100,000 spectators gathered at Wembley Stadium to hear the words of its charismatic leader, Fr Patrick Peyton. A key component of the crusade mission was encouraging the family to say the rosary together every day, which it espoused under the mantra 'The Family that Prays Together Stays Together'. Aside from the distinctly 'pre-conciliar' connection between Catholic ideals and traditional family values that Alana Harris has explored in relation to this movement, the Rosary Crusade epitomised the reassertion of a certain type of formalised but also communal prayer that was to become increasingly obsolete in the following decades.[45] When asked how her prayer life had changed, Katherine's first response was: 'Well I ditched the rosary! Vatican II was a big boost for my faith in that way!'[46] Other interviewees spoke of their distaste for the rosary's repetitiveness: 'It was so boring! The main challenge was making sure my sister didn't make me laugh in it.'[47]

It was not just boredom that typified the interviewees' memories of the rosary, but a deeper problem with the form of religiosity that it represented. Georgina described it as a way of 'controlling your mind and time through repetition' and this psychologically oppressive interpretation of the rosary was echoed by many respondents:[48]

> I remember thinking, not too long ago, maybe just fifteen years ago, that this is a waste of my time and God's time. It does not relate to my life, my self, in any way.[49]

We see the term 'self' appear again here – the issue that many Catholic women developed with the rosary and formalised prayer in general was its inability to relate to their individual lives. There were interviewees for whom the rosary remained an important part of their worship. Sorcha still said the rosary on a weekly basis, explaining that as a child she 'never used to think too much about it'. Since her children had grown up she had started devoting each decade [one 'Our Father', ten 'Hail Marys' and one 'Glory be to the Father'] to a member of her family, often one of her grandchildren. 'It means more to me that way, I concentrate harder … it makes it something real to me.'[50] Even amongst those who continued to say the rosary, its meaning had been augmented by a personalisation in their later marriage. The compulsion to take ownership of prayer, to link it to personal, subjective experience represented a defining feature of Catholic women's religious development.

While the 'self' provided the object of many of the interviewees' changing religiosities, the word 'questioning' was often used to describe the process through which this self was realised. For Marian, her 'questioning' was a point of pride and reflected the strength of her faith compared to her more 'orthodox' mother:

> My mother, actually didn't have the same, didn't have as much faith as me and therefore didn't question as much as me, to question you must have faith.[51]

In keeping with her 'liberal' Catholic identity, 'questioning' was interpreted by Marian as not only an enabler but also the consequence of a quantifiably stronger faith. A number of the interviewees spoke of their mothers not being able to question in the way they had. In this way, the interviewees positioned themselves as the pivotal generation in the development of women's Catholicism – the group that permanently dismantled an infantile, restrictive form of religiosity. They spoke of how women encountered more resistance to 'questioning' than men. Katherine recalled asking a question at a prayer group in the late 1960s and being told by one of the leaders of the group ' "not to worry or else you'll get in a muddle". I said "I don't mind getting in a muddle!" That was the point!'[52]

In the course of many of the 'liberal' interviewees' later marriage, their Catholic faith had become thought of as a set of questions rather than answers. This transition was often remembered in a positive, liberating light, as the process that resurrected their dwindling Catholic affiliation. Implicitly tied up with this 'liberation', though, was the erection of a conceptual divide between their religious beliefs and sense of self. Throughout the interviews their religiosity was defined as an 'aspect', 'side' or 'part' of their lives. Teresa's use of the phrase 'prayer life' was indicative of the active compartmentalisation that many of the liberal interviewees employed when discussing their religiosity.[53] When I explained at the start of our interview that I was interested in uncovering the reciprocal links that exist between religious and sexual experiences, she intervened with: 'But there aren't many links if it's all in compartments … It only informs it in a negative way.' She went on to explain that her faith could only survive by 'completely separating my faith out from myself'.[54] 'Compartments', 'categories' and 'separations' were key terms that the liberal interviewees drew on when composing their narratives of personal religious development.

In direct contrast, Elizabeth stressed how she could never compartmentalise her sexual and religious experiences. When she spoke of her 'repulsion' at the idea of the pill distorting her 'body's natural rhythms', I asked whether it was more of a physical rather than spiritual issue that she had with it. She stressed emphatically that the two could not be separated: 'Well I think they were one and the same thing, you mustn't compartmentalise.'[55] Elizabeth was the first 'orthodox' interviewee I had spoken to and my line of questioning was evidently tailored to a 'liberal' response. She returned to the language of compartmentalisation later in the interview: 'I've never felt that my life is compartmented ... I've not divided anything up and I'm not divided with my faith either because I am just one person.'[56] This discourse of 'compartmentalising' or 'categorising' was a key point of divergence between the 'liberal' and 'orthodox' interviewees. Just as with the 'self', both sets of women used the term, but with directly opposing attitudes towards it.

For many liberal Catholic women, later marriage saw their faith move into a new conceptual space. It was a space that was defined by two key features. It stood outside their sense of self, a set of abstract questions and codes to be interrogated by this central agent. It was also a space that was juxtaposed to the physical, profane demands of sexuality. In many ways, the interviewees' testimony seems to substantiate Charles Taylor's philosophical postulations. The idea of 'expressive individualism', whereby religious beliefs needed to fit in with the quest for personal self-discovery, was a conspicuous presence in almost all the interviews.[57] The apparent virtues of this liberated state were not unanimously subscribed to, though, with the interviewees critiquing, challenging and problematising its apparent virtues. In a post-1960s setting, a 'liberation narrative' became an unavoidable discourse for Catholic individuals, providing a point of reference within and against which their religious identities could be defined.

If this section has remained couched at a level of discourse, the next uses the interviewees' testimony to reconstruct that enigmatic elixir of the oral historian – lived experience. It moves on to provide a closer examination of the moments within which these religious and sexual changes occurred, focusing on a topic that was at the centre of every interview without exception: birth control.

Changes in contraceptive morality

The advent of affordable, effective means of birth control has been frequently identified as the defining feature of a 'sexual revolution'. In her seminal book *The Long Sexual Revolution*, Hera Cook argued that the introduction of 'reliable contraception' was a 'substantial improvement, amounting to a transformation, in the lives of English women over the past two centuries'.[58] Cook maintained that the pill in particular offered women in England a previously unparalleled means of separating sex from procreation: 'It increased the control of fear and allowed a greater experience of pleasure and increased emotional aspirations.'[59] This association between the pill and the idea of a 'sexual revolution' was echoed in the interviews. When asked what the term 'sexual revolution' meant to them, both 'liberal' and 'orthodox' interviewees promptly spoke of the pill: 'Well it was all bound up with the contraceptive pill', 'The pill was very important I think.'[60] Bridget never used the pill herself and opposed it on religious grounds, but recognised that 'the change it has wrought for women has been absolutely revolutionary, oh yes, revolutionary'.[61] Although Lara Marks points out that it is now commonplace for the pill to be identified as the 'catalyst of the revolution', it seems the matter of birth control holds a position of particular, inflated significance in Catholic women's image of post-war history.[62]

At the heart of the personal sexual and religious changes that the 'liberal' interviewees described was the subject of birth control. The decision to use artificial means of contraception was remembered by many interviewees as the key that unlocked their 'sexual self'. Of the twenty-seven individuals spoken to, twenty-one took up contraception during their marriage, having previously abstained from it for religious reasons. For nineteen of the interviewees, this decision was one that was not taken until later marriage. It was the defining factor that marked a break in their marital narratives. The following section explores how these personally and historically ground-breaking decisions were made, paying a close attention to the explanations that the interviewees emphasised.

In accordance with Cook's assertions, the decision to take up artificial means of birth control was remembered as one that greatly increased the experience of sexual pleasure. Just under half of the interviewees explained that they did not have an orgasm until after taking up artificial means of birth control, in most cases the pill. Lynn explained that:

> I didn't find my sexual power, orgasm, until I had made the decision to go on the pill. So that's maybe an interesting point for you ... but that was in the seventies, that wasn't in the sixties.[63]

The 1970s are now increasingly regarded as the decade in which the headline-grabbing innovations of the 1960s infiltrated the everyday lives of 'ordinary' men and women. As Emily Robinson and her co-authors have shown, the decade saw many in Britain express greater desires for and expectations of personal autonomy and self-fulfilment.[64] The pill offered Catholic women a means of satisfying these desires, of finding power: in Lynn's words, of finding 'sexual power'. Lynn emphasised how much of an 'inhibitor' the fear of pregnancy had been in her early marriage, claiming that 'I'm sure a lot of women my age would tell you that.'[65] Katherine tried the pill when she was in her mid-thirties, but finding that the 'chemicals didn't agree' with her, started using condoms. Again emphasising the positive experiential impact of contraception, she found that 'sex was so much more pleasurable after that. The fear had gone and it became a completely different experience.'[66]

The significance of the decision to use artificial means of contraception was found not simply in the heightened sexual pleasure it enabled, but also the fundamental rupture it signified in the relationship between the interviewees' Catholic religiosity and sexual morality. For many Catholics, it was the first time they had knowingly contravened the Church's official teaching:

> It was the starting point really. I remember thinking, if the Church is wrong about this, it could be wrong about other things.[67]

The subject of birth control therefore stood at the cornerstone of the 'liberal' interviewees' life stories and their continuing religious identities. The way these changes in contraceptive theology have been explained by various intellectual authorities reveals much about how the religious and the sexual have been understood in a post-war setting.

Just as for David Lodge's characters hell suddenly disappeared in the 1960s – 'it was there one minute and gone the next' – so contraception went from being 'intrinsically evil', to not 'intrinsically evil' for large swathes of Britain's Catholic community in an equally abrupt and definitive manner.[68] Almost all of the liberal interviewees stressed two distinctive features of this shift. One: that they entirely and earnestly believed in the early years of their marriage that artificial means of birth control were sinful and would prevent them from achieving salvation. Their change in attitude was not the realisation of a repressed belief in the legitimacy of contraception that had always been harboured in some way, and I will not be probing into the realms of their subconscious or even unconscious with an amateur psychoanalytical flashlight. Two: the change itself was remembered as strikingly sudden; all the liberal interviewees acknowledged a longer period of 'questioning' that varied in length from a few weeks to over a decade, but the decision itself was defined by a resolute immediacy. In the following section, we will interrogate the interplay between these gradual and transient factors, between the temporal and the linguistic explanations that the interviewees identified.

The testimony of the interviewees suggests that historians need to accommodate the temporal, emotional and experiential components of these highly subjective decisions. As we have seen, intellectual appraisals of personal religiosity tend to privilege the discursive over the experiential. From Émile Durkheim at the start of the twentieth century through to Peter Berger at its end, social scientists have continually attributed changes in religious belief to the operation of liberating ideas and languages.[69] Despite his intention to break away from pejorative sociological readings of religion, Brown's model of 'discursive Christianity' is also predicated on this discursive approach. The women I spoke to acknowledged the importance of the new ideas they came across in the 1960s, but their testimony placed an emphasis on the actual moment within which these changes occurred. Oral history allows us to revisit these moments, mapping the physical locations they occurred within and the feelings they were constituted by. As we have seen in the previous chapter, material and emotional aspects of intimate experience received surprisingly little attention in the Catholic birth-control debate of the 1960s. When attempting to understand Catholic women's shifts in personal religiosity, the questions of where and when may be just as valuable as why and how.

To help us get at the intricacies of Catholic women's contraceptive changes, the testimony of a single interviewee will serve as a 'telling case'. This interviewee's memories will serve as a springboard from which to discuss those of the other interviewees. The difference between a 'telling' case and a 'typical' case has been outlined by Dorothy Sheridan, Brian Street and David Bloome in their analysis of qualitative material gathered for the Mass Observation Project:

> The search for a 'typical' case for analytical exposition is likely to be less fruitful than the search for a 'telling' case in which the particular circumstances surrounding a case serve to make previously

obscured theoretical relationships suddenly apparent. Case studies used in this way are clearly more than 'apt illustrations'. Instead, they are means whereby general theory may be developed.[70]

As such, the following excerpt has been selected not simply because it illuminates aspects of Catholic marital experience, but because it provides a unique insight into the way this experience has been, and can be, understood by intellectual observers. At this point, I would like to introduce Anne. Anne had eight children between 1950 and 1965, the first born when she was twenty. She described herself as a practising 'liberal Catholic' who attended church on a Sunday all her life. Anne lived in a few small towns in the south of England and described her background as 'working class'.[71] Up to the point in the interview that we will be attending to, our discussion had largely consisted of Anne detailing the great pain and suffering she had experienced while using NFP. She spoke of the 'immense emotional and physical frustration' that she and her husband felt in the periods when they could not have sex. She also spoke of the resulting pressure and lack of spontaneity felt when they could, which led to instances of impotence, premature ejaculation and an inability for both partners to climax.[72] Although she explained that more often than not sex was 'fabulous' and 'very physically satisfying' throughout her marriage, by the time Anne had had her eighth child, the fear of another pregnancy was leaving her in a state of 'perpetual turmoil in her own bedroom'.[73] When I asked Anne why she had not used a form of contraception, she stated simply 'Well, I thought it was wrong. I thought it was completely wrong.'[74]

Anne recalled speaking about her contraceptive troubles in confession at some point in the middle of the 1960s. The priest encouraged her to go on the pill. I commented that it must have been rare for a priest to give advice that explicitly contravened the Church's existing teaching, but Anne stressed emphatically that it was not rare at all – such was the prevailing belief that a change in the Church's teaching was imminent. I then asked Anne how she responded to this advice, and whether she did go on the pill. This was her response:

> I didn't at that time. I should think it was nearly a year before I really got there. And it ... I read everything I could read. I just read around, I've never not been a reader. And ... I read and I prayed, I prayed in agony. I don't think, I don't think anybody

can know the agony that women who wanted to be true to God, true to their beliefs went through. And I can remember exactly when I changed my mind. I was kneeling saying my prayers in the evening, by my bed, as I used to at that time, and I was thinking when we get into bed we're going to make love, I knew it, I just knew it ... and ... I thought ... I cannot remember the words ... but I was really tormented ... and then I suddenly had a flash – 'don't worry, forget it, don't worry, don't worry any more about this ever, about this, this ...' and I never have since. And I went straight to the doctor and asked to go on the pill.[75]

What kind of questions should the historian be asking in order to try and understand how changes in personal religiosity, like the one presented in Anne's rather startling recollection, related to their wider historical context? By that I do not simply mean which questions should be asked in the interview, but the intellectual frameworks within which this piece of testimony should be placed.

The use of the word 'flash' to describe the very moment of her change suggested both a suddenness and a sense of enlightenment. The link between secularisation narratives and a language of illumination is one that has been observed many times before. For Brown, it was the newly available ideas and discourses of 'sexual liberation' that provided British women with the necessary language to abruptly reject Christian moral codes and see the light.[76] Anne did speak of the reading she did to try and help her make sense of the situation she was in. She referenced the work of a collection of progressive Catholic writers that had emerged in the 1960s who were attempting to marry the discourses of sexual liberation with Catholic thought. Writers like Jack Dominian, an eminent relationship psychologist and Catholic layman, presented a new theology on married love that valued the centrality of healthy sexual expression to a loving and godly marriage. These authors argued that there were legitimate grounds in existing Catholic teachings to see the use of contraception as a means to facilitating such a union.[77]

How much weight should we grant these new languages of Catholic morality in bringing about Anne's change then? Certainly, this emergent culture introduced Anne and many Catholic women of her generation to an unprecedented set of questions about the authority of the Church in matters of sex. Lynn spoke of the importance of reading Jack

Dominian's book *The Church and the Sexual Revolution* (first published in 1967) to her own sense of 'liberation': 'The theology of pleasure being part of God's design and sexual intimacy being conducive to a lasting marriage ... that was crucial.'[78] Having completed a PhD in feminist literature herself, Lynn engaged comfortably with the language of cultural theory. She went on to reflect on the role of 'discourse' in bringing about her change: 'I didn't even have the discourse ... you can't express things if the discourse is not available to you.'[79]

However, many of the interviewees stressed that they did not come across the work of Jack Dominian or any of the other liberal Catholic theologians until well after the 1960s. Indeed, for a large majority of the interviewees, these theological writings were not properly engaged with until after they took up artificial means of birth control. Patricia explained that:

> I was sort of ... aware of Dominian's stuff at that time [the 1960s], people were talking about him, but I didn't really sit down and read it for myself until much later, in the eighties at least, after I'd been on the pill for almost ten years.[80]

The general feeling was that the work of these authors confirmed existing beliefs rather than forged them in the first place. Joan stated that 'I think Jack Dominian's ideas confirmed what I already knew to be the case. It helped me fit things together, but I had already made my mind up.'[81] Even for those that did read Dominian's work in the 1960s, they did not elaborate much on his writings. Mary was typical in the way her responses became notably brief when probed about the topic:

> DG In the 1960s, bound up with the ideas of Vatican II, 'liberal' Catholics were talking about a new theology on married love, sex being about conjugal love as much as it is about procreation ...
> Mary Yes, well of course it is.
> DG I was wondering if you can remember whether you were aware of authors like Jack Dominian in the 1960s?
> Mary Oh yes yes, I know him.
> DG And you read his work in the 1960s?
> Mary Yes yes absolutely, and I was aware of the writings of your grandfather.

DG Yes he was producing similar stuff. I was wondering about how these new ideas about the Church's teaching on sex changed your views on things like contraception?
Mary It confirmed ideas I already had. What we had decided.
DG Did you read this literature a lot?
Mary I suppose a bit.[82]

We should recognise that like Mary, Anne also did not directly attribute her change to these 'liberal' writings. She did not actually spend much time talking about the progressive Catholic authors or their ideas at all, even when explicitly prompted later in the interview.[83] It may well have been a flash of wording that marked her shift in attitude, but before this flash, Anne flagged up the fact that she 'cannot remember the words.'[83] This could be interpreted as the consequence of a failing memory, but it could also be seen to reflect the aspects of this moment that Anne saw as significant. It seems peculiar that Anne would not remember the wording of her revelation when her memory was proficient enough to specify many other details about this and other experiences from the time. What I am suggesting is that the selections that are present in Anne's recollection of this 'flash' reveal the limited role of linguistic and abstracted discourses and emphasise the centrality of the temporal and emotional moment of experience. The questions that were raised by writers like Jack Dominian in the form of words and text still needed to be answered by Catholic women in the bedroom.

Foucault's seminal contributions to the history of sexuality provide another framework through which to understand Anne's testimony. Foucault maintains that Christianity did not introduce specific rules of sexual morality, such as an opposition to things like polygamy, homosexuality and the separation of sex and procreation (these ideas predated the emergence of organised Christianity, Foucault tells us), but introduced instead certain procedures of self-regulation for inculcating these moral codes. He describes these mechanisms as 'technologies of the self'; processes such as internalisation, alerting one's self to one's own weaknesses and the compulsion to perpetually confess a hidden truth of the self.[84] These processes offer a useful way of thinking about Anne's change – despite being fully conscious of the progressive theology on contraceptive morality that was available to her, the act of rejecting the Church's teaching was described as an internalised moment of self-articulation. Anne could only reject the Church's teaching by discarding the processes through which she governed and policed herself. She actually started using the word 'self' for the first time in the interview when talking about the period after her change. She recalled lying in bed on the night *Humanae Vitae* was published with her husband Paul, who Anne stressed always left contraceptive decisions up to her, and being asked what she was going to do. She explained to him that she had made her decision and 'believed in her whole self' that she was right – she maintained that she has not felt any guilt or remorse about her contraceptive behaviour since her moment of revelation.[85]

Do these recollections point to a historicised change in the way these 'technologies of the self' worked? This is an interesting question certainly, but there are a few problems with a Foucauldian reading of Anne's testimony. Foucault maintained that these procedures could only function through what he called the 'figure of the pastorate' – a spiritual authority who monitored and directed the moral well-being of society.[86] Anne's disregard for the authority of her pastor, the priest, was clear to see – even when she was explicitly told to go on the pill in confession, it was over a year before she actually made her decision. Foucault's approach may offer a useful alternative to the pervasive, 'top-down' model of power relations in which Catholic women are continually positioned as inert victims, but there is still a sense that they are being 'acted upon' rather than 'acting'. The external institutions and structures that are usually identified as the forces of governance are simply replaced by internalised, discursive regimes. Just as Brown's model of a 'cultural revolution' rendered Catholic women the irrational others of a secularising modernity, so a Foucauldian framework equally relegates the agency of religious individuals to a mere function of discourse.

The problem with privileging the discursive over the experiential when trying to explain a change in religious belief is that the essence of what an individual is stressing can be overlooked; in this case, the great physical and emotional suffering that Catholic women went through when attempting to keep to the Church's teaching. As Anne stated, 'I don't think anybody can know the agony that women who wanted to be true to God, true to their beliefs went through.'[87] In their efforts to intellectualise and textualise the decisions of Catholic women, the frameworks offered by Foucault and Brown down play the role of corporeal and emotive sensibilities. As we saw in the first chapter, the central hierarchy's attempt to 'know the agony', or at least the lived experiences, of Catholic women in the 1960s also overlooked these intimate aspects of personal experience. Surprisingly, this was even true of 'liberal' Catholic authorities who advocated a change in contraceptive doctrine. The next chapter on Catholic women's experiences during early marriage demonstrates how oral history, can resurrect these neglected drivers of personal and collective change.

Before this, though, I want to focus on what Anne did emphasise about this shift. Her testimony stressed a sudden, temporal moment of revelation. She chose to specify the time and space within which this moment occurred: 'And I can remember exactly when I changed my mind. I was kneeling saying my prayers in the evening, by my bed, as I used to at that time.'[88] When thinking about getting into the bed she was praying next to, sexual thoughts encroached on her religious reflections. The experiential proximity of sexual and spiritual activities in terms of time and space, provided not just the environment but also the very catalyst for Anne's change in thinking. I asked all the interviewees where and when they prayed and where and when they had sex in the early years of their marriage, and almost without exception they identified evenings and the bedroom as the settings for both. Anne spoke of starting to see her bedroom as a place of 'frustration and stress', and that she would often begin to feel this anxiety as it got dark.[89] Indeed, the thermometer and graph that Anne used to calculate her fertility was kept in the top draw of her bedside table alongside her Bible and rosary. If tensions and negotiations between spiritual and sexual activities occupied similar physical spaces for Catholic individuals, then decisions to reject the Church's teaching on contraception should be understood in the context of this material proximity.

Anne was not alone in speaking of the time and space in which sexual activities occurred; a remarkable number of the first set of interviewees specified these details when recalling contraceptive behaviour. In response, I began actively asking about 'where' and 'when'. It was as if these concrete details gave their memories a tangible framework from which to work. Certain neuroscientists would insist that human memory inherently looks to these stabilising points of reference, but the interviewees' tendency to dwell on time and place also spoke of the historical setting within which these shifts in contraceptive practice were lived and understood.[90] The spaces which accommodated contraceptive decisions were themselves constituent parts of these choices.

In more recent years, Catholic authorities have picked up on the spatial significance of the bedroom. A 2009 book published by the orthodox-minded Catholic Truth Society encourages couples to pray before sex, including a special prayer to help couples 'purify their intentions' amidst pre-coital passions. The 'Prayer Before Making Love' implores God 'to place within us love that truly gives, tenderness that truly unites, self-offering that tells the truth and does not deceive, forgiveness that truly receives, loving physical union that welcomes'.[91] It is impossible to say whether this prayer would have had any effect on the contraceptive practices of Anne and her 'liberal' Catholic contemporaries, but it does suggest that the bedroom rather than the pulpit or pew had become recognised as the real battleground for competing contraceptive moralities in late-modern England.

By later marriage, Catholic women had more time and space to consider their religious and sexual aspirations than ever before in their married life. Furthermore, they were living through a historical moment when religious contemplation, notably personal prayer, was concentrated into smaller and more specific spaces than it had been just twenty years earlier. They grew up in a world where religious ritual punctuated their days – when they woke up, before meals, at public functions – while many of the places they inhabited were graced with Catholic imagery – schools, women's groups, even many workplaces. By the late 1970s, though, many of these dedicated religious times and spaces had dissolved. Catholic women's religiosity had been forced into private spaces, private spaces which were also the domain of sexual activity.

In line with the movement away from traditional, communal forms of worship towards a personalised religiosity as described earlier in this chapter, the intimate space of the bedroom became increasingly viewed as the primary site for spiritual expression. By later marriage, other places of religious activity had either ceased to function in the same way or decreased in relevance. Lydia recalled that:

> When I was growing up we used to say a prayer in the classroom at the start of every lesson, you know, it was always there. And even when we were first married I used to pray with the kids on the way to school, say grace round the dinner table before all our meals. And of

course that was when going to church meant a lot more to me, it was the House of God. They all seemed to drift away later, it was all saved up for my nightly prayers in my bedroom.[92]

Nightly prayers in the bedroom were a popular practice amongst Catholic women, both housewives and those who had taken up paid employment in later marriage. As religious practice retreated from the public realm, so the bedroom emerged as a vital space within which these new, private religiosities could work.

Catholic couples' bedrooms were often adorned with more religious regalia than any other room in the house. Elizabeth kept a phial of holy water on her dressing-table beside her make-up and hairbrushes, while many of the interviewees had a crucifix nailed to the wall over their marital bed.[93] With Jesus' eyes cast down over the scene of sexual activity, religious reminders peppered the intimate landscape of Catholic marriage. Doreen had been taught by her mother to kneel and say her prayers by her bed every night, with her hands clasped together and her elbows resting on the bed. She stopped kneeling beside her bed at 'some point in her forties', saying her prayers when she was 'in bed, just as I went to sleep. After sex if it had happened.'[94] Even within the confines of the bedroom, prayer and sex were being pushed into closer proximity by later marriage. The top drawer of Anne's bedside table was typical for many Catholic women practising NFP. With thermometers, graphs, pencils, instruction manuals and tubs of Vaseline nestled amongst rosaries, bibles and prayer books, these spaces epitomised the confrontation and attempted conflation of sexual science and Catholic thought in the post-war decades. The sexual and the religious closeted away together, removed from the prying eyes of children and visitors and yet afforded a place of privilege alongside the marital bed.

Later marriage was typified by an increase in time available for the 'personal'. Just as Claire Langhamer has shown how women in the post-war period could pursue leisure activities more easily after their children had grown up, so sexual and religious concerns could also receive more attention at this point.[95] June spoke of how her evenings 'seemed to become longer' in her mid-forties.[96] Without the task of feeding and putting to bed young children, Catholic women found themselves with more time to not only have sex, but also contemplate the intricacies of their beliefs. Mary reflected on the spiritual significance of this time of the day:

> I suppose it's practicality – you're free from the hustle and bustle of the day. But there's also something else – it's also about the dark setting in, sleep drawing near. You think back on the day and put things in a different light … I've started reading a bit of the Bible every evening now.[97]

Many of the interviewees spoke of the evening and night as a time that brought to mind questions of faith. Angela reflected on how the moments before sleep brought into focus the mortal dimensions of her faith:

> Before you slip of into silence or sleep, so way after sex, so I say … I tell you what I often do, I say a little 'Hail Mary'. Because I've seen a lot of suffering, and death – and that's the best bit. 'Now and at the hour of our death' because who knows what's going to happen to you … and so I'm, I just put myself into the hands of God and I say I'm sorry if I've slipped up, that's a very Ignatian thing to say, you say sorry to cover your tracks, I'm sorry if I slipped up, I hope I sleep well, I'm not a long prayer, I pray succinctly but sincerely, and I sleep well.[98]

For some interviewees, the increased time available in evenings prompted them to think about matters of sexual morality specifically. Mary explained that:

> [T]he evening was when I did most of my thinking about these things [the Church's stance on contraception]. It just happened that way as I grew older, that was when I really started to think about things properly, to reflect on what I really thought.[99]

Weekends were also freed up from the demands of various family duties. Sunday had always been a particularly busy day for Catholic mothers in the early years of their marriage, with Church attendance in the morning followed by the preparation, eating and washing-up of Sunday lunch. Sunday evenings were dedicated to getting the family ready for the week ahead, with little time or energy left for sex. Lydia recalled that once her children had reached their late teens, her Sundays had become 'suspiciously tranquil', and with this, a day free for 'amorous time-wasting'.[100] Brown has argued that Sunday was a 'pious' day for the 1950s household, remembered as a space for 'feminised family-time' – walks in the park, board games and visiting elderly relatives. He maintains that this culture was irrevocably destroyed by women's sexual liberation, making it 'a day like any other'.[101] The interviewees did speak of a shift in their Sunday routines and a resulting increase in the opportunities for sex, but it was a shift that was less about an ideological rejection of 'pious femininity' and more a practical time alleviation made possible by the contraction of domestic duties. It also remained a day that was hardly 'like any other' – many of the interviewees described a Sunday that retained its distinctiveness, a day of 'restfulness', even 'boredom', but one devoted to decidedly 'different' pursuits from the rest of the week.

Given the increased time and space that became available for religious and sexual activity in later marriage, it is little surprise that so many Catholic women were to reconsider their stances towards artificial contraception at this stage. Expanded physical and temporal opportunities encouraged a new form of personal theological contemplation. Bridget insisted that she 'simply did not have the time to even think about things like family planning' in her early marriage – 'births just happened and we got on with it'.[102] June, who we have seen became sexually awakened when she had an affair in her mid-forties, explained that:

> I did not have many expectations early on, but then when you have a bit more time and space to sit back and consider things, you begin to realise what you're missing. That's the point, you need the time and space.[103]

The interviewees' sexual aspirations increased in later marriage, a trend that would seem to mirror broader societal changes in female sexuality as described by the likes of Hera Cook. However, the interviewees were again to consider this less a consequence of a raised 'sexual consciousness' brought about by a liberating ideology and more a practical matter of time and space. It was these physical, earthly aspects of everyday experience that were emphasised in their narratives of sexual change.

We have seen that the 'liberation' narratives that the interviewees recounted were predicated on a process of compartmentalisation, an active separation between the religious and the sexual. The culmination of this process was, more often than not, the decision to reject the Church's prohibition of artificial contraception, a decision which was made as religious and sexual activities were being physically forced together like never before. The spatial and temporal grouping of the religious and the sexual was a phenomenon that certainly predated the post-war. The bedroom and evenings had been the principal site of sexual activity for centuries while prayer had been progressively removed from the industrial 'working day' since the eighteenth century.[104] The tie between the two speaks of the perennial nature of the questions they address – questions relating to life and death, human interaction, selfhood and the body.

But there was also something peculiarly 'modern' about the secluded, personalised spaces within which these questions were being confronted during the post-war years. It has been widely observed that religion retreated from the 'public' realm in the years after the 1960s.[105] Conversely, historians such as Jeffrey Weeks have detailed the paradoxical fate of sex in this period, becoming at once a popularised, ubiquitous topic while at the same time being confined to the 'private' – a matter for the individual behind closed doors.[106] Oral history allows us to see how Catholic women's contraceptive behaviour was affected by these cultural developments in ways that might not otherwise seem clear. But this was not simply a story of shifting lines between the public and private. The emphasis that the interviewees placed on time and place when remembering their changes in contraceptive practice reflected their will to communicate the centrality of material, lived experience. They were eager to show how their beliefs on the morality of birth control were inexplicably bound up with day-to-day living, and they appealed to time and space as a means of reinforcing this connection.

This attention to the temporal and spatial dimensions of lived experience seems to chime with two recent intellectual trends: what Harry Cocks has described as the 'spatial turn' in the history of sexuality and the long overdue emergence of what Jennifer Scheper Hughes has dubbed 'a materialist theory of religion'.[107] As historians like Matt Cook and Matt Houlbrook have sought to demonstrate that 'sexuality and identity are inseparable from the material networks and spaces that they inhabit', so practitioners of religious studies have attempted to combat the 'near absence of the body as an interpretive analytic' and instead 'take seriously both the material conditions and conditioned-ness of human existence as well as the material consequences of embodied religious belief and practice'.[108] Concurrent with these trends, there has been an attempt to do away with approaches to both sex and religion that obsessively pursue 'meaning', and treat them instead as lived moments of experience. As Colin Jones argued at his plenary lecture at the 2014 Social History Society conference, historians have made a totem out of causation which has prompted them to overlook the chaotic, sometimes unthinking aspects of human behaviour.[109] This observation is particularly true of scholars of religion. Surely the point is that meaning and causation are embedded *in* quotidian, mundane existence rather than there marking a dichotomy between the two. The memories of Catholic women allow for a reconstruction of the spatial and temporal materiality that framed everyday existence. They therefore offer an important means of rethinking the way contraceptive morality is understood. Historians and commentators in the Catholic birth-control debate have all too often overlooked the interdependency of religious experience and meaning.

Catholic beliefs on the body were formed by an interaction between physical, material structures and theological ideologies, both of which, as this chapter has shown, changed and mutated through the course of the twentieth century. As the interviewees moved through their marriages, they increasingly felt the clergy were incapable of relating to the physical, embodied dimensions of marital sexuality. The next section demonstrates how later marriage saw this experiential disparity come to a head, as the moral authority of priests in matters of sex was irreversibly undermined.

The declining authority of the clergy in sexual matters

> I can remember going to the priest at my Parish at the time and saying 'I'm really struggling with this [NFP]. What can we do?' And you know what he said? He told me to offer it up! And I remember thinking you have no idea, absolutely no idea what I am talking about. I mean he was sympathetic, but it occurred to me at that moment that he was literally the last person on earth who could relate to what I was going through![110]

'Offering up' physical suffering as a sign of pious devotion was an abiding memory of many of the interviewees' religious education – one recalled being instructed by a sister at her convent that 'if you have a headache or something you don't complain, you offer it up to Our Lord, suffering is good for you'– but by the middle of the 1960s this form of 'sacrificial spirituality' had largely fallen out of favour. Paula Kane has shown how this element of Catholicism was taken to an extreme in the cult of the 'Victim Soul', where specific individuals, often women, were 'chosen by God to suffer in order to alleviate the suffering of others and to diminish the effects of sin'.[111] As Kane demonstrates, this highly gendered form of ascetic Catholicism gained an understated popularity in the 1950s, but fell away dramatically after Vatican II. It comes, then, as little surprise that Patricia was so incredulous at being told to 'offer up' her sexual suffering by her priest in 1979. It epitomised the insularity that lingered in certain strands of the clergy, betraying an imperviousness to developments not only in mainstream secular culture but also within the Catholic community.

Patricia's testimony was typical in two ways. First, the timing of her change in attitude towards the clergy, occurring in later marriage after a prolonged period of using NFP. As we saw was the case for Anne, a handful of the interviewees had disregarded the authority of their parish priest in the early stages of their marriage. For some this came even earlier – Marian explained that she never had any confidence in priests after the seminarians at her boarding school made the students 'donate' their bacon rations to them during the war.[112] For the large majority of the interviewees, though, the clergy, much like the teachings of the central Church, remained a respected source of moral and spiritual guidance up until the later phase of their marriage. Second, Patricia's testimony was typical in the emphasis she placed on her priest's inability to 'relate to' or understand her sexual experiences. Although the interviewees spoke of a gradual process of questioning steadily eroding their youthful deference, much like Anne's rejection of the contraceptive doctrine, they often recalled a specific moment or instance when their admiration for the clergy crumbled. Teresa recalled hearing a sermon in which the priest blamed the declining rate of vocations to the priesthood on women's 'reluctance to procreate the human race'. A woman in the congregation stood up and left in protest, and Teresa herself was sorely tempted to do the same. She explained that 'it was at that point I realised who these men were. I never held them in the same esteem again, or any esteem really.'[113]

One of the clearest manifestations of the clergy's weakening moral authority was the dramatic decline in confessional attendance. John

Cornwell has argued that the sacrament of confession, a defining feature of Catholic liturgy before the war, had become largely obsolete for a high proportion of Catholics by the late 1970s.[114] Many of the interviewees attended confession regularly in their youth and early marriage, but stopped between the ages of forty and sixty. Joan found it impossible to give the priests any credibility: 'I just stopped thinking what they had to say had any relevance to me.'[115] If Catholic priests had, by and large, ceased to hold an autocratic, coercive form of power decades, perhaps even centuries earlier, the demise of the confessional in the years after the 1960s represented the dissolution of a more subtle form of authority. Priests ceased to function as the 'pastor' for Catholic women – no longer the moral shepherd in possession of a privileged, spiritual knowledge. It became clear that the Catholic clergy were among a select few in society who actually lacked a particular kind of knowledge.

Sex was at the centre of Catholic women's rejection of both the confessional and clerical authority in general. Katherine stated that, 'Well it was all about sex really. I stopped going because I couldn't bear speaking to my priest about that kind of thing!'[116] June explained that as her marriage moved on, she felt increasingly 'uncomfortable speaking about sex with those celibate men, very, very uncomfortable. I didn't say to him the things I would say to you.' I asked June why this was and she explained that 'they'd probably be aroused hearing these sort of things. Even from an old woman.'[117] The distinction she made between me, an actively heterosexual man, and a priest offers an insight into the widespread mistrust of clerical attitudes to sex that predated even the recent child abuse scandals. The fact that June was happy to divulge intimate details about her sex life to me, and felt assured that I would not be aroused by them, suggested that it was not the priest's gender that was the problem. It could have been my younger age or the academic nature of my interest in the subject that gave me a heightened legitimacy. Either way, celibacy was clearly at the heart of June's and many other Catholic women's growing reticence to speak about sex with priests. The decline of the confessional has generally been interpreted as a product of a Vatican II-inspired 'liberation', where the moral authority of the clergy was fundamentally challenged by a democratising ideology.[118] Alongside this story of shifting power dynamics, the decline of the confessional also spoke of the Catholic Church's alienation from the body as a site of knowledge. Transcendent answers were no longer seen to be an appropriate response to what were increasingly thought to be material questions of embodied experience.

The fact that priests were entirely bereft of marital sexual experience became increasingly apparent to Catholic women as their own married lives moved on. This was a point that almost all the interviewees repeatedly returned to in the interviews. Before I had even asked my first question, Marian had diagnosed the problem with the priesthood in this way:

> The main thing is because they rejected the earthly experience, they grew up in theory. You don't live in theory, theoretically you don't live in theory, and practically you don't.[119]

Many of the interviewees came to our meeting armed with a similar message – the clergy could not possibly understand or hold any moral authority on sex, particularly female sexuality, as they had not experienced it themselves. Indeed, certain priests may have been less ignorant of the experiential nuances of sex than they would have wanted us to believe. Of the twenty-seven interviewees, no less than five spoke confidently of knowing parish priests who had had affairs with parishioners, with several others alluding to similar rumours that they could not confirm to be true.[120] These stories were rarely recounted with anger or outrage, but rather a sense of exasperated pity. Celibacy was viewed as an 'unnatural' state which both attracted and generated moral deviancy.

While parish priests at a grassroots level gradually lost their position of pastoral authority in Catholic women's lives, the central hierarchy was to see an even more dramatic fall from grace. For many of the interviewees, their 'frustration' and 'exasperation' with the hierarchy turned to 'anger' and 'disdain' in later marriage:

> Weak old men! All men! I agreed for a long time but when I saw the coronation of the Pope, this last pope [Pope Benedict XVI] on television, the serried ranks of old men, almost all white, I just … If you go to weekday Mass you hardly see a man, it's the women who do things.[121]

Alongside the preponderant issue of gender, there was also a sense that the central hierarchy was even more removed from the daily experiences of Catholic couples than the local parish priests. Lynn pointed out that:

They are locked away in their ivory towers in the Vatican, they don't know anything about the Catholic people. They are so removed from normal existence; they couldn't begin to understand things like sex. At least the parish priests are there, on the ground level, meeting and talking to the laity every day.[122]

By later marriage, the experiential distance between Catholic women and the celibate clerical officials of the Holy See had become abundantly apparent and prompted many of the interviewees to reject the Church's moral authority outright.

Certain Catholic authorities of the time, and today, have contended that it is not necessary to have lived through a particular experience to be able to take a position, or indeed act as a source of guidance, on it.[123] Indeed, this apriorism was the epistemological precept on which clerical authority in sexual matters had been based for centuries. However, as we saw in the last chapter, this idea was being challenged inside the walls of the Vatican in the 1960s. The very existence of the Papal Commission for Birth Control indicated that the Catholic hierarchy was acknowledging new, extrinsic sources of sexual knowledge. In the context of these seemingly progressive developments, *Humanae Vitae* was interpreted as a rejection of not only Catholic women's bodily autonomy, but also the value of their lived experience. This latter indictment became increasingly apparent to Catholic women as their marriages moved on; it was something that took the time and space of later marriage to fully crystallise. When it did, their form of Catholic devotion would never be the same again.

Conclusion

Academic studies of female sexuality tend to devote more attention to younger than older women.[124] Brown's work focused on 'young women caught in the throes of a sexual revolution', while the sociological investigations of the Papal Commission for Birth Control also showed little interest in married women beyond their mid-thirties.[125] Numerous reasons for this heightened interest in early as opposed to later female sexuality could be suggested – it speaks of the 'male gaze' that continues to frame intellectual assessments of femininity as well as the persistence of fertility as the primary determinant of women's sexual function. Even when the experiences of older married women have gained attention, marriage has been treated as a single homogeneous life-cycle stage. The interviewees' memories show that the sexual experiences of Catholic women in post-war England were defined by a clear and distinct break. It was 'later marriage' that witnessed transformatory changes in their religious beliefs, sexual behaviour and sense of identity. Acknowledging this break provides the foundations for a fuller picture of the 'personal' when considering Catholic women's sexual experiences.

This chapter has highlighted the centrality of later marriage to the formation of Catholic women's 'liberal' religious identities. It was a life-cycle stage where the clerical hierarchy's authority in sexual matters, particularly contraceptive morality, was irreversibly broken. The direction of causation between experience and authority is vitally important. The authority of the clergy was not simply undermined by a Vatican II-inspired ideology of democratisation, but also by the experiences that Catholic women lived through in their early married life. Changes in Catholic power dynamics were driven by physical, embodied experiences rather than being directed by intellectual and theological elites. This chapter has also demonstrated how these 'liberal' Catholic identities were forged through an active recategorisation of the religious and the sexual. It was often not until after the end of the 1960s that the separation between these two domains of knowledge along material lines took hold in the personal theologies and everyday experiences of Catholic women. The next chapter delves back into Catholic women's early marriage, uncovering the emotional and embodied sensibilities which induced these moments of personal transformation.

Notes

1 M. Anderson, 'The Emergence of the Modern Life Cycle Stage in Britain', *Social History*, 10 (1985), pp. 69–87.
2 Childrearing itself was an activity which changed over time. For more discussion of this see S. Humphries and P. Gordon, *Labour of Love: The Experience of Parenthood in Britain, 1900–1950* (London, 1993).
3 L. Botelho, 'Old Age and Menopause in Rural Women of Early Modern Suffolk', in P. Thane and L. Botelho (eds), *Women and Ageing in British Society since 1500* (Oxford, 2001), pp. 43–66.

4 This tendency provided the motivation for Pat Thane's research, see Thane and Bothelo, *Women and Ageing*.
5 Doreen, interviewed 11/08/2012.
6 P. Summerfield, *Reconstructing Women's Wartime Lives: Discourse and Subjectivity in Oral Histories of the Second World War* (Manchester, 1998), pp. 9–16.
7 Brown discusses the similarities and divergences (which Brown interprets as merely a matter of semantics) between Taylor's and his own model of 'cultural revolution': C. Brown, *The Death of Christian Britain: Understanding Secularisation, 1800–2000* (Cambridge, 2000), p. 194.
8 A good example of this emerging historiography of the 1970s is E. Robinson, C. Schofield, F. Sutcliffe-Braithwaite and N. Thomlinson, 'Telling Stories about Post-War Britain: Popular Individualism and the "Crisis" of the 1970s', *Twentieth Century British History*, 28:2 (2017), pp. 268–304.
9 K. Plummer, *Telling Sexual Stories: Power, Change and Social Worlds* (London, 1995), p. 123.
10 Although none of the interviewees had read Brown's work prior to the interview, I ended each interview by mapping out his model of historical change and asking for the interviewees' opinion of it.
11 For example Sorcha, interviewed 09/01/2014; Georgina, interviewed 22/11/2012.
12 A number of critiques of 'sexual liberation' emerged in the late 1980s and early 1990s from various intellectual standpoints. For examples and surveys of these critiques, see S. Seidman, *Embattled Eros: Sexual Politics and Ethics in Contemporary America* (London, 1992); J. D'Emilio and E. Freedman, *Intimate Matters* (New York, 1988); A. Giddens, *The Transformation of Intimacy* (Oxford, 1992); N. Rose, *Inventing Our Selves: Psychology, Power and Personhood* (Cambridge, 1996).
13 G. Jantzen, *Becoming Divine: Towards a Feminist Philosophy of Religion* (Manchester, 1998), p. 89.
14 N. Rose, *Governing the Soul: The Shaping of the Private Self* (New York, 1989).
15 M. Kimmel, 'John Gagnon and the Sexual Self', in M. Kimmel (ed.), *The Sexual Self: The Construction of Sexual Scripts* (Nashville, TN, 2007), p. vii.
16 W. Gagnon and J. Simon, *Sexual Conduct* (Chicago, 1973).
17 Ibid.
18 Elizabeth, interviewed 08/02/2014.
19 Margaret, interviewed 29/09/2013.
20 Ibid.

21 A. Offer, *The Challenge of Affluence: Self-Control and Wellbeing in the United States and Britain since 1950* (Oxford, 2006), p. 1.
22 Elizabeth, interviewed 08/02/2014.
23 Brown, *Death of Christian Britain*; Lynn, interviewed 12/04/2012.
24 Lynn, interviewed 12/04/2012.
25 Sarah, interviewed 04/09/2016.
26 June, interviewed 20/02/2013.
27 Ibid.
28 Anne, interviewed 24/03/2012.
29 Mary, interviewed 02/10/2013.
30 Ibid.
31 M. Foucault, *The History of Sexuality*, vol. 1 (London, 1976), pp. 51–74; T. Laqueur, *Solitary Sex: A Cultural History of Masturbation* (New York, 2003).
32 Elizabeth, interviewed 15/07/2013.
33 Lydia, interviewed 20/03/2013.
34 H. Cook, *The Long Sexual Revolution: English Women, Sex and Contraception 1800–1975* (Oxford, 2004), p. 304; M. Hornsby-Smith (ed.), *Catholics in England 1950–2000: Historical and Sociological Perspectives* (London, 1999), p. 7.
35 The emergence of a specifically 'modern' sense of self has also been located in the first half of the twentieth century. For example, Matt Houlbrook has explored the relationship between understandings of selfhood and a burgeoning fictional culture in the 1920s. M. Houlbrook, '"A Pin to see the Peepshow": Culture, Fiction and Selfhood in Edith Thompson's Letters, 1921–1922', *Past and Present*, 207 (2010), pp. 215–249.
36 'Heightened reflexive self-awareness has converged with the growth in the significance of sexuality, creating the conditions for a highly self-conscious sense of sexual subjectivity and opportunities for endless sexual self-telling' S. Jackson, 'The Sexual Self in Late Modernity', in Kimmel, *The Sexual Self*, pp. 3–15.
37 Doreen, interviewed 11/08/2012.
38 Plummer, *Sexual Stories*, p. 123.
39 C. Taylor, *A Secular Age* (Cambridge, MA, 2007), p. 473.
40 Ibid., p. 636.
41 Teresa, interviewed 04/04/2012.
42 Ibid.
43 Ibid.
44 Katherine, interviewed 14/07/2013.
45 A. Harris, *Faith in the Family: A Lived Religious History of English Catholicism, 1945–1982* (Manchester, 2013), p. 134.

46 Katherine, interviewed 14/07/2013.
47 Ibid.
48 Georgina, interviewed 22/11/2012.
49 Mary, interviewed 02/10/2013.
50 Sorcha, interviewed 09/01/2014.
51 Marian, interviewed 26/09/2013.
52 Katherine, interviewed 14/07/2013.
53 Teresa, interviewed 04/04/2012.
54 Ibid.
55 Elizabeth, interviewed 15/07/2013.
56 Ibid.
57 Taylor, *A Secular Age*, p. 473.
58 Cook, *The Long Sexual Revolution*, p. 1.
59 Ibid.
60 June, interviewed 20/02/2013; Sorcha, interviewed 15/04/2013.
61 Bridget, interviewed 16/04/2013.
62 L. Marks, *Sexual Chemistry: A History of the Contraceptive Pill* (London, 2001), p. 1.
63 Lynn, interviewed 12/04/2012.
64 Robinson et al., 'Telling stories about Post-War Britain', pp. 268–304.
65 Lynn, interviewed 12/04/2012.
66 Katherine, interviewed 14/07/2013.
67 Sarah, interviewed 04/09/2016.
68 D. Lodge, *How Far Can You Go?* (London, 1980), p. 113.
69 É. Durkheim, *The Elementary Forms of the Religious Life*, trans. Carol Cosman (Oxford, 2001); P. Berger, *The Sacred Canopy: Elements of a Sociological Theory of Religion* (New York, 1967).
70 D. Sheridan, B. Street and D. Bloome, *Writing Ourselves: Mass Observation and Literacy Practices* (Cresskill, NJ, 2000), p. 107.
71 Anne, interviewed 24/03/12.
72 Ibid.
73 Ibid.
74 Ibid.
75 Ibid.
76 Brown, *Death of Christian Britain*.
77 J. Dominian, *The Church and the Sexual Revolution* (London, 1967).
78 Lynn, interviewed 12/04/2012.
79 Ibid.
80 Patricia, interviewed 03/05/2013.
81 Joan, interviewed 19/09/2013.
82 Mary, interviewed 02/10/2013.
83 Anne, interviewed 24/03/2012.

84 M. Foucault, 'Pastoral Power and Political Reason', in J. Carrette (ed.), *Religion and Culture: Michel Foucault* (New York, 1999), pp. 135–154.
85 Anne, interviewed 24/03/2012.
86 Foucault, 'Pastoral Power and Political Reason'.
87 Anne, interviewed 24/03/2012.
88 Ibid.
89 Ibid.
90 A. Eichenbaum, *The Cognitive Neuroscience of Memory* (Oxford, 2002).
91 Catholic Truth Society, *Prayer Book for Spouses* (London, 2009).
92 Lydia, interviewed 20/03/2013.
93 Elizabeth, interviewed 15/03/2013.
94 Doreen, interviewed 11/08/2012.
95 Langhamer, *Women's Leisure in England* (Manchester, 2000), pp. 133–186.
96 June, interviewed 19/11/2013.
97 Mary, interviewed 02/10/2013.
98 Angela, interviewed 07/01/2014.
99 Christina, interviewed 06/01/2014.
100 Lydia, interviewed 20/03/2013.
101 C. Brown, *Religion and Society in Twentieth-Century Britain* (London, 2006), pp. 5, 28.
102 Bridget, interviewed 16/04/2013.
103 June, interviewed 20/02/2013.
104 Callum Brown documents the removal of prayer from the working day, *Death of Christian Britain*, pp. 145–169.
105 For example, see G. Davie, *Religion in Britain since 1945: Believing without Belonging* (Oxford, 1994).
106 J. Weeks, *Sex, Politics and Society* (London, 1981).
107 H. Cocks, 'Approaches to the History of Sexuality since 1700', in S. Toulanlan and K. Fisher (eds), *The Routledge History of Sex and the Body: 1500 to the Present* (Abingdon, 2013), p. 48; J. Scheper-Hughes, 'A Materialist Theory of Religion: The Latin American Frame', *Method and Theory in the Study of Religion*, 24 (2012), pp. 430–444.
108 M. Houlbrook, *Queer London: Perils and Pleasures in the Sexual Metropolis, 1918–1957* (Chicago, 2005); M. Cook, *London and the Culture of Homosexuality 1885–1914* (Cambridge, 2003); Scheper-Hughes, 'A Materialist Theory of Religion', p. 430.
109 C. Jones, 'SHS Conference Plenary Lecture' (2014). Addressing the conference after Jones' lecture, the society's chairman, Malcom Chase, was to ask whether we were seeing the emergence of a 'quotidian turn'.
110 Patricia, interviewed 03/05/2013.

111 P. Kane, '"She Offered Herself Up": The Victim Soul and Victim Spirituality in Catholicism', *Church History*, 71 (2002), p. 116.
112 Marian, interviewed 26/09/2013.
113 Teresa, interviewed 04/04/2012.
114 J. Cornwell, *The Black Box: A Secret History of Confession* (London, 2014).
115 Joan, interviewed 10/09/2013.
116 Katherine, interviewed 14/07/2013.
117 June, interviewed 20/02/2013.
118 M. Hornsby-Smith, *Roman Catholic Beliefs in England: Customary Catholicism and Transformations of Religious Authority* (Cambridge, 2009), pp. 61–62.
119 Marian, interviewed 26/09/2013.
120 It should be acknowledged that this proportion reflects the fact that the sample was made up of individuals who tended to be very involved in parish communities and Church organisations.
121 Teresa, interviewed 04/04/2012.
122 Lynn, interviewed 12/04/2012.
123 For example, this principle was the basis of Ford and Grisez's minority report to the Pope.
124 This tendency provided the motivation for Pat Thane's research, see Thane and Bothelo, *Women and Ageing*.
125 C. Brown, 'Sex, Religion, and the Single Woman c.1950–75: The Importance of a "Short" Sexual Revolution to the English Religious Crisis of the Sixties', *Journal of Social History*, 22 (2011), pp. 189–215.

· 4 ·

Sexuality in early marriage

We first met June in the previous chapter; we saw how it was not until her early forties that her marriage went 'off the rails', as she became aware of her and her husband's 'sexual incompatibility' and had an affair. The following excerpt from our interview offers some insight into the sexual difficulties that June encountered in her early marriage, while also introducing a number of the key themes this chapter addresses:

> DG Do you want to talk about your experience of using natural family planning?
> June Right, disastrous. In fact, this is very personal – when I went to the hospital, when I thought I was expecting Matthew two months after we were married, I was examined and I was still a virgin, so that shows how efficient we were at sex. So a second virgin birth! And the consultant deflowered me I think is a polite way of putting it, without asking my permission!
> DG (pause) Can I ask how that happened, you conceived Matthew …
> June Well you have a little hole, when you're menstruating you have a little gap, don't you, in the hymen I suppose it is, my husband must have had very strong spermatozoa as he managed to make me pregnant through the hole.
> DG Without coitus …
> June Well we had coitus but I don't suppose he went in very far, I mean we were so ignorant in those days, we've written to each other since and apologised for the mess we made of each other's life and you know he said we just didn't know what we were doing and the Church was such a hindrance we couldn't experiment, it was just so rigid.[1]

The revelation of a second 'immaculate conception' was certainly unexpected, which goes some way to explaining my failure to pick up on June's unsettling disclosure that her consultant 'deflowered' her without permission. It is a regret that I did not think to ask about this at the time, but it was also clear that June did not see this as the main point of her story.

June's recollections serve as a particularly poignant entry point to this chapter on early marriage for two reasons. First, the acute ignorance of sexual anatomy that marred her first sexual encounter was an increasingly rare phenomenon amongst young Catholic couples in 1960s Britain. This was, in part, a consequence of wider societal shifts in sexual culture, including a 'democratisation' of sexual knowledge described by the likes of Lesley Hall and Roy Porter, but also a direct response to the rapid expansion of specifically Catholic marriage preparation initiatives.[2] Although the Catholic Marriage Advisory Council (CMAC) was founded in 1946, it remained, in the words of marriage guidance historian Jane Lewis, a 'small and rather closed organisation' until the early 1960s, when it rapidly transformed into a professional, internationally recognised organisation.[3] Alongside the CMAC's advances, a number of sex manuals specifically aimed at Catholics were produced in the early 1960s that offered frank and detailed guidance on the biological mechanics of sex. *Preparing for Marriage* (1962) included a chapter on 'First Times' that would have proved particularly useful to June and her husband.[4] June was one of only six respondents not to have consulted any form of sexual guidance before her marriage, a fact that reflected both her geographical location (June was from a small town in the north of England and the core of the CMAC's centres were still concentrated in London and the south-east) as well as her wariness of the distinctly middle-class character of its counsellors and clients. This chapter begins by examining how Catholic sexual instruction emerged as a distinct field of expert knowledge in the post-war decades, extending its reach to almost all sections of the Catholic community. It assesses the understanding of female sexuality that was constructed by these experts and the effect this had on Catholic women's marital experiences.

Second, June's response epitomised the way that many of the interviewees conflated the Church's teaching on contraceptive morality with its wider approach to sex. My question was about her experience of practising NFP, but her response almost immediately turned to her own sexual naivety and the Church's culpability for this. She did not start to practice NFP until after the birth of her third child, over five years after this incident. The interviewees' overriding memory of early marriage was of their sexual interests being denied or frustrated by their Catholic beliefs in one way or another. We have seen that for many of the interviewees, later marriage witnessed a moment of 'liberation' or 'enlightenment' in which their religious beliefs on sexual behaviour, notably contraception, were permanently disrupted. They emphasised that this moment was driven by years of physical and emotional struggle rather than being brought about by an emancipatory ideology. The second section of this chapter explores these years of struggle, using the interviewees' testimony alongside contemporary source material to reconstruct Catholics women's everyday experience of using NFP.

For almost all the interviewees, 'early marriage' was a distinctive life-cycle stage which ran from engagement to the end of childrearing. Again, as with 'later marriage', the timings of this life-cycle stage varied from person to person and shifted over time. The interviewees universally spoke of early marriage as a period that was typified by the 'busyness' and 'constant activity' of raising a young family. A cartoon published in the *Catholic Herald* in 1968 by John Ryan (of Captain Pugwash fame) humorously portrayed the archetypal Catholic woman in early marriage (Figure 1). Surrounded by a hoard of young children, she explains to a bespectacled researcher that she does not have the time to read encyclical letters. While on one level the cartoon satirised the class dynamics of the Catholic birth-control debate, it also highlighted the all-consuming nature of raising a young, and large, family. Many Catholic women found that it was only after the daily demands of motherhood had diminished that they were afforded the necessary time and space to reflect on the significance of *Humanae Vitae*.

All bar two interviewees had not had sex before they were wed, a proportion that, if Michael Schofield's survey data is to be believed, was not as far out of kilter with the rest of society as might have been thought.[5] In this sense, early marriage was not necessarily a specifically Catholic experience; elements of it would have been familiar to many women living in post-war Britain. Young Catholic women did, though, encounter a very particular set of concerns and questions relating to their faith. The interviewees' memories of early marriage were defined by a tension between the physical, bodily concerns of sexuality and the

Figure 1 John Ryan cartoon published in the *Catholic Herald*, 2 August 1968

transcendent, ethereal domain of religious beliefs. Amidst the daily pressures that this schism exerted on them, they did not forgo their faith or relationships, but pursued creative 'tactics' that allowed them to negotiate these dissonant demands. It was out of these tactics that they eventually reformulated their religious identities and realised their full 'selves'. If later marriage saw the 'culmination' or 'realisation' of a process of recategorisation between the religious and the sexual, then it was the everyday experiences of early marriage that set this process in motion. Ultimately, the chapter demonstrates how a conceptual separation between the sexual and the religious took hold in the postwar decades, shaping the way early marriage was contemporaneously experienced and also retrospectively understood by Catholic women. Rather than simply being defined by binaries of repression/liberation and authority/autonomy, the cleaving of sex and religion worked along deeper, material lines.

Catholic marriage preparation

The interviewees were of a generation whose sex lives were subjected to an unparalleled level of attention from Church institutions. Disciples of the theorist Michel Foucault would claim that the Catholic Church had always policed sexuality through the clerical gaze of the confessional, but it had never provided much in the way of formalised premarital instruction.[6] The very concept of 'marriage preparation' had not featured in Catholic thinking before the war and was still unfamiliar to much of the laity by the early 1960s – the first chapter of the 1962 marriage guidance manual *Preparing for Marriage* is titled 'Why Prepare?' and reads:

> The first question many people ask when preparation for marriage is mentioned is, Why prepare? They declare that their parents and grandparents did not have books or attend courses for engaged couples, yet they did very well for themselves and their families.[7]

The manual pointed out that:

> Marriage today is more difficult a venture than it was in times past ... Marriage is a natural state, but the complexities of modern

society are such that our natural instincts and intuitions are not enough to guide us. We need to learn how to meet the demands of contemporary life, without despoiling real values, or interfering with our true nature.[8]

We can see how a traditional Catholic rhetoric of the 'natural', articulated here through phrases like 'natural instincts' and 'our true nature', remained an important aspect of the way marriage preparation was marketed. The extract also indicates how Catholic authorities were becoming increasingly concerned that the 'complexities of modern society' were making marriage, and particularly sexuality, an area that required renewed attentions. Throughout the 1960s, this awareness of a new, 'modern' understanding of sexuality was a conspicuous presence in the rhetoric of Catholic marriage guidance experts, papal commission members and even the Pope himself.

The most pointed expression of this concern can be seen in the CMAC's rapid expansion in the 1960s. At its initiation in the mid-1940s, the CMAC offered private counselling for couples and was largely confined to the London area. By 1968 it had moved into sex therapy services, education and medical work, with fifty-nine centres across Britain. The CMAC's most popular service was the Preparing Engaged Couples for Marriage course, which provided Catholic couples with information and guidance on a range of aspects of marriage, with a particular focus on sexual matters. The course marked a major reorientation in the Church's approach to sexual instruction – the central hierarchy had previously made it clear that the only individuals in a position to advise married couples on questions of sex and family planning were members of the clergy, in consultation with a doctor if necessary. A 1951 memorandum to the CMAC's counsellors confirmed the circumscribed nature of their role; they were to give information about NFP (which had been first endorsed by the Pope in an address to midwives earlier that year) but never to advise on whether or not to actually use the method.[9] The CMAC training manual *Preparing Engaged Couples for Marriage* (*PECFM*) indicates that by the mid-1960s counsellors were being fully entrusted with the responsibility for directing Catholic couples' contraceptive choices and sexual behaviour.[10]

This extension of counsellors' jurisdiction coincided with a shift in clerical attitudes towards the CMAC. Ex-CMAC chairman John

Marshall pointed out in our interview that in the 1950s parish priests remained generally sceptical of marriage guidance in principle, opposing the very idea that married love could be 'taught' or 'counselled'.[11] The Catholic clergy's widespread acceptance and promotion of the CMAC's work in the early 1960s represented a reversal in clerical attitudes towards both lay participation and the very concept of marriage guidance. Support for the CMAC amongst the English clergy was such that an annual training conference was set up to inform parish priests of the CMAC's services and to educate them in the latest approaches to sexual instruction. The first, in 1960, was attended by 188 priests; by 1964 there were over 400.[12] Just as Jane Lewis has shown to be the case for secular institutions during the 1960s, the Church recognised sex to be a legitimate site for expert intervention, a subject that could be taught and learnt, studied and understood.[13]

In the following three sections, the CMAC's internal correspondence and counsellor training manuals are used alongside the interviewees' recollections to explore the relationship between prescription and practice. Twenty of the twenty-seven interviewees used the CMAC's services at one point in their married lives. However, many found the advice that they received in their early marriage lacking in some way. For a handful of 'liberals', this was simply a consequence of the organisation's need to 'toe the party line' when it came to birth control. But as other interviewees pointed out, clients were generally aware that this would be the case before they visited the CMAC. In keeping with the wider intellectual climate of the 1960s, the CMAC's guidance on sexual behaviour was rigorously scientific, but the interviewees found that it paid little attention to the emotional and spiritual aspects of married love. In this sense, the CMAC's construction of female sexuality shared many similarities with that of the papal commission. Representatives of both groups neglected the personal, intimate aspects of sexual experience in their efforts to engage with 'modern' notions of healthy sexual expression. Underpinning this failing was an implicit separation between the religious and the sexual, with the sexual defined as something biological and the religious as a transcendent matter removed from the body's earthly mechanics.

The CMAC valued sexual knowledge as more than just a helpful aid to engaged couples, but as a necessary prerequisite for successful marital relations. A section in *PECFM* was devoted to explaining the different ways in which men and women achieve orgasm, stressing the importance of specific sexual 'knowledge':

> If one wants to give happiness to one's partner in marriage it is necessary that one should know something about the essential details. Good intentions are not enough, one must have sound knowledge.[14]

The point that 'good intentions are not enough' suggests that it was the marital duty of each member of the couple to 'give happiness to one's partner'. This indicates that the CMAC had a firm idea of what constituted good or healthy sex, a target that could only be realised through the correct knowledge of the human body.

The CMAC went beyond this in its genuflection to a modern body of sexual expertise. It became apparent that engaged Catholic couples were often more concerned with receiving sexual advice than any other aspect of the eight-week marriage preparation course; counsellors Quentin de la Bedoyere and his wife Irene would end their seminars explaining that the following week might be dealing with 'sex and religion' but they might also be looking at 'finance in marriage' so as to ensure full attendance for both. Despite Quentin and Irene's best efforts, reports from the decade indicate that the attendance for the 'Sex in Marriage' seminar far outstripped that for any other class.[15] The CMAC responded to the Catholic community's growing demand for sexual guidance by introducing specialist 'sex therapy counsellors' to augment its existing personnel. These individuals were specifically trained for dealing with 'sexual difficulties', a move that was believed to be a direct response to the publication of Masters and Johnson's research in 1966.[16] John Marshall explains that their specialist status was largely derived from their medical training and that couples often found the regular CMAC counsellors equally, if not more adept at dealing with questions of intimacy.[17] In 1972, the sex therapy counsellors were phased out by the CMAC on the grounds that the regular counsellors' 'human approach' could adequately cater for the emotional issues that were being raised. This zeal to acknowledge sexuality as its own field of knowledge, requiring its own form of expertise, represented a persistent feature of the way Catholic authorities approached the changing status of sex in the 1960s. In bringing in and training specific sex therapy counsellors, the CMAC marked out sexual problems as an area of marriage that demanded special attention.

Although the CMAC favoured the non-directive approach to counsellor training that had been developed in the UK by the secular author John Wallis, it actively encouraged a particular way of talking about sex. It is apparent from *PECFM* that much thought had gone into the way in which sexual knowledge should be imparted by CMAC representatives.[18] Headings such as 'Language', 'Style', 'Jokes', 'Use of Drawings' and 'Common Mistakes' were all separately addressed in the textbook that outlined the desired approach to discussing sex.[19] The use of humour represented an important facet of a counsellor's presentational style. In a section devoted to jokes, the manual read:

> Mild witticisms to ease the tension with laughter are essential, set piece jokes tend to fall flat and belly laughs should be avoided; both tend to emphasise rather than diminish embarrassment.[20]

The use of light comedy to ease tension and create a comfortable environment in which to discuss sex represented a popular technique for corresponding secular agencies. Alex Comfort's *The Joy of Sex* (first published in 1972) pointed out that:

> The amount of laughter you have [when talking about sex], is evidence for, not against the seriousness of your communication. If you have this, the laughs never fail, because sex is funny.[21]

Gentle humour served to acknowledge the stigma that still surrounded sex in the 1960s, particularly within the Catholic community, and ensured that sexual issues were not blown out of proportion by the counsellors or couples. It should be noted that this approach was the product of conscious and considered directives from within the CMAC rather than being left to the counsellor's discretion. The section devoted to 'Jokes' spent over two pages outlining the appropriate use and misuse of humour when dealing with sexual subjects. These attentive guidelines contradicted the CMAC's commitment to a non-directive form of counsellor training. As the CMAC's director, Fr Maurice O'Leary, acknowledged, at times it could prove difficult to reconcile this non-directive approach with the rigid set of moral principles set out by Catholic doctrine. The CMAC's counsellors were afforded a high level of autonomy in almost all aspects of their counselling, but sex remained a topic that was closely governed.

The CMAC's understanding of female sexual pleasure

Just as the papal commission's discussion of female sexuality involved a reversal in the central hierarchy's approach to Freud, so the CMAC's work in the 1960s represented a similar turnabout for distributors of Catholic sexual advice. Marriage guidance provided by Catholic authorities before the 1960s tended to be sceptical of, if not downright hostile towards, psychoanalysis. A collection of frequently asked questions for Catholic couples, first broadcast on radio by Frs Rumble and Carty and then published in a booklet, set out the 'Church's' opinion of Freud in 1938:

> As a system, Freudian psychoanalysis must be rejected as false and most pernicious … Psycho-analysts have fallen into absurd exaggerations, and their pretence to furnish a new basis for all human activities in art, education, morality and religion must be utterly rejected. Most loathsome is his over-emphasis of sex.[22]

And of Freudian approaches to psychotherapy:

> Even as a therapeutic treatment of neurosis psychoanalysis is dangerous. The discovery of the harmful element in psychic life does not mean the cure. Often a complete re-education of the patient is necessary. The Catholic confessional has all that is good in psychoanalysis, but with safeguards unknown in this pretended new science.[23]

Two decades later, it was apparent that official Catholic marital 'experts' had completely reversed their attitudes to psychotherapy and Freud in particular. CMAC counsellor Quentin de la Bedoyere described his training in the early 1960s as 'highly Freudian' and the guidance in counsellor training manuals was grounded in a distinctly psychotherapeutic vocabulary.[24] As the Freudian school became widely critiqued in psychological circles in the early 1970s, so the CMAC replaced this approach with the 'skilled helper system' and looked to the more accommodating framework provided by Jungian theory. The 1960s were, though, a peculiar point of union between Freud's understanding of human nature and the sexual discourses of Catholic authorities.

The subject of the female orgasm was addressed directly and rigorously within CMAC seminars. Figure 2 shows the graph that counsellors were encouraged to use to illustrate the different sexual responses of men and women. The paragraph below detailed the 'problems' that could come about if a woman did not reach orgasm:

> She will be left in a state of suspended animation having been roused to a certain extent but not satisfied. If this state of affairs occurs as a regular feature of marriage it can be detrimental to both physical and psychological health. What is to be done about it? Obviously the man must be slowed down and the woman speeded up until the two coincide.[25]

Sexual pleasure was considered to be a constitutive aspect of a woman's well-being, a well-being articulated in terms of 'physical' and 'psychological' health. Counsellors instructed married couples on techniques to ensure the correct mood was created for intercourse, offering advice on 'Settings', 'Timing' and 'Foreplay'. They were also trained to encourage the husband to 'prolong' intercourse so as to achieve the ultimate objective of the mutual climax. Although there was no explicit distinction made between a clitoral and vaginal orgasm, it was stressed that caressing of the clitoris was 'perfectly right and normal in proper marriage'. The clitoris was described as a 'very important organ' and information on the 'Stimulation of the Clitoris' was detailed under the heading 'Intercourse' rather than 'Foreplay'.[26] The CMAC's counsellors were trained to provide candid and frank instructions for achieving the female orgasm as if it were nothing less than a biological certainty.

The CMAC actually placed more of an emphasis on the importance of women's 'sexual response' than corresponding secular agencies in the 1960s, with a National Marriage Guidance Council (NGMC) training manual informing counsellors not to 'get caught up with questions of the female orgasm, this is ... specific to individual women and can often become a point of obsession rather than fulfilment'.[27] The NGMC's approach reflected an increasing awareness that some women were feeling guilty for not achieving orgasm, as well as a sensitivity around its own lack of scientific expertise. In comparison, the CMAC's approach chimed with a notion of marital 'mutuality' that was more in vogue at the start of the century. Robert Irwin among others has shown that the call for an erosion of sexual ignorance, a preoccupation with sexual technique (notably the man being slowed down so as to achieve female satisfaction) and the valorisation of the mutual orgasm were all being promoted by various sexual authorities in the first half of the twentieth century. For Irwin, this form of mutuality was ushered in by the influence of first-wave feminism, second-wave sexology and the trauma of the First World War.[28] In this sense, the CMAC was over a generation behind early sexologists such as Marie Stopes in its discussion of the female orgasm, but the very fact that the topic represented a legitimate area of discussion for a Catholic institution should be viewed in the context of the Church's longstanding silence on the subject. *PECFM* showed a meticulous, almost fastidious commitment to redressing the Church's previous ambivalence towards the libidinal interests of married women.

The CMAC was eager to employ scientific modes of communication wherever it could – the graph in Figure 2 not only functioned as a useful visual aid for the counsellors, but provided a sense of authority on sexual matters that drew from its seemingly empirical basis. The *PECFM* seminar on 'Sex in Marriage' began with the group labelling a diagram of the human body, an exercise that ensured all the participants had a certain level of knowledge of human anatomy, but also served to establish the

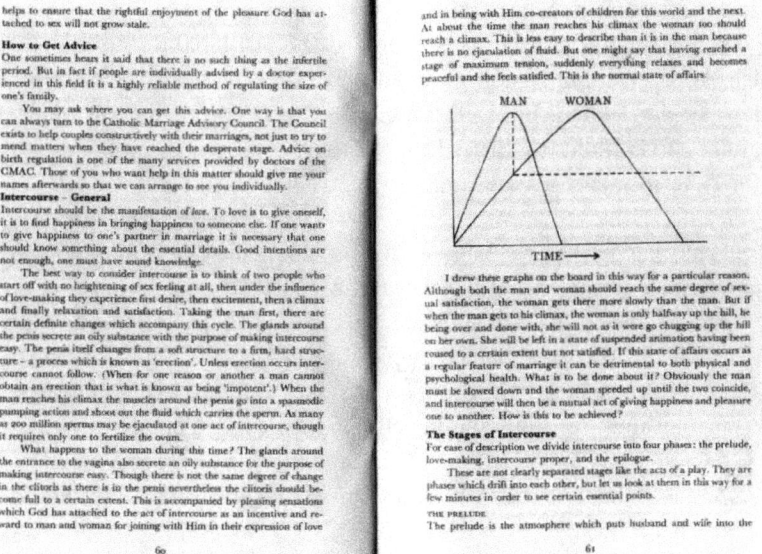

Figure 2 Extract and graph illustration from *Preparing Engaged Couples for Marriage*, CMAC training manual (London, 1969)

terminology that would be used throughout the seminar. As we shall see in the following chapter, the necessity of this exercise was, to some extent, an indication of the limited nature of sexual education provided in Catholic schools during the 1940s and 1950s. *PECFM* comprehensively listed the terms that should be used when discussing bodily parts, explaining that:

> Scientific terms that lay people are going to meet should always be used, but bracketed with the vernacular equivalent only when appropriate. Thus 'womb-or-uterus' is used as one word every time that organ is referred to – qualifying phrases like 'the womb or as we call it the uterus' serve only to exasperate the informed and patronise the ignorant.[29]

In this way, medical terminology was actively encouraged as the principal language with which to discuss marital sexuality. Even the way *PECFM*'s narrative was structured mirrored the scientific process, with each chapter divided into sections titled 'Aims', 'Method' and 'Summary'. The CMAC's approach to marital sexuality demonstrated a reverence for the scientific, borrowing liberally from the vocabulary and methodological apparatus of the medical sciences.

While scientific discourses provided the principal resource that the CMAC drew on in its communication of sexual advice, there were certain tensions when counsellors attempted to integrate the 'spiritual' language of Catholic teachings into this narrative. For example, consider the description of sexual intercourse outlined in *PECFM*:

> What happens to the woman at this time? The glands around the entrance to the vagina secrete an oily substance for the purpose of making intercourse easy. The clitoris should become full to a certain extent. This is accompanied by pleasing and joyous sensations which God has attached to the act of intercourse as an incentive and reward to man and woman for joining Him in their expression of love and in being with Him co-creators of children for this world and the next. At about the time the man reaches his climax the woman too should reach a climax.[30]

The spiritual aspect of married love was dealt with exclusively in the fourth sentence, clearly distinguishing it from the medical descriptions of the body's processes. The colloquial tone that was encouraged throughout *PECFM* was dropped at the end of this sentence, with the phrase 'this world and the next' seemingly lifted directly from a liturgical prayer. The sentence structure also set it apart from the rest of the passage; when describing the sexual act the sentences were short and to the point, whereas the sentence in question was lengthy and long-winded in its description of sex's celestial virtues. This tension between the medical language used for sexual instruction and the spiritual discourses required to communicate Catholic teachings on marital love represented a recurrent motif in *PECFM*'s narrative. As we shall see, this tension did not escape the attentions of the CMAC's clients.

Catholic women's opinion of the CMAC's advice

After sharing some of my initial research with one of the interviewees, she commented that she 'remembered well' being presented with the graph from *PECFM* in her marriage preparation seminar almost fifty years ago. In a written correspondence between us, Veronica recalled that:

> A woman said – 'couldn't she just act up?' From the men including the speaker came a wave of 'no no, honestly, nothing false, openness in marriage' and the discussion veered from the issue. Later in the ladies cloakroom the assembled women burst out laughing in support of the person who had suggested acting up. Do you not think there has to be some mystery between men and women?[31]

Veronica's recollections provide an insight into the way the CMAC's rigorously empirical understanding of 'sexual response' did not always correlate with the performative dynamics and gendered expectations that shaped marital relations. In my response to Veronica, I told her that her anecdote reminded me of a scene from the recently aired TV series *Masters of Sex* (2013). Purporting to be based on 'real events', the drama series depicted the work of the pioneering sex researchers William Masters and Virginia Johnson in the late 1950s. In this particular scene, the eminent sexual scientist Dr Masters was baffled by the revelation that a woman had simulated her orgasm – he simply could not understand why she would ever want to do this.[32] Both instances seemed to perfectly encapsulate how the empiricism of mid-century sexual science was intimately tied up with an almost exclusively masculinist perspective on the body. The valorisation of the 'mutual orgasm' drove women to 'act up', which in turn denied them their own physical pleasure, so I concluded. However, in her reply Veronica shared with me the slightly different meaning she took from her story:

> But I had in mind a different scene: instead of saying oh, you're home rather early, she says hi, here's your welcome home hug.[33]

My own interpretation had emphasised the wife's physical frustration at not being satisfied, but Veronica had taken a more optimistic reading of 'acting up'. She viewed it more as a means of loving cooperation rather than deception. It appears I equally displayed the tendency of male intellectual investigators of female sexuality to focus on 'the orgasm' and physical response rather than the complex interpersonal dynamics of married love. The interviewees' memories shine a light on the intimate negotiations that went on in Catholic marital bedrooms, negotiations for which the CMAC and my own initial questioning made little provision.

While the interviewees' evaluations of the CMAC's sexual advice were often determined by existing views of the Church's teaching on birth control, there was a comment common to both 'liberal' and 'orthodox' women. 'Doreen' described the CMAC's seminars as 'very, very anatomical', while 'Katherine' recalled that 'It was all extremely clinical. It [sex] was something to learn from a textbook, like a school for love.'[34] Another Catholic woman recalled that she was eager to gain an insight into the sexual act, but the CMAC's detached and somewhat impersonal form of sexual guidance was epitomised by the fact that her own parents were counsellors: 'I mean, talk about a difference between the rhetoric and the reality!'[35] It seems the positive and emotional aspects of sex were communicated in a diagnostic language that neglected something of the spiritual for these Catholic women.

The CMAC's failure to recognise the fullness of women's sexual experience could be placed in a continuum with the Church's traditional indifference, perhaps even opposition, to female sexual expression. Elements of this tradition lingered in the CMAC throughout the postwar decades. June recalled finding sex very painful in her early marriage, especially when her husband would first enter her. When she visited a CMAC counsellor to ask for help in the early 1970s, she was informed that she should use KY jelly to 'ease entry'.[36] This particular counsellor's advice seemed to suggest that a woman's role in sex was primarily about satisfying male or procreative interests (or at least this was how June interpreted it), reflecting an understanding of sex which had dominated Catholic thinking up until the war. However, it would be misleading to present this as an overriding feature of the CMAC's working beyond the 1960s. Episodes like that cited by June were extremely scarce in the interviews, and the counsellor's advice in this instance directly contravened the training the counsellors were receiving. As Alana Harris has pointed out, the majority of the counsellors were themselves women, a real oddity for an imprimatured Church institution.[37]

At the heart of the CMAC's shortcomings was less a straightforward issue of gender as it had been for Church representatives in the first half of the century – when women were often deemed undeserving of or irrelevant to sexual fulfilment per se – and more a matter of how women's sexual fulfilment was constructed. In their zeal to present frank and scientific sexual guidance, the CMAC's counsellors overlooked the emotional and spiritual aspects of married love. Sex had become considered a matter of empirical 'truth', a rendering which the philosopher Michel Foucault has identified as a key feature of a distinctly 'modern' understanding of sex.[38] The CMAC's understanding of female sexuality, much like that of the Papal Commission for Birth Control, was therefore a product of its wider historical environment. The question Veronica posed at the end of our correspondence illuminates an important dimension of this environment: 'Do you not think there has to be some mystery between men and women?'[39] Veronica may have been referring to a specific situation of marital communication, but the observation that underpinned her question resonated profoundly with the themes of this book. The understanding of sexuality that the CMAC and Catholic authorities more broadly constructed in the 1960s worked to deny the mysteries of sex. In a late-modern context, a widespread distrust of the enigmatic, the peculiar and the unspoken developed in dominant approaches to sexuality, and served to sever sex from questions of religious belief.

The next section moves forward from the marriage preparation which Catholic women received to look at their contraceptive behaviour during early marriage. Particular attention is paid to the emotional sensibilities that were bound up with these decisions and practices. Retrospective oral testimony holds an unparalleled capacity to uncover these often overlooked sensibilities, underlining the poverty but also historical specificity of the CMAC's highly clinical approach to subject.

The experience of practising NFP

From 1951 when the method was approved by the Pope, up until the mid-1980s when it began to significantly wane in popularity, a large proportion of Britain's Catholic population were to practise NFP at some point in their marriage.[40] It was a distinctly post-war marital experience that spoke of Catholicism's complex and sometimes fractured relationship with modernity. The heavy use of scientific apparatus and concern for the economics of the family showed an unprecedented engagement with secular thinking, while the renewed devotion to the 'natural' and the almost ascetic demands made on the body seemed increasingly anachronistic to many outside observers. Catholic couples everyday, or more accurately every night, experience of practising NFP therefore represents a critical point of enquiry for this book. It embodied Catholic women's daily negotiation of the spiritual and the sexual, the moral and the material, at a time when these categories were themselves blurring and disintegrating.

Alongside the testimony of the interviewees, the following section draws on a collection of letters sent to Professor John Marshall, my grandfather, in his capacity as a CMAC medical officer and author of guidance manuals on the method.[41] Over a period of forty years, he corresponded with over 10,000 individuals. The private correspondence offers a unique window into contemporary opinions of the method and allow us to measure these against the interviewees' present-day recollections. A selection of the correspondences was published in a small book in 1995.[42] Marshall, writing as a medical authority and hailing from a background in neurological research, prided himself on taking a 'scientific approach' that allowed the statements 'to speak for themselves'.[43] His accompanying commentary did little more than summarise the points made. As one reviewer stated, it was 'written with empathy and compassion but without question or judgement'.[44] While the statements are still presented here as they were first written, my 'historical approach' makes no claims to be 'scientific'. Furthermore, it is a historical approach which acknowledges and even celebrates the 'question and judgement', selections and interpretations that are brought to bear on the material. The differing frameworks within which my grandfather and I place these statements is a testament to our divergent disciplinary backgrounds, but also to the wider historical setting within which these backgrounds were formed. A valorisation of the empirically scientific and a positivist mistrust of methodological relativism were distinctly post-war traits when confronting the sexual and religious aspects of human experience. As the last line of my grandfather's book proclaims: 'They [married Catholics] must, as did the correspondents in this book, make known their experience, so that ultimately truth will prevail.'[45] I am less interested in pursuing any singular 'truth', and more in the manifold, sometimes conflicting, personal 'truths' that the statements signify.

It was generally half an hour into the interview that I asked the interviewees about their experience of using NFP. This often prompted a shift in the emotional tenor of our dialogue:

DG Could you talk about the experience of using NFP?
Teresa– (sighs) Well we've used it all our lives and I think it's just … (breaks into tears for two minutes) … it's just… exasperating in one sense.[46]

Up to this point in the interview, Teresa had reminisced about her youthful 'innocence' in a light and jovial tone. When we moved on to talk about sex, she quickly became upset. Teresa was married in the spring of 1968 amidst a climate of much expectancy within the Catholic community following the leak of the papal commission's final report. She explained that the only reason she and her husband Michael had started using NFP was because they 'didn't expect to be using it long'.[47] However, when the Pope reasserted the Church's prohibition of artificial means of contraception three months later, they decided to grapple with the method a little longer. In the end, they continued practising NFP for over twenty years, interspersed with sporadic periods of using the pill. She explained that she never felt completely comfortable with defying the Pope, but that it was primarily her husband's 'scruples', which Teresa attributed to his strict education from Benedictine monks, that meant they always returned to 'natural' means. Although Teresa stressed that these decisions were always 'mutually agreed through discussion', she was unlike the majority of the interviewees in that it was her husband who took a dominant role in contraceptive decisions.[48]

Teresa detailed the physiological difficulties they encountered with the method:

> One of the consequences of the safe period for us, used to be premature ejaculation, which was sort of, obviously disappointing for me, but frustrating and disappointing for him. And then, the whole notion of going more slowly, because of the pressure of the safe period made things difficult, and then sort of in later years, then the other thing is, as he gets older ... you get a degree of, it's harder to maintain an erection.[49]

Just under half the interviewees spoke of experiencing premature ejaculation in the 'safe' period at some point. This was also a relatively common occurrence among my grandfather's correspondents:

> Although I find on the first marriage act after a lapse of approximately three weeks I cannot control the flow of my semen which occurs immediately as my penis enters the vagina, nevertheless I am able to continue until my wife is satisfied.[50]

The physiological language which was used by this man was typical of the letters from the 1960s and 1970s, particularly those written by men. It seems that medical terminology provided a more favourable means of disclosing personal information that could be seen to undermine notions of 'masculine virility'. A popular technique for combating premature ejaculation was 'going slow', but, as Teresa found, this had the potential to offer a less than satisfying experience for both parties. One interviewee stated that:

> I never orgasmed during the safe period, we took it slow to help, but as soon as he started to get a head of steam it was all over. Too much pent up you know.[51]

As well as detailing the physical problems of abstinence, it should be noted that these quotations do suggest a heightened concern for the wife's sexual satisfaction (although exactly how the man writing to my grandfather managed to achieve this 'satisfaction', or indeed gauge it, was not made clear).

Impotence was not only a problem that developed in later marriage as it did for Teresa's husband, but also marred the early years of marriage for some couples struggling with NFP.

> The reading of the thermometer alone caused the sex to be far from spontaneous. As time went on, I sometimes found I was unable to have an erection during the safe period, but often had them when sex might result in an unwanted conception.[52]

As well as the pressure that ensued from needing to 'make the most' of the infertile time, the very notion of a 'safe' period was itself de-eroticising. It was a space associated with clinical language, medical apparatus and cold doctors' rooms. Its 'safeness' was the antithesis to everything the dominant liberationist construction of sex claimed to be about – excitement, spontaneity and self-expression. Conversely, the 'unsafe' period became distinctly eroticised for many couples, a phenomenon that we will explore in more depth in the next section.

For women in particular, the 'unsexiness' of the safe period was not only psychological, but grounded in the physical and bodily routines that accompanied the method. As the husband above pointed out, the reading of the thermometer did cause sex to be less than spontaneous for both partners, but women also had the accompanying procedure to go through. This was all the more trying for some women as the prescriptive literature made a point of stressing that rectal recording was preferable. The image in Figure 3 shows an illustration of the discrepancies that could occur between oral and rectal recording presented by the manual *The Infertile Period: Principles and Practices*. The manual therefore instructed medical representatives guiding couples on the method that:

> The best method of recording is rectally ... Recording the temperature rectally is not difficult. Lubricating the bulb of the thermometer with a little Vaseline enables the tip to be easily inserted and three minutes' recording ensures reliable reading. If this method is routinely recommended as the normal procedure most women have no objection to it.[53]

A number of the interviewees found the act of rectal recording unpleasant, with one stating that:

128 *The Pope and the pill*

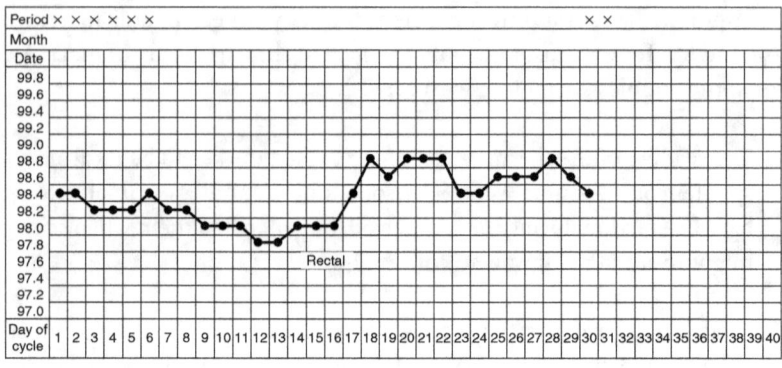

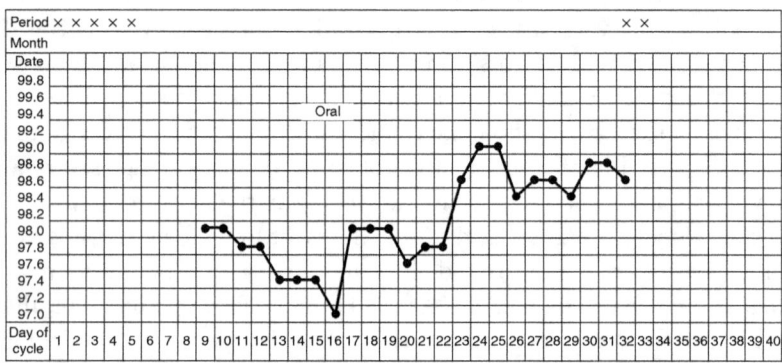

Figure 3 Graph detailing the different readings possible from rectal and oral use of a thermometer when practising NFP, from J. Marshall, *The Infertile Period: Principles and Practices* (Baltimore, MD, 1963)

> I really didn't like it – you could never fully separate doing that in the mornings from what you did that evening.[54]

The aesthetic similarities between rectal recording and the sexual act was an unsettling aspect of NFP that only the wife fully encountered. Filling in the chart, hardly a titillating experience in itself, was also invariably the job of the wife. Mary explained that:

> Well yes I did it all. Filling in the graph, with a pencil and ruler, taking the temperature obviously. He [her husband] never took any interest in that side of things.[55]

Although NFP manuals emphasised the 'mutual cooperation' that was needed from both parties for the method to work, the main responsibility for its execution lay with the wife. While a number of historians have spoken of the pill as a 'revolutionary' challenge to gendered notions of contraceptive responsibility, the interviewees tended to view their role in NFP as more of a burden than emancipation.[56]

The process of remembering encouraged some interviewees to rethink their views on the morality of NFP. The interview provided a dedicated space within which to consider the emotional implications of the method, one that may not have existed before this point. Bridget was a particularly interesting example. She identified as 'orthodox', explaining that she had always believed 'in the Church's teachings pretty much in toto … and I make no excuses for that'.[57] She practised NFP after her second child for the remainder of her 'sexual years'. She accepted that NFP had been 'tough', but went on to say that 'so is getting up every morning … this is life when you are a mother'.[58] In this way, Bridget remembered NFP as another aspect of her maternal labour during early marriage, a part of daily routines and duties alongside tasks such as 'making the children's breakfast'. She spoke of the method making sex more 'special' and drew on a sensualistic allegory to elucidate her point:

> It's like when you have a box of chocolates, I love chocolates and I would want to eat the whole of the top layer, but it's not the best thing. I appreciate them more when I haven't had it for a while.[59]

The idea that NFP enhanced the sensual experience of sex by limiting coital frequency was a key feature of the way the method was advertised by Catholic authorities. One correspondent echoed this sentiment:

> Strangely enough, my husband, who is not a Catholic, feels that the enforced self-control is a good thing – he says we will never get tired of one another as a result of over indulgence![60]

It should be noted that aside from Bridget, none of the other interviewees subscribed to this opinion of the method, even those 'orthodox' Catholics who kept with it throughout their married lives. As the interview with Bridget developed, she also intimated that she may have been less happy with the method than her chocolate box analogy had suggested.

> DG The method was advertised as being spiritually beneficial to the couple as well. Did you find this to be the case?
> Bridget You're making me think now, at the time we didn't have time for spiritual soul searching or scratching the wound or whatever … but there was not so much to take out and look at, and hold up to the light, you know, fidget with. You're actually making me look into that younger self, well I only perhaps express it that way now … when I've only just got it out to look at myself.[61]

It was clear that Bridget was grappling with her own life story in the course of the interview. My questions were opening up new lines of thought which had not existed in her early marriage. We get here an insight into the time constraints that made 'spiritual soul searching' almost impossible in early marriage, but also the stoicism, the sense of 'getting on with things', which typified many of the interviewees' depiction of the lifecycle stage. She went on to say that in the last five years she had started to question her belief in the Church's teaching on contraception:

> Do I want this recorded? (pause) I actually think it [contraceptive morality] is between God and the person now. And therefore, if the person next to me approaches the altar of God with his or her belief that they are approaching God, who am I to say well you haven't had it blessed by the correct, ordained priest. Yes, possibly the Church has had some very strict rules, where … perhaps I'm trying to say that I believe in the essence, but sometimes there has to be some broader look. … So I've come to that and I don't think you'd have heard me say that when I was twenty-five![62]

Although it was more a matter of doctrinal infallibility that Bridget was talking of here, she went on to admit that she 'would have been happy if *Humanae Vitae* had been different'.[63] It was not only her life story that Bridget was reworking in the course of the interview, but through this, her beliefs on the morality of birth control and the nature of papal authority.

In both the contemporary correspondence with my grandfather and the interviewees' retrospective recollections, there was a real emphasis on the physiological, bodily repercussions of practising NFP.

The interviewees' memories, however, included far more discussion of the emotional effects of the method than the correspondence from the time. Teresa detailed the impact of the method on her relationship:

> So it sort of affected our relationship, inevitably. And we've ... erm ... (breaks into tears) it's been erm ... great sorrow really, a sorrow about what might have been, er because when you were in bed together, and you want to have sex and you can't have sex, I mean that for ... but then you, or certainly we, moved to a stage when it's easier to cope with if you don't get close, and you want sex, it's a self-protection, you know.[64]

It was not only anger and pain that Teresa expressed in the interview, but a real sense of loss:

> When I think of the years we have lost, the years we could have been happy ... it was not until the 1980s when we sought out counselling that we started to come back together.

In the early years of her marriage, a period often remembered as the most amorous by couples, Teresa was forced to sacrifice intimacy with her husband in an attempt to negotiate her spiritual and sexual imperatives.

The correspondents' use of physiological language was hardly surprising given that they were addressing a medical practitioner in formal, written dialogue. References to the method's effect on the couples' interpersonal relationship were rare, but not entirely absent:

> The main difficulty is not abstinence alone, but how to maintain a loving relationship while 'repelling' any advances made. I find myself in the very unpleasant role of 'watchdog' ... Looking back now, I realised that what I really needed was advice about how to use this method without damaging our relationship but I did not explain or even realise this at the time.[65]

The CMAC's marriage preparation as well as the NFP training manuals did not offer much guidance for coping with the psychological or emotional tensions that NFP could exert on a couple. Physical or 'libidinal' frustrations were dealt with, as were 'spiritual aspects', but always separately and with little attention to the interpersonal issues that often accompanied the method.⁶⁶ It is important to note that this correspondent was also 'looking back', much like the interviewees. She did not even realise that she required help with the delicacies of marital communication in the earlier stages of her marriage. As we saw in the opening of the last section, the first job of marriage preparation initiatives at the start of the 1960s was to introduce and justify the need to prepare in the first place, to prepare preparation. It seems that the emotional, interpersonal consequences of NFP only fully came to light through the act of remembering. The hustle of day-to-day living in early marriage, coupled with a sexual culture that invariably assumed sexual problems to be physiological, meant that these aspects of married love were often overlooked in personal and intellectual evaluations of NFP.

This correspondent's anxiety over 'repelling' the advances of her husband hinted at the potential for an unsettling dynamic to develop in the relationship. Similar situations were spoken of in the interviews, but a lack of consent was never insinuated.⁶⁷ Angela's husband was abroad for work for months at a time; she explained that trying to tell him, ' "Sorry, not till next Thursday" would have been absurd'. Although she did describe him as the 'boss' in the relationship, Angela emphasised that her husband never 'pressured' her into anything she did not want to do.⁶⁸ However, she was also aware that her own situation was not representative of the entire Catholic population:

> 'Conjugal Love' won't make sense to women in the North, the wife of someone working on the shipyard. On a Saturday night he will be half cut, and he wants his Saturday night. If you try to say no you would be hit about. There can be a lot of violence in sex, some people like violence in sex.⁶⁹

Angela's views on the relationship between sex and violence are explored more fully in the following chapter. She displayed here a consciousness of the class and geographical specificity of her own experience. Her assertions were informed by her work as a CMAC counsellor in the north of England and therefore represent a very specific interpretation of working-class culture. The northern, industrial Catholic community, particularly concentrated in towns like Liverpool, Manchester and Bolton, is somewhat under-represented in the sample – an oral history study of Catholic marriage in these locations would offer a useful means of exploring Angela's claims more thoroughly. Her comments do reflect a relatively widespread belief that periodic abstinence was more suited to the 'mutuality' which was seen to typify middle-class marriages. When the interviewees did speak of NFP's propensity to heighten tensions around the question of 'conjugal rights', it was always in a way that distanced the subject from their own personal experience. Whether this was because of a reticence to disclose sensitive, even incriminating information or because there was nothing to disclose is unknown.

Despite the frustrations and conflicts that many of the interviewees faced while practising NFP, none of them abandoned their Catholic identity or marital relationship. The vast majority continued to wrestle with the method until at least their late thirties. How should this be understood? The simple answer would be found in the texts that advocate a psychoanalytical reading of Catholicism; that guilt and scrupulosity compelled the couples to continue with a practice that flew in the face of their physical, bodily interests.[70] Such a view was typified by Vincent Broome's scathing response to *Humanae Vitae*, referenced in the Introduction, which expressed pity for the 'countless number of simple-minded people' who were to be victims of the Church's dogmatic rule. However, alongside a story of religious indoctrination shackling instincts and intuitions, a more optimistic account of individual creativity, resistance and agency emerged. The interviewees' testimony therefore encourages us to reframe the question we ask of their memories – what tactics did Catholic women employ to negotiate the dual demands of spirituality and sexuality? The word tactics rather than strategies is used advisedly. It borrows from Michel de Certeau's distinction between the two. In *The Practice of Everyday Life*, De Certeau spoke of 'strategies' as being produced by institutions and structures of power such as the state, businesses, scientists and the Church, while individuals act in environments defined by strategies by using 'tactics'.[71] Andrew Blauvelt elucidates Certeau's denotation of 'tactics' in this way:

> Certeau's investigations into the realm of routine practices, or the 'arts of doing' such as walking, talking, reading, dwelling, and cooking, were guided by his belief that despite repressive aspects of modern society, there exists an element of creative resistance to these strictures enacted by ordinary people … Tactics are employed by those who are subjugated. By their very nature tactics are defensive and opportunistic, used in more limited ways and seized momentarily within spaces, both physical and psychological, produced and governed by more powerful strategic relations.[72]

Catholic women were the subject of a peculiar set of 'strategies' in the 1960s; their mental and material environments were being increasingly shaped by the new 'producers' of modernity such as sexual science and consumer culture, but the Church continued to provide the codes and structures that determined their sexual morality. The next section explores the tactics that Catholic women employed during their early marriage to work around, within and against these often conflicting imperatives.

Tactics for dealing with penetrative abstinence

The period of abstinence from penetrative intercourse varied from couple to couple depending on the woman's fertility cycle, but generally ran from four to ten days per month. Critics of the method argued that a woman was most responsive to sex during and around ovulation, a point that was exhaustively debated by medical representatives within the papal commission. As we saw in Chapter 2, a vast corpus of sociological data was collected by both sides to substantiate their cases. These debates tended to centre on whether medical evidence could be sought to establish the anatomical nature of the 'rhythmicity of desire'.[73] Whether there were physiological grounds to these criticisms or not, the correspondents spoke of the 'unsafe' period as a time of heightened desire:

> I think I am probably one of those people who experience maximum desire around the time of ovulation, as at these times I usually experience insomnia and intense physical restlessness.[74]

There were also men who found themselves particularly aroused during the 'unsafe' period:

> I find it very hard to abstain. I have a very beautiful, loving wife and during the unsafe period I seem to find her more desirable than at any other time of the month.[75]

The female correspondent spoke of 'ovulation' while the male correspondent used the phrase 'unsafe period', reflecting the different levels of bodily involvement of the husband and wife. One male interviewee spoke of sex during the unsafe period as 'forbidden fruit – and all the more desirable because of it'.[76] It was not only men who eroticised the very idea of the 'unsafe' – a number of the female interviewees spoke of there being something appealing about defying the imposed chastity, using terms like 'dangerous', 'naughty' and 'adventurous'.[77] Regardless of whether it was understood in physiological or psychological terms, the 'unsafe' period was a time of almost irresistible temptation for many Catholic couples. The compulsion to explain this temptation as a biological phenomenon was typical of the post-war Catholic sexual culture.

Coitus interruptus (or 'withdrawl') was spoken of surprisingly rarely. It was generally viewed as 'ineffective', 'messy' and morally indistinguishable from the use of condoms or the pill – a 'contraceptive mentality' was seen to remain. ('June, interviewed 20/ 02/ 2013'). The most commonly used tactic for coping with periods of abstinence was masturbation. The vast majority of the interviewees spoke of participating in mutual masturbation, where one partner manually stimulated the other, while around half also spoke of solitary masturbation. The dwindling and yet selectively gendered social stigma that still surrounds solitary masturbation could have accounted for this discrepancy, but it is more likely that mutual masturbation was a preferred recourse for Catholic women. As well as having sensual and emotional benefits, it was a more practically viable option for Catholic women in their early marriage: 'Well I might have [masturbated alone], but where and when? No there wasn't the time or space for that sort of thing.'[78]

The Church continued to teach that masturbation was a sin in itself as it could not fulfil procreative ends, but unlike contraception, this teaching was not publicly reasserted by the central hierarchy at any point during the interviewees' lives. In fact, a newly sympathetic theology towards the 'naturalness' of masturbation had growing support within the lay and clerical population. Writing in 1965, Jack Dominian spoke of masturbation as a way of exploring sexuality in its immature state, stressing the importance of compassion and understanding when considering its intrinsic morality.[79] A judgement was still made of the act, but this now appeared in pathological rather than moralistic terms.

As Katherine's anecdote below suggests, by the mid-1960s many parish priests at a grassroots level were downplaying the immorality of masturbation:

> Funnily enough, talking about masturbation, when we moved in here [1964], there was a talk from the priest about questions about

bringing up children. I was in the audience and there was a lot of Irish people there, and one woman asked (puts on Irish accent) 'Father, Father, what do you say to your boy if he masturbates?' He said 'Masturbation? It's like picking your nose!' He said, 'if he sits in the corner all day doing it he's got a problem, but otherwise everybody does it'. And everyone was 'gasps' (chuckles) … so that was good.[80]

As well as giving an insight into a sexually progressive strand within the English clergy, this story also highlighted the theological 'orthodoxy' that was seen to permeate the Irish immigrant population. There was also opposition to a more sympathetic view of masturbation within the English Catholic community. A sex manual called *Choices in Sex* (1970) had its imprimatur removed after complaints about its treatment of masturbation from the Catholic Priests Association (CPA), a relatively small clerical society in England and Ireland with deeply conservative convictions.[81] The CPA claimed the booklet intended to 'rob them [the readers] of their priceless Catholic faith or corrupt the integrity of their moral lives' and the public debate that accompanied the dispute filled the letters pages of mainstream British broadsheets as well as the Catholic press.[82]

Resistance to a more sympathetic view of masturbation was not simply the preserve of an 'orthodox', clerically led minority, but something that many Catholics grappled with internally on a daily basis. One female correspondent informed John Marshall:

It is only fair to say to you that I have very regretfully been self-abusive and masturbating.[83]

The phrase 'self-abuse' and the confessional tone that accompanied this comment were indicative of an attitude to masturbation that has become largely obsolete amongst present-day Catholics. The majority of the interviewees were quite uninhibited when speaking of masturbation, but looked back on their earlier marriage as a time when this would not have been the case. Joan explained that she 'always felt terrible after, I just thought it was wrong'.[84]

Many interviewees were of the belief that they had had more 'scruples' about solitary masturbation than their husbands. Rosie said she masturbated on her own during periods of abstinence when 'it all got too much', and although they had not expressly spoken about it, was 'quite sure' that her husband also did:

> Rosie I'm sure that my husband had no idea that I was worrying about things like that, because I never told him, I'm sure he never had thoughts like that at all.
> DG As in had scruples?
> Rosie Yes, although he'd been educated in a monastery, but men are different.
> DG Do you think then the scruples are more of a feminine thing?
> Rosie Yes I do, and in fact I've met people who now are my age who still suffer from scruples, which is terrible, it's a terrible burden that the church put on us, it was unforgivable really, and I think a lot of people are … I think I was retarded spiritually; I was still a seven-year-old until I was in my forties.[85]

The gendered sense of sexual guilt that many of the interviewees communicated resonated with Brown's description of 'pious femininity'.[86] Catholic women often carried this burden with them well beyond the 'sexual revolution' of the 1960s. There were also cases of sexual guilt being more of an issue with the husband than the wife. We saw in the last section how Teresa's husband had been more scrupulous than her about the morality of contraception and the same was the case for masturbation:

> Teresa And then of course, not so much for me but for Martin, enormous sexual frustration, because masturbation's wrong as well isn't it, you know just … he used to really try and do the right thing, and there were all things he's been told and he's internalised, as wrong, and I was saying I just don't think this was all wrong.
> DG Did you say this to Martin?
> Teresa Yes, about actually loving each other you know, I just don't believe it's wrong, of course he didn't want to believe but he couldn't get away from it. He would have loved to have believed something different.[87]

Catholic teachings actually allowed greater room for a woman's stimulation outside of penetrative intercourse than for a man's. The popular theologian Christopher West offered this translation of Pope John Paul II's writings on the matter:

> Since it's the male orgasm that's inherently linked with the possibility of new life, the husband must never intentionally ejaculate outside of his wife's vagina. Since the female orgasm, however, isn't necessarily linked to the possibility of conception, so long as it takes place within the overall context of an act of intercourse, it need not, morally speaking, be during actual penetration.[88]

This reading of the Catholic doctrine is not without contest, but what West was suggesting was that if a man was to ejaculate before his wife had reached orgasm, it would not be unlawful for the man to then stimulate his partner by either mouth or hand to bring her to orgasm. There was no mention of this in the NFP training manuals from the time and no interviewees recounted a corresponding experience (although they weren't asked about it either). Although this is not the same as masturbation during the 'unsafe period' (which includes no procreative intent and is therefore deemed unlawful outright) the example illuminates the differing materialities of the male and female orgasm.

Teresa may have seen her husband's scruples as being rooted in his monastic education, but for men as conscious of doctrinal intricacies as Martin was, the act of 'spilling the seed' would have served as a physical reminder of the Church's insistence on sex's procreative function.

Along with manual masturbation, the interviewees spoke of other sexual practices that helped them ease the frustrations of the 'unsafe period'. Oral sex was relatively commonplace:

> Oh yes we used to do that, some men can only be stimulated with a bit of oral sex you know. But yes we started doing that more in the unsafe period and that helped.[89]

Doreen pointed out that there was 'something different about oral sex, less mechanical, more loving'.[90] In this sense, oral stimulation offered a different kind of intimacy than that of manual masturbation. Doreen was specifically speaking of fellatio here, but she and many of the interviewees recalled that their partners 'often reciprocated'. Some interviewees expressed an aversion to oral sex on aesthetic grounds, but none had had a moral issue with the practice based on religious grounds. Anal sex was spoken of less frequently, but was something that a handful of the interviewees explored specifically as a means of coping with the safe period: 'I don't think we would have tried it had it not been for the safe period. It wasn't really for us in the end.'[91] Another interviewee recalled that they 'discovered' the practice during an 'unsafe' period, and finding it 'quite enjoyable', ended up intermittently practising it throughout their marriage despite giving up on NFP in their mid-thirties.[92]

Perversely, the Church's dictates on contraception were encouraging couples to turn to new sexual activities that were equally, if not more, condemned by traditional Catholic teaching. Over half the interviewees expressed an aversion to the physicality of anal sex, but unlike oral sex, there were also interviewees who took moral issue with the activity. Katherine was very candid about the sexual activities she 'experimented' with, including mutual masturbation and oral sex, but stated clearly 'I didn't go in for sodomy.' She was not alone in using the phrase 'sodomy' in response to my asking about 'anal sex'.[93] This was a discourse that clearly remained an integral part of a certain Catholic generation's understanding of sexual morality.

It was not always physical acts of sexual release that were used by Catholic women to deal with the periods of abstinence. An unexpected tactic was the use of humour. Lucy explained that she and her husband 'dealt very badly' with the 'unsafe' period, and so they enlisted the help of a third party:

Lucy We had a very large teddy bear, you know the kind of thing you win at the fair, which we sometimes used to keep us apart at 'unsuitable' times.
DG Really, how big was this teddy bear then?
Lucy Oh enormous! (chuckles)
DG Did it work?
Lucy It was just for fun. We would go to bed and the bear would be in the bed. It would be a bit of a laugh.[94]

Lucy stressed how the bear helped diffuse tensions at bedtime, but also provided something to hold on to when contact with her husband would have been 'too much to handle'. This creative tactic was an exception to the stories of the guilt-laden conflict that defined many of the interviewees' early marriage. It also pointed to the limited recourses available to Catholic women when attempting to mediate the demands of their libido, relationship and religious beliefs. She recalled that a friend of hers 'trained her dog to growl at her husband when he approached her at "unsuitable" times'.[95] The efficacy of these alternative tactics should not simply be measured by their success at upholding abstinence, but also in their capacity to keep the couple together and Catholic.

The use of teddy bears and growling dogs were the only tactics employed by the interviewees that did not contravene the Church's official teachings in some way (at the point of writing). In the early years of marriage, some of the interviewees saw illicit sexual release, be it from masturbation, oral sex or anal sex, as a 'lesser evil' than artificial contraception, but the majority spoke of it as something that just 'happened':

> There wasn't much of a decision, it would just happen. Afterwards I always regretted it, thinking this is a sin, but it never stopped it happening again. We were compelled by our bodies if you like.[96]

This quotation epitomised the way the interviewees described their sexuality as an instinctive, visceral force that drove their behaviour, with the phrase 'it would just happen' reinforcing the sense of unthinking determinism. Although the interviewees remembered their actions as almost inevitable concessions to 'natural instinct', at the time many believed that they were committing grievous sins.

For Catholics wanting to alleviate the ensuing guilt, the next logical step was to confess to a priest. Joan pointed out that she was fully aware that she would recommit the sin even as she knelt in the confessional. Although this would have defeated the integrity of her confession, she still continued to confess masturbation throughout her early marriage: 'it made me feel better for a bit. You had to play the game.'[97] The allusion to a game was apt. David Lodge described Catholic morality as being like a game of snakes and ladders:

> The name of the game was Salvation, the object to get to Heaven and avoid Hell. It was like Snakes and Ladders: sin sent you plummeting down towards the Pit; the sacraments, good deeds, acts of self-mortification, enabled you to climb back towards the light.[98]

In early marriage, Catholic women were often conscious of the contradictions and paradoxes that governed the game they were playing, but still could not free themselves from its confines. As was the case for the characters in Lodge's book, the movement away from this mentality happened at different speeds for different interviewees, but almost always involved a rejection of the confessional as a source of moral absolution.

In the course of many of the interviewees' early marriages, confession ceased to function as a vehicle of celestial reconciliation and became instead a space within which to gauge the Church's position on matters of personal morality, particularly questions of sex. Katherine used to confess masturbating her husband during periods of abstinence, but made sure she sought out the 'right sort of priest' for it:

> The word around was if you wanted to go to confession, you went to Fr Andrew. Franciscan, he was easy (chuckles) when it was a 'How Far Can You Go?' sort of thing.[99]

Katherine's comments indicate just how variable clerical attitudes to sex and masturbation were in the 1960s, even within the same locality.[100] However, it was her trusted confessor of choice who ended up breaking her lingering devotion to the sacrament of confession:

> I remember going to confession to talk about masturbating my husband when it wasn't the safe period. Then I found out that he himself was having an affair with someone in the Parish! (chuckles) You know, I thought, bloody hell, I've been confessing this to him while he's … I'm not saying everyone's the same but it rather put me off my confession. I think that that liberated me a bit.[101]

At the start of many of the interviewees' early marriages, confession was an important part of the tactics they employed for negotiating spiritual and sexual demands. It was still a space in which matters of religion and sexuality could meet and be mediated under the watchful gaze of the clergy. As they moved through this life-cycle stage, though, episodes like the one that Katherine recalled not only undermined the moral authority of the clergy, but also encouraged Catholic women to see their sexual behaviour as something that bore little relation to matters of faith.

With the confessional no longer representing the same space of spiritual expression that it had for the interviewees' parents' generation,

I was interested to hear how prayer helped the interviewees deal with the strains and difficulties they experienced with NFP. However, the interviewees did not bring this up of their own volition, and so I started asking specifically about the role of prayer; did they pray for strength during the 'unsafe' period, for guidance with questions of sexual morality or for forgiveness when they believed themselves to have sinned? Again, I received very little response. A number of the interviewees talked of starting to pray about these matters in their later marriage – we have heard how Anne 'prayed in agony' in the lead-up to her moment of 'liberation'.[102] But it seems that in early marriage, sexual issues were either deemed an unsuitable topic or simply did not factor in Catholic women's thinking at the moment of prayer: 'No not really. I didn't really think to, you don't pray about things like that do you.'[103] This mental separation between prayer and matters of sex was made all the more problematic by the shared physical spaces which they inhabited. Marian explained to me that religious practice and sex could not coexist in the same spaces:

> Marian If you take your beads before you got to bed, it's a death-knell to the marriage. We used to say our rosary when the children were still up at 6, yes we would kneel down then too.
> DG Why would it be a death-knell to your marriage?
> Marian (pause) Well because, not many men would say it was that proper to have intercourse with someone who had just, who was still, just said a prayer. You go to pray yeah – give yourself a bit of a break.
> DG Did your husband ever say that to you?
> Marian No, no I knew it. Things don't have to always be said for people to know.[104]

Marian's comments encapsulated the tensions and contradictions that defined Catholic women's daily negotiation of sexual and religious imperatives; the two were at once both physically tethered and yet mentally separated. Her notion of a sexually conducive mood and environment, shaped primarily by her interpretation of her husband's wishes, could not accommodate the intrusion of religious sentiment. Furthermore, religious sentiment represented the 'death-knell' for intimate marital relations, the direct antipode to a liberated, masculinist construction of healthy sexual expression. In this sense, the break between the religious and the sexual was a recategorisation of lived experience as much as knowledge.

The tactics that the interviewees employed to deal with the strains of practising NFP were almost always physical. They spoke of using masturbation, both mutual and solitary, oral and occasionally anal sex to deal with the periods of abstinence, rather than prayer and confession as the advice literature encouraged. Abstinence brought about physical frustrations that were alleviated by physical means. The interviewees' early marriages were remembered as a time when they worked to appease the visceral, instinctive urges of the 'sexual self' that would eventually be set free in their later marriage. Marian's comments prompt us to think again of the shared times and places that sexual and spiritual activities inhabited in Catholic women's early marriage. She spoke of needing to consciously take a 'break' between sexual and religious practices, to actively construct a spatial and temporal barrier between the two. It was the material proximity of spiritual and sexual activities which brought into focus the conceptual tension between the two.

Conclusion

The prevailing memory that many of the interviewees had of their early marriages was of pain, suffering and disquiet. At the time, the bustle of family life, a lack of heightened expectations and a stoic outlook encouraged Catholic women to 'get on with things', as Bridget put it. It was the experiences of later marriage that brought into focus the extent of the physical and emotional hardship they underwent with NFP. This retrospection does not delegitimise the value of the interviewees' memories, though, but opens up otherwise obscured emotional and sensual aspects of sexual intimacy. It is this facet of oral-history research which could help reframe the way the 'personal' is constructed within Catholic debates about contraceptive morality. The material contained in the middle section of this chapter provides a starting point for such an undertaking. Catholic women's memories, when treated with the appropriate methodological provisions, highlight the messy, varied and highly subjective processes through which meaning and experience interact.

The separation of sexual and religious sensibilities which occurred in the liberal interviewees' later marriages was rooted in the everyday experiences of their early married life. It was a conceptual divide which did not simply work at the level of discourse, but shaped the concrete, material spaces that sexual and religious activities occupied. Marian's assertion that praying in her marital bed would have been the 'death-knell' for her marriage epitomised the way this separation affected the cultural geography and routines of quotidian existence.[105] Indeed, it was the shared physical spaces that the two inhabited which often forced Catholic women to seek out new and creative tactics for dealing with the ensuing conflicts. Their role in actively negotiating spiritual and sexual demands allowed them to maintain their Catholic affiliation, while laying the foundations for the 'liberal' identities that they would go on to adopt. This chapter has emphasised the agency that both 'liberal' and 'orthodox' Catholic women exercised in their early years of marriage, despite the array of mental and material structures that framed their existence. The final chapter moves back in to Catholic women's pre-marital sexualities, but does so not to seek an explanation or root cause of their marital behaviour. Early life is treated as a constitutive rather than formative life-cycle stage. In so doing, the significance of the experiences documented in the chapters thus far are not undermined, but recognised as lived moments affected by what oral historians would call human agency, what Catholics would understand to be free will.

Notes

1. It should be noted that I generally used the term 'sex' in the interviews rather than 'coitus'. This was June's term and so I ended up adopting it here. June, interviewed 20/02/2013.
2. R. Porter and L. Hall, *The Facts of Life: The Creation of Sexual Knowledge in Britain* (New Haven, CT, 1995).
3. J. Lewis, 'Private Counselling versus Public Voice, 1948–68', in J. Lewis, D, Clark and D. Morgan (eds), *Whom God Hath Joined Together: The Work of Marriage Guidance* (London, 1992), p. 74.
4. J. Marshall, *Preparing for Marriage* (Baltimore, MD, 1962).
5. M. Schofield, *The Sexual Behaviour of Young People* (London, 1965), pp. 148–149, 216, 254.
6. C. Taylor, *The Culture of Confession from Augustine to Foucault* (New York, 2009).
7. Marshall, *Preparing for Marriage*.

Sexuality in early marriage   145

8   Ibid.
9   'Decisions Reached on Preparation for Marriage and Pre-Marriage Advice to be Given by Counsellors' (11 April 1951), Marriage Care Papers, unarchived collection, London/Nottingham. Accessed with permission from Terry Prendergast, Marriage Care Chief Executive. The Pope's endorsement of NFP was given at addresses of 29 October 1951 to the Italian Catholic Union of Midwives and 26 November to the National Congress of the Family Front and the Association of Large Families, National Catholic Welfare Conference, Washington, DC.
10 Catholic Marriage Advisory Council, *Preparing Engaged Couples for Marriage* (London, 1967).
11 J. Marshall, interviewed 12/05/2011.
12 J. Marshall, *Fifty Years of Marriage Care* (London, 1996), p. 60.
13 Ibid., p. 25.
14 CMAC, *Preparing Engaged Couples*, p. 60.
15 'Attendance', file 'Reports 1960–1969', Marriage Care Papers.
16 Marshall, *Marriage Care*, p. 33; J. Marshall, interviewed 12/05/2011.
17 J. Marshall, interviewed 12/05/2011.
18 CMAC, *Preparing Engaged Couples*.
19 Ibid., pp. 53–55.
20 Ibid., p. 54.
21 A. Comfort, *The Joy of Sex* (New York, 2002), p. 191.
22 L. Rumble and C. M. Carty, *Radio Replies by Frs Rumble & Carty* (St. Paul, MN, 1938), p. 261.
23 Ibid., p. 263.
24 Q. de la Bedoyere, interviewed 20/06/2011.
25 CMAC, *Preparing Engaged Couples*, p. 61.
26 Ibid., p. 64.
27 National Marriage Guidance Council, *Marriage Guidance* (London, 1968), p. 16.
28 R. Irwin, '"To Try and Find Out What Is Being Done to Whom, by Whom and with What Results": The Creation of Psychosexual Counselling Policy in England, 1972–1979', *Twentieth Century British History*, 20:2 (2009), p. 176.
29 CMAC, *Preparing Engaged Couples*, p. 53.
30 The 'joyous sensations' are 'attached' to the sexual act, suggesting sex was essentially a procreative act to which pleasure was appended. This understanding of sex was consistently upheld by the Church right up until *Humanae Vitae*, when the 'hierarchy of values' reversed this order. Arguments about the 'primary' and 'secondary' function of sex – the ordering of procreation and pleasure – was central to the Catholic birth-control debate in the 1960s. As stated in the

Introduction, this book is not interested in rehashing the well-trodden theological binaries of these contests. I am more interested into how these dichotomies mapped on to a deeper process of categorisation. CMAC, *Preparing Engaged Couples*, p. 60.
31 Correspondence with Veronica, 15/09/2013.
32 *Masters of Sex*, series 1, Showtime (2013).
33 Correspondence with Veronica, 15/09/2013. The written nature of this source should be taken into account when considering Veronica's position. She had more time to 'compose' her response than would have been the case for the interviewees. This would account for the fluidity of expression, but could also been seen to direct the meaning of her reflections.
34 Doreen, interviewed 11/08/2012; Katherine, interviewed 3/05/2012.
35 Teresa, interviewed 04/04/2012.
36 June, interviewed 20/02/2013.
37 A. Harris, 'Love Divine and Love Sublime: The Catholic Marriage Advisory Council, the Marriage Guidance Movement and the State', in A. Harris and T. West (eds), *Love and Romance in Britain, 1918–1970* (New York, 2015), pp. 188–244.
38 M. Foucault, *The History of Sexuality*, vol. 1 (London, 1976), p. 56
39 Correspondence with Veronica, 15/09/2013.
40 G. Jones and D. Nortman, 'Roman Catholic Fertility and Family Planning: A Comparative Review of the Research Literature', *Studies in Family Planning*, 34 (1968), pp. 1–72.
41 For more information about my relationship to my grandfather, see the section on 'Religious history and the personal' in Chapter 1.
42 J. Marshall, *Love One Another: Psychological Aspects of Natural Family Planning* (London, 1995).
43 Ibid.
44 J. Judge, 'Review of *Love One Another*', *The Tablet*, 25 May 1996.
45 Marshall, *Love One Another*, p. 122.
46 Teresa, interviewed 04/04/2012.
47 Ibid.
48 Ibid.
49 Ibid.
50 Marshall, *Love One Another*, p. 43.
51 Sorcha, interviewed 09/01/2014.
52 Marshall, *Love One Another*, p. 43.
53 The manual did go on to recognise that 'some women have strong psychological objections to the rectal route of recording'. J. Marshall, *The Infertile Period: Principles and Practices* (Baltimore, MD, 1963), pp. 46–48.

Sexuality in early marriage 147

54 Georgina, interviewed 22/11/2012.
55 Mary, interviewed 02/10/2013.
56 For an example of such a reading of the pill's emancipatory function for women, see H. Cook, *The Long Sexual Revolution: English Women, Sex and Contraception 1800–1975* (Oxford, 2004); for a discussion of the gendered notions of contraceptive responsivity before the 1960s, see K. Fisher, *Birth Control, Sex and Marriage in Britain, 1918–1960* (Oxford, 2006), pp. 189–237.
57 Bridget, interviewed 16/04/2013.
58 Ibid.
59 Ibid.
60 Marshall, *Love One Another*, p. 59.
61 Bridget, interviewed 16/04/2013.
62 Ibid.
63 Ibid.
64 Teresa, interviewed 04/04/2012.
65 Marshall, *Love One Another*, p. 48.
66 Angela, interviewed 07/01/2014.
67 Historians such as Joanna Bourke have shown how understandings of consent and marital rape underwent significant changes in the post-war period. This large and highly sensitive subject falls beyond the immediate bounds of this book, but the Catholic experience would make for a valuable area of future research. J. Bourke, *Rape: A History from 1960 to the Present Day* (London, 2008).
68 Angela, interviewed 07/01/2014.
69 Ibid.
70 L. Pyle (ed.), *Pope and Pill* (London, 1968), p. 116.
71 M. de Certeau, *The Practice of Everyday Life*, trans. Steven Rendell (Berkeley, CA, 1984).
72 A. Blauvelt (ed.), *Strangely Familiar: Design and Everyday Life* (London, 2003), p. 20.
73 For a contemporary survey of medical debates about the 'rhythmicity of desire', see Marshall, *The Infertile Period*, p. 101.
74 Marshall, *Love One Another*, p. 34.
75 Ibid., p. 45.
76 Frank, interviewed 18/12/2012.
77 Lydia, interviewed 20/03/2013; Teresa, interviewed 04/04/2012; June, interviewed 20/02/2012.
78 Lydia, interviewed 20/03/2013.
79 J. Dominian, *The Church and the Sexual Revolution* (London, 1967).
80 Katherine, interviewed 14/07/2013.
81 Q. and I. de la Bedoyere, *Choices in Sex* (London, 1970).

82 *Catholic Herald*, 10 August 1969, p. 2.
83 Marshall, *Love One Another*, p. 50.
84 Joan, interviewed 19/01/2013.
85 Rosie, interviewed 11/09/2012.
86 C. Brown, *The Death of Christian Britain: Understanding Secularisation, 1800–2000* (Cambridge, 2000), pp. 9–17.
87 Teresa, interviewed 04/04/2012.
88 C. West, *Good News about Sex and Marriage: Answers to Your Honest Questions about Catholic Teaching* (New York, 2000), p. 88.
89 Angela, interviewed 07/01/2014.
90 Doreen, interviewed 11/08/2014.
91 Teresa, interviewed 04/04/2012.
92 Sorcha, interviewed 09/01/2014.
93 Katherine, interviewed 14/07/2013.
94 Lucy, interviewed 08/02/2013.
95 Ibid.
96 Doreen, interviewed 11/08/2012.
97 Joan, interviewed 19/01/2013.
98 D. Lodge, *How Far Can You Go?* (London, 1980), pp. 6–7.
99 Katherine, interviewed 14/07/2013.
100 Andrew Greeley's survey of the American clergy indicates that a 'sexual revolution' occurred in their attitudes to contraception; by 1965, 49 per cent of parish priests stated that they disagreed with the central Church's teaching on the matter, almost exactly the same percentage as in the lay community. Although there was no comparative research undertaken in Britain, Leo Pyle has collected much anecdotal evidence in the form of letters to bishops, parish sermons and newspaper reports that suggest the attitudes of the British clergy were not dissimilar, A. Greeley,' The Sexual Revolution in the Catholic Clergy', *Review of Religious Research*, 14 (1973), pp. 91–100; L. Pyle (ed.), *Pope and Pill* (London, 1968).
101 Katherine, interviewed 14/03/2013.
102 Anne, interviewed 24/03/12.
103 Sorcha, interviewed 09/01/2014.
104 Marian, interviewed 26/09/2013
105 Ibid.

• 5 •

Early life and pre-marital sexuality

The final chapter of this book looks at Catholic women's sexual and religious development in the years that preceded their marriages. For all the interviewees bar one, this period did not involve any penetrative intercourse. For the vast majority, there was also little to no genital activity of any kind with a partner, while only six spoke of solitary masturbation. This period in the interviewees' lives was most distant to them at the point of interview, but, for reasons outlined in the first chapter, I do not want to get snagged on questions surrounding the 'reliability' of their memories. Nor am I interested in debating the definitions of terms like 'childhood', 'youth' and 'adolescence'; others have theorised over the parameters that should be drawn around these descriptors.[1] Indeed, the tendency to focus on the intricacies of this period in a person's life, particularly in relation to sexual and religious development, is itself one that will be historicised here. The experiences of an eight-year-old Catholic girl were, of course, very different from those of an eighteen-year-old, but the interviewees tended to remember their sexual development in a way that drew them together under the banners 'early life', 'upbringing' or 'before marriage'. 'Early life' is therefore treated as both a life-cycle stage which Catholic women lived through as well as a subject which has been debated, defined and understood by different individuals and institutions. As has been the case throughout this book, the chapter demonstrates that there was a close relationship between the two – the personal, lived experiences of young Catholic women and the broader, intellectual understandings of the life-cycle stage.

Early life, whether described in terms of childhood, adolescence or youth, has been endowed with an inflated significance by academics assessing personal religiosity in the post-war. In academic texts and the wider imagination, childhood has been placed at the centre of 'rationalist' explanations of religious belief.[2] Catholicism, to a greater degree than any other belief system, ideology or source of identity, has become understood to be the product of indoctrination or psychological programming in a person's early life. The quotation 'give me a boy until he's seven and I'll show you the man', often attributed to St Francis Xavier and commonly associated with the Jesuits, has been regurgitated in countless attacks on Catholic belief in the last fifty years.[3] This reading of early life is historically specific; the final section of the chapter details how it was informed by the ascendency of popular psychoanalytical thought in the immediate post-war years. In this sense, the chapter builds on the work of Matthew Thomson, which, in the words of one reviewer, 'develops a growing emphasis on the mid-20th century as a crucial moment in the development of thinking about childhood … and in the increasing importance of psychological ways of thinking in popular debate'.[4] The intention here is to cut 'early life' down to size in academic accounts of religious life stories. By treating childhood as a constitutive rather than determinative life-cycle stage, the complex meanings and motivations behind religious and sexual identities can be brought in to focus.

The association between religion and infantilism was a conspicuous presence in the interviews; some interviewees adopted elements of it while others actively resisted the link.[5] The latter group were eager to emphasise the agency they exercised within their own religious upbringings. They often spoke out against the indictment that their Catholicism had been imposed upon them in their childhood. Some even singled out specific public figures that represented and espoused this form of militant secularism. The final section moves on to consider how psychoanalytical interpretations of childhood belief affected the interviewees' approach to parenting. Although they readily imparted Catholic theology to their offspring, religious ideals were almost entirely absent from their sexual guidance. The book concludes by reflecting on what this approach to parenting can tell us about the shifting relationship between sex and religion, and how the interviewees envisioned this relationship developing in the future.

While the interviewees stressed a sense of agency in their early religious life, they also emphasised their relative 'innocence' and 'sexual ignorance' compared to not only girls of today, but also their male and non-Catholic peers.[6] This was often a trait that they were conscious of at the time. The second section of the chapter explores how the interviewees' gender and Catholicism intersected to shape their understanding of sexuality in adolescence. It uses Brown's notion of pre-sixties 'pious femininity' as a starting point from which to assess the gendered expectations that surrounded the politics of courtship, chastity and desire.[7] The interviewees' interpretation of their 'innocence' did not always accord with Brown's story of imposed suppression. Instead, many remembered the climate of innocence and naivety that pervaded their early sexual development with a sense of ambivalence and even nostalgia. The interviewees' experiences of marital sexuality clearly affected the way this period was remembered. Some saw their youthful sexual ignorance as the root cause of the troubles they experienced in marriage, while for others these troubles incited them to view their youth with a wistful longing. Their memories of this period would have undoubtedly been shaped by more recent sexual experiences, but this does not make their interpretations any less insightful. The tone, mood and emotions that accompanied the interviewees' recollections of early life offer an insight into how this life-cycle stage was experienced at the time, as well as the interpretive filter they developed subsequently.

This chapter begins with a discussion of the sexual education that was available to Catholic women in the post-war decades. The interviewees were of a generation who received little to no formal sexual education. The first section therefore attends to the multiform and ad hoc sources of sexual knowledge that young Catholic women sought in the years immediately surrounding the war (late 1930s to 1950s). What was apparent was that no correlation existed between the form of sexual education received in adolescence and the eventual religious belief system taken up in adulthood. Attributing a Catholic woman's eventual 'orthodox' or 'liberal' Catholic identity, or any other aspect of their beliefs, to their sexual education is therefore misleading.

The middle of the 1960s witnessed a sudden proliferation of Catholic sexual education initiatives (a little too late for most of the interviewees). Catholic schools started providing sex education provision and manuals began appearing in the bedside tables of, generally liberal-minded, Catholic teenagers. There was an underlying commonality in the way these initiatives were framed by progressive Catholic authorities and the way the interviewees remembered their own sexual education. The most recurrent theme that ran through the interviewees' testimony was the idea that their sexual education had been an act of self-revelation or discovery, something that 'just happened' or was 'naturally in them'.

A discourse of the 'natural' was central to the way they made sense of their sexual development. Although the Catholic sexual educators of the 1960s were of the opinion that sex needed to be taught rather than just discovered, they too shared this conception of sex as a 'natural', instinctive entity. The chapter therefore begins by introducing an idea which runs throughout: that changes in Catholic understandings of pre-marital sexuality were the consequence of a much deeper shift in the way sex and religion were categorised.

Catholic sexual education

The sexual education provided to Catholic adolescents underwent rapid and substantial change in the post-war years. Growing up in the decades immediately surrounding the war, the vast majority of the interviewees received no formal sex education at all, let alone from Catholic sources. It was not until the middle of the 1960s that authorities within the Church, Catholic schools and affiliated organisations began to move into this area. As Lutz Sauerteig and Roger Davidson have demonstrated, sexual education became a major point of contest across European societies in the 1960s.[8] Informed by the theories of Wilhelm Reich, the 'sexual repression' of childhood was increasingly seen as a 'major cause of human cruelty', an indictment that moved beyond the circles of leftist and progressive 'sex radicals' into the popular consciousness.[9] The emergence of Catholic sexual education initiatives was therefore a response to developments in secular culture, while also reflecting a growing awareness from within the Catholic community that more needed to be done to educate the younger generation.

As well as tracing the emergence of 'formal' Catholic sexual education in the post-war years, this section also explores the more diffuse, ad hoc forms of sex education to which young Catholic women were exposed. The interviewees spoke of sourcing sexual knowledge from their parents, peers, media, cultural representations and the 'natural world'. Indeed, the 'natural' was a key discourse used by the interviewees when making sense of their sexual development. Among the variable sources that the interviewees identified, there was no correlation with their eventual religious identities, sexual morality or contraceptive practice. In this way, the sexual education that Catholic women received should not be viewed as determinative of their ensuing religious identities, but a lived component of a particular life-cycle stage.

For Catholics going through their teenage years before the 1960s, the parental home served as a leading source of sexual knowledge, although rarely in the form of expressed dialogue. Only one of the interviewees spoke of receiving 'the talk' from her mother:

> It was when I had my first period, she sat me down and did the birds and bees thing. Maybe I should have already known about things but I think this was the first time I put things together.[10]

Generally though, the interviewees spoke of learning from their parents without being actively taught by them. Leonie explained that she learnt from 'example':

> I could see them together, and how they were with each other. And I suppose that's how I learnt about men and women, romantic love. I think I just made the natural connection between that and the things I learnt in biology.[11]

The 'natural connection' that Leonie spoke of was typical of the way the interviewees made sense of their sexual education. Her testimony suggested a distinction between questions of gender and love, which she learnt from her parents, and sex, which was a matter of biological mechanics. Crucially, it was left to her to make a connection between the two rather than this connection being made for her.

It was often in the family home that Catholic girls would be introduced to the subject of birth control. Catholic girls' schools did not offer any formal sex education in the 1950s, let alone anything that dealt with questions of contraception. Their mothers therefore often represented the first point of contact with the matter. Sorcha came from an 'academic family' who 'had always spoken out against the Church's teaching on artificial means'. Although her mother never explicitly commented on her own practice to Sorcha directly, Sorcha explained that she could tell from the spacing of her siblings' births that her mother was using 'some form of apparatus'.[12] Sorcha's mother was a rarity among the interviewees' parents' generation in that she was willing to defy the Church's teaching well before the birth-control debate took off in the public realm during the 1960s. Despite this example in her early life, Mary chose to grapple with NFP at the start of her marriage, only moving on to the pill in her forties. While the interviewees were introduced to the morality of birth control by their parents, their eventual contraceptive behaviour was not determined by these examples.

Penny was the only other interviewee who was aware that her mother had used artificial means, but gleaned this knowledge in a very different way:

> I remember as a twelve-year-old finding a book, about family planning and, not that at that age did it dawn on me that that was something the Church said you shouldn't do, but I was a bit fascinated that it was hidden, you know it was hidden, my mother liked reading, but this was hidden. And later as I got older I realised this must have been a problem for her, my mother, because during those fertile years she stopped going to church, later she went back, after the menopause she went back again, but she was quite a long time when she didn't go.[13]

The culture of secrecy that surrounded birth control in the immediate post-war years was a key difference between the settings of the interviewees' marriages and that of their parents' generation. Penny's mother's decision not to go to Mass while she was using artificial means, or at least Penny's reading of this decision, was one that reflected a different understanding of devotional practice, when the prospect of receiving communion in a state of mortal sin would keep individuals away from Church all together. Where the interviewees negotiated spiritual and sexual demands by reformulating their personal beliefs on birth control, Penny's mother was of a generation who were thought to have been compelled to sacrifice Mass attendance.

Penny's fascination with her mother's concealed book epitomised the restricted but also diverse avenues of sexual knowledge that were available to Catholic teenagers in the 1940s and 1950s. It was the 'hidden' nature of the book that aroused her interests initially, but it was only at a later stage that she could fully appreciate the significance of what it contained. Catholic teenage girls were often left to discover and interpret sex in their own ways. The gaps and silences that continued to pervade Catholic attitudes to adolescent sexual education in the 1950s ensured that Catholic teenagers encountered sex for the first time in idiosyncratic and often highly personal ways. The advent of formal Catholic sexual education in the late 1960s went some way to limiting this variability.

The exchange of information within peer groups has frequently been cited by historians as a leading, if not formative, source of sexual information for young people in the twentieth century.[14] The interviewees were split into two camps in this respect – just over half of the sample said that they spoke about sexual matters in depth with friends at school, while the remaining half stressed that they hardly spoke of sex at all until they left school. The type of school that was attended would have undoubtedly affected this, but there was no clear correlation in terms of mixed/single sex, state/private or Catholic/non-Catholic school (twenty-one of the twenty-seven interviewees attended a Catholic school, of whom twelve attended a convent school). What was apparent from the interviews was that Catholic teenage girls often considered themselves and their Catholic friends more 'innocent' or sexually 'ignorant' than non-Catholic girls:

DG Did you talk about sex with your friends at school?
Teresa Not much no. Girls didn't talk about that sort of thing … there would be no in-depth conversations, we were Catholic girls. Catholic girls didn't do that sort of thing. I knew that others did, but it wasn't for us![15]
Patricia We were so naive. I remember being aware that other girls were different in that way. At other schools they talked about sex. We did talk about some things like the boys we liked and that sort of thing. But not sex, not us Catholic girls.[16]

Catholicism was central to many of the interviewees' social networks when they were growing up in the 1950s. With their friendship groups often drawn from schools, parish communities or Catholic localities, 'sexual innocence' was a trait of collective as well as individual identity. As Kate Fisher and Simon Szreter's oral history research has indicated, gendered expectations about sexual naivety were not specific to the Catholic community in pre-1960s Britain.[17] Nevertheless, young Catholic girls perceived themselves to be less informed than their non-Catholic counterparts on account of their religious identity.

The interviewees primarily understood their sexual education as something that occurred 'naturally'. Many struggled to recall exactly how and when they first learnt about sex, but they often spoke of it 'just happening' or 'being part of nature':

> You learn about the birds and the bees, but really it's just in you. You don't learn it, it's just your body. It's just natural isn't it?[18]

This discourse of the 'natural' appeared in a particular form in the recollections of one interviewee who spent part of her early life in a rural location:

> During the war I was evacuated on to a farm, and I don't know if you've ever seen a stallion have a go, but I can tell you, the length of his penis is to be marvelled at. It's a wonderful sight! It really is! So from that onwards ... if you're on a farm you know exactly how it's done.
> It must follow since we are all animals that's the way it is.[19]

Angela took her sexual education from the 'natural world' in a very direct way. It was not just a knowledge of anatomical procedures that she developed on the farm, but also notions of gendered desire:

> Again I would refer you to the natural world. Most animals have to fight before they get any sex, you look at stags. In Africa you have the lion kingdom, there's a lot of competition, and competition can turn into violence. I'm not recommending it, I'm just saying that it occurs.[20]

Angela's belief that elements of violence were inherent in sex led me to ask about sadomasochism – which she viewed as 'not wrong' but a malady that she felt compassion for – and then to broach the subject of rape:

> DG In terms of the allegory with animals and the 'force' that is used in sex, is there any links between that and rape, and how does that sit with your religious beliefs?
> Angela The allegory is difficult, I don't want to make a big thing of the animal kingdom, but after all we are animals. You seem to think in terms of the male being an aggressor, but I can assure you there's an awful lot of 'come on', 'I'm ready for it' from the female point of view. Particularly lions, the lioness goes out looking for men because she knows she shouldn't mate with her party. What do you think all these hen parties are doing, they're going out,

looking for it in our present day culture. These short skirts, what are they doing?[21]

Angela pointed out that I was assuming a dynamic of male activity and female passivity. She went on to say that:

> This always comes up in rape cases, a judge will say she was looking for it, he paid for her drinks and then she comes on all 'Oh I don't want it' and he feels like he's being short changed. To come back to God's plan in it, if we think of God being like some sort of love, obviously we are programmed, we need a long time to educate and nurture a child. So I think it's God's plan to have a stable and loving relationship in order to bring up the next generation.[22]

We see here a marriage of Catholic creationism and Darwinian evolutionary psychology. At the centre of Angela's understanding of sex was the function of procreation and the idea of the 'natural'. The traditionally gendered notions of what Camille Paglia would label 'sexual personae' were premised on this confidence in the profane animalism of human nature.[23]

Catholic girls who grew up in a rural setting were habitually exposed to material examples of what they would later understand to be 'the facts of life'. Indeed, 'the facts of life' was a phrase that Angela and a number of other interviewees used repeatedly when discussing their sexual education – 'facts' suggesting an absolute, empirical set of laws governing sexual response. Angela's reflections epitomised an interpretation of human sexuality that ran through many of the interviewees' testimonies. Sex was understood to be a biological phenomenon that worked on what Charles Taylor would call a 'horizontal plane' – a manifestly 'knowable' set of instincts and responses that were removed from the 'vertical' concerns of theological meaning and morality.[24] Although Fisher and Szreter's discussion of sexual education in youth and childhood makes passing reference to a 'facts of life' discourse, it did not represent the central trope in their interviewees' narratives that it did in the testimony of my Catholic respondents.[25] An emphasis on the empiricism of sexual knowledge may have been, in part, a reflection of wider societal understandings of sex in the 1940s and 1950s, but it chiefly spoke of a specifically Catholic experience.

The vast majority of the interviewees were of the last generation not to be the target of coordinated Catholic sexual education initiatives. In the middle of the 1960s, a number of manuals and pamphlets were produced by various Catholic authorities with the intention of educating young people. One of the earliest such publication was *Choices in Sex*, written by married couple Quentin and Irene de la Bedoyere. The pamphlet's front cover (Figure 4) immediately established the light and casual tone in which sex was to be discussed throughout the booklet. Gently satirical cartoons were used to illustrate the points that were made in the text, and small jokes and anecdotes peppered the pamphlet's narrative. The image of the man and woman on the front cover stressed similarities between the genders rather than differences, with the couple sharing comparable haircuts, facial features and heights.[26] Mutuality represented a major theme in the text of the pamphlet, and the image of the husband and wife seems to affirm this commitment to gender equality. Martin Richards and Jane Elliot state that 'advice books in the 1960s stressed openness, sharing (mutual orgasms) and closeness in sex' and these themes were replicated in Catholic publications.[27] Although continuing to uphold traditional Catholic teachings on the morality of marriage, monogamy and birth control, the form and style with which these messages were communicated to young Catholics were entirely new.[28]

Choices in Sex and similar sex education publications were not simply the work of individual Catholic authors removed from the Church; they were approved by the clerical hierarchy in the form of an imprimatur (a seal given by a clerical authority which affirmed that a publication accorded with Catholic doctrine). Or at least they were initially. As we saw in the last chapter, *Choices in Sex* had its imprimatur removed amid complaints about its content from certain members of the Irish clergy. The pamphlet's author explained that:

> The main problem that was levelled against the book was in its approach to sexuality. I believe young people are not always in the habit of obeying the rules, and the purpose of *Choices in Sex* was to get people actually thinking about their own sexual morals.[29]

It was this non-didactic approach to sexual morality that was criticised by members of the CPA. Indeed, it is now difficult to comment on the specifics of the *Choices in Sex* quarrel as it eventually led to a libel case about the imprimatur process itself.[30] Catholic organisations and

Figure 4 Front cover of a sexual advice manual aimed at young Catholics, Q. de la Bedoyere and I. de la Bedoyere, *Choices in Sex* (Dartford, 1964)

agencies attempted to police the sexual discourses directed at the young in the 1960s, and the resulting contests moved beyond mere rhetoric in some cases. In this sense, it is clear to see that the internal conflicts that existed within the Catholic community represented significant

Figure 5 Front cover of a Catholic marriage guidance manual, Q. de la Bedoyere, *My Wife and I Don't Agree* (Dartford, 1972)

divisions. As Hugh McLeod has argued, these internal schisms cannot be disregarded when assessing Catholic change in the post-war.[31] It is also evident though, that these conflicts were not exclusively formulated within the confines of the Catholic world, but were the product of an interaction between secular and religious developments.

Sex education also arrived in Catholic schools at the end of the 1960s. The subject had been touched on in the interviewees' biology lessons before this point, but there was nothing that went beyond a clinical detailing of reproductive mechanics. Wendy, one of the youngest interviewees, was fifteen in 1969 and remembered her convent school bringing in its first sex education initiative for her year. A married woman addressed the class, answering questions from the students in a question-and-answer format. Wendy did not know how the woman was qualified for the role beyond her marital status, but remembered her to be a 'glamorous' woman who even smoked a cheroot in their first session (for which she had been reprimanded by the head teacher, she later told the class). Wendy pointed out that she did not learn much that she did not know already in the sessions in terms of the bodily processes.[32] The advice that was given always accorded with Catholic teachings on sex, marriage and birth control – there was no learning how to put a condom on, for example, as there were in corresponding sessions in some non-Catholic schools.[33] The sessions did, though, open up new avenues of discussion, with questions about the sensuality and feeling of the sexual act alongside more specific questions such as 'can you have sex with a bra on?'. This openness was a development from the only other form of sex education that Wendy's school had provided up to this point – a booklet called *My Dear Daughter* that had been given to her at the age of ten. Wendy remembered it dealt with genital hygiene, informing her:

> Don't imagine that it's wrong to see or touch yourself in this way [when cleaning the labia], just say a prayer to Our Lady afterwards.[34]

The sense of guilt and shame that had traditionally coloured Catholic advice on the body was not present in the new sex education initiatives that were emerging by the end of the decade.

A thorough assessment of the impact that these new sex education initiatives had on individual women is beyond the bounds of this project's sample. It is likely that, like Wendy, many still garnered sexual knowledge from other sources, as Catholic women had done before such initiatives existed. The initiatives did, though, reveal much about the way that 'sexual progress' was conceptualised within the liberal Catholic movement. Jack Dominian's book *The Church and the Sexual Revolution* (first published in 1967) saw sexual education as a vital undertaking for the Church. Dominian noted that the advances in the subject of sexuality in the last two centuries had 'almost entirely occurred outside the Christian tradition and often encountered opposition from it', listing, 'sexual education, women's emancipation, the drive to bring procreation under human control, the psychological and scientific study of sex and an emphasis on the beauty and goodness of sexuality' as being the principal developments in the field.[35] For Dominian, 'sexual education' and through this the 'sexual revolution' itself were distinctly secular phenomena which the Church needed to 'engage with' or 'respond to'. Implicit in his definition of sexual education was the idea that a healthy, liberated form of sexuality was somehow foreign to the realm of the religious. This rendering of 'modern' sexuality was common to many 'liberal' Catholics working in the 1960s, including sex education advocates, CMAC marriage guidance counsellors and members of the papal commission.

Two main themes have come out of this study of Catholic sexual education. First, that there was no clear correlation between the form of sexual education received in adolescence and the eventual religious belief system taken up in adulthood. Catholic women growing up in the years immediately surrounding the war drew their sexual education from a range of sites and sources; attributing their views on birth control or sexual morality to this process is inaccurate. The second theme relates to the way sexuality was conceptualised by both the interviewees when remembering their own sexual education and also the new Catholic sexual educators at work in the late 1960s. There existed an underlying commonality between the two. The interviewees viewed their sexual education as a 'natural' process – a form of self-revelation in which a hidden, innate force manifested itself. This naturalised understanding of human sexuality was equally present in the 'liberal' Catholic sex education initiatives that emerged at the end of the 1960s. The idea that sexual knowledge was a scientific, biological area of expertise was resolutely championed by Catholic sexual educators, just as it had been by 'liberal' members of the Papal Commission for Birth Control. It seems this discourse has now been firmly established as a dominant way of conceptualising the relationship between sex and religion, shaping the way the interviewees made sense of their own sexual development in early life.

Desire and gender in Catholic adolescence

A dissolution of the gendered codes and expectations that surrounded sexual desire has been identified as an integral feature of post-1960s Christian decline. Brown argues that in response to the disruption of war, a strong connection between femininity and piousness was forged in 1950s Britain to restabilise the nation along traditionally gendered lines. The magazines that teenage girls read, the clothes they wore, the music they listened to, the parenting and schooling they received all converged to create a climate in which young women were expected to be chaste, pure and 'good':

> [T]hey were still expected to seek their femininity from a religious-based coda which, however liberated from conversionism, was still tied to an evangelical vision of the 'good woman'.[36]

Central to this culture was the idea that female sexual desire was to be mistrusted and suppressed:

> By the 1950s organised Christianity had become characterised by the support of a harsh and vindictive state apparatus that oppressed many pleasures without reason, and hurt the lives of many young people – especially women and gays.[37]

According to Brown, the 1960s witnessed a revolutionary shift as the connection between femininity and piousness was decisively severed, leaving women free to express sexual desire in an open and healthy way. To some extent, the testimony of the interviewees bore out Brown's model. They spoke of the importance of 'purity' and 'goodness' being impressed upon them in their upbringings during the 1940s and 1950s. They also spoke of becoming increasingly conscious of their relative naivety when compared with boys and also non-Catholic girls. There were, though, mixed interpretations of this innocence. Some interviewees saw it as a form of oppression that denied them healthy sexual expression – an interpretation that corroborated Brown's picture of 'pious femininity'. Others, however, looked back on the period with wistful nostalgia, lamenting the loss of a time when the complications and troubles of sex did not exist. This section examines the gendered responsibilities and expectations that were attached to the development, negotiation and management of pre-marital sexual desires. The interviewees' memories of their early lives were shaped by subsequent experiences, but this should not be seen to undermine the historical value of their testimony. Retrospection affords us a privileged insight into the way memory and experience interact in the production of meaning.

All the interviewees bar Michaela (who no longer identified as a Catholic believer by her late teens) did not have sexual relations of any kind before their marriage.[38] Amidst the plethora of debates and discussions that surrounded the Catholic Church and its approach to sex in the twentieth century, the prohibition of pre-marital sex was never really questioned. The interviewees largely concurred with the Church's line on pre-marital sexuality. We saw in the last chapter how Teresa and her partner had great difficulties with their sexual relationship, but she still subscribed to the Church's teaching on the sanctity of marriage:

> I mean sex before marriage was an absolute no-no, and we all accepted that, we thought it was wrong, so if you're a Catholic that wasn't an issue.
>
> I haven't changed my mind on that. The sanctity of marriage and all that, it makes sense. If you believe in a Catholic God, I think you believe that sex is sacred and reserved for marriage.[39]

Three interviewees did express dissent on the question of pre-marital sex. Sorcha, for example, spoke of the importance of 'knowing your partner physically' before marriage. She explained that without this foreknowledge, a couple would have to go through a period of 'working out how sexually active you were going to be with someone'.[40] Her concerns for 'sexual compatibility' were not common amongst the interviewees, though. Sex and marriage were generally considered to be tethered by a divine providence that overrode any need for bodily familiarity.

Resisting the temptation to have sex before marriage was more difficult for some Catholic women than others; those courting non-Catholic men had to justify their beliefs to their sometimes less than sympathetic partners. Patricia recalled having to explain to a man she was seeing of 'no particular faith' that she did not care what he thought he could offer her, 'it had to beat eternal salvation'.[41] None of the interviewees spoke of feeling a pressure that they were uncomfortable with, and it should be noted that Patricia's man of 'no particular faith' made his case based on the pleasure he believed Patricia would experience. Even in all-Catholic couples though, the responsibility for maintaining a state of chastity worked along distinctly gendered lines. A number of the interviewees remembered having to come up with new and inventive ways of keeping their partners' advances at bay. At the age of eighteen Penny started courting her eventual husband Harry – she recalled the 'alone time' they shared when she visited him in his naval barracks:

> When we were getting a little too amorous, I would pull on his ear. Gently, you know, as a joke, but to say 'stop there'. That was our tactic for keeping ourselves in check … I knew that was my job and so did he. I quite liked it, it was like a little game we played.[42]

There were some exceptions to these gendered responsibilities. Teresa recalled that resisting sexual urges was as much her eventual husband Michael's prerogative as it was her own:

> DG Were you excited about the prospect of sex?
> Teresa Well yes you get all sorts of sexual feelings when you're courting, we had to pull back at times.
> DG Was it more your responsibility to do this, the pulling back, or a mutual thing?
> Teresa No it was a mutual thing. Our faith was important to both of us, we were both regular, we were both traditional Catholics as it would be described then, you know, we were both regular Sunday Mass goers.[43]

Teresa was a rare interviewee who did not feel in some way that it was more her than her partner's responsibility to maintain the couple's chastity. This responsibility was not always viewed as a burden by Catholic women – for some it represented a sense of empowerment, while for others like Penny it was remembered as a playful negotiation of gender roles.

The gendered expectations that surrounded the maintenance of pre-marital chastity were not new to adolescent Catholic girls, but a continuation of the sexual climate they had grown up in. Catholic girls growing up before the 1960s were generally expected to be pure, innocent and uninformed when it came to sexual matters. Lynn spoke passionately about how the notion of female sexual desire was actively suppressed in her childhood:

> In the fifties when I was brought up, sex wasn't mentioned, OK, the idea of the Catholic girl was to be pure, and pure meant not to have any ideas about sex, the word didn't even come … pure meant virgin, that was what it meant, so the sin against purity was to have sex. We couldn't even read novels, 'dangerous reading' … so I couldn't even read novels like *Madame Bovary*.
>
> Not just sexual, passion, I mean the idea that was really kept away from us was that a woman could be passionate and could physically enjoy sex. That was not on. So anybody, a married woman enjoying sex … the idea was not acceptable. I mean girls were not told that there was something in it for them.[44]

Lynn's depiction of 1950s Catholicism corroborated Brown's analysis of Christian womanhood. As Mary Eaton has detailed, Catholic girls were encouraged to think of themselves as the 'children of Mary', with an associated emphasis on virginal purity.[45] Marian devotion was a central aspect of the interviewees' religious upbringing, but was often a source of consternation at a later stage in their life:

> I look at Mary now, and I think, this right here is the problem with the Catholic Church. Why does she need to be a virgin? I feel very uncomfortable about her position now.[46]

As we have seen, it was not until the middle of the 1960s that the central Catholic hierarchy engaged with the idea of female sexual pleasure, as lay papal commission members, CMAC counsellors and Catholic sex manual authors worked to relay the values of a 'sexual revolution' culture to a Catholic audience. Catholic girls going through adolescence before this time were taught that sexual desire was itself an unfeminine sensation; sex had nothing 'in it for them'.

The image of hell was central to the gendered understandings of sexual morality that were impressed on young Catholics in the 1940s and 1950s. Rosie spoke of the guilt she felt as she began to have 'fantasies' in her teenage years – she was taught to believe that to think about sex was a sin in itself:

> Rosie We were burdened with this instruction about impurity and how wrong it was, and it was always a serious sin we were told, you were going to Hell! I'm sure that my husband had no idea that I was worrying about things like that, because I never told him, I'm sure he never had thoughts like that at all.
> DG As in a fear of hell?
> Rosie Yes, although he'd been educated in a monastery, but men are different. They didn't get the same guilt placed upon them when it came to sex.[47]

Michaela saw both sex and ceasing to believe in Hell as crucial aspects of her disaffiliation as a teenage girl:

> As a child it was quite scary really, very clear threats and consequences of doing wrong which was particularly directed at girls. My brother never got the same sort of thing. I remember very clearly that the whole business about purgatory, I can't remember what the word is, but you get time off purgatory, you could do Stations of the Cross seven times, you know, say certain prayers and you'd have less time in purgatory. And it seemed ridiculous eventually.[48]

If Hell disappeared in the 1960s as Lodge claimed, then this was perhaps more of a relief for Catholic women than for Catholic men. Their sexual upbringing had been punctuated by regular and persistent threats of eternal damnation.

Kate Fisher's oral history research suggests that the maintenance of an uninformed, innocent feminine persona may not have been specific to Catholics in the 1950s, but a part of a wider sexual culture. She shows how women, particularly working-class women, worked to uphold the appearance of ignorance when it came to things like contraceptive knowledge, in an attempt to maintain their 'passive' feminine identity.[49] However, the interviewees were eager to stress that their Catholicism set them apart from their peers in this respect. Sorcha remembered being aware of her 'difference' from non-Catholics in her school-days, but not fully realising the extent of her 'innocence' until university:

> DG Were you conscious at the time of being more innocent than other non-Catholic girls?

> Sorcha Oh yes, yes definitely, going to university was quite a shock, I was not really mature at seventeen, not your average maturity. I think that was quite a feature of girls going to Catholic schools … single-sex Catholic schools anyway. I was immediately much more aware that some people were much more sexually aware and promiscuous than me. My room-mate was so much more mature, I was quite threatened by her. I didn't really discuss sex issues with her, she seemed on a different planet really when it came to that.[50]

The interviewees who did go to university were thrown abruptly into a new and challenging sexual culture, but were also exposed to new practical opportunities for meeting boys and pursuing sexual activities. Those who did not go to university tended to continue living at home, which offered limited opportunities for meeting boys. Whether attending university or not, the interviewees became increasingly aware in their teenage years that their Catholic upbringings had set them apart from non-Catholics when it came to matters of sex.

Sorcha recalled that she did feel 'physical desires awakening in her' during her school-days, but that she did not articulate these thoughts to anyone else, even her close friends. In an attempt to get the interviewees thinking about the development of their early sexual desires, I asked them about whether they had a favourite Beatle:

> DG Did you have a favourite Beatle?
> Sorcha Yes I thought the Beatles were quite exciting, definitely. I wasn't the sort of teenager who fell in love with pop stars – some of my friends were like that. I did like dancing though. But I didn't talk much about sex with friends. I can remember hardly any discussions with my friends about sexuality.[51]

Sorcha went on to reflect on her friendship group's lack of discussion about sex:

> It's amazing we did have discussions about all kinds but I didn't even with my close friends talk about what they actually did on the sexual front, which is a bit strange really … It was more being aware … we had a close-knit group of five friends – all Catholics bar one … I didn't actually discuss it, that's really weird.[52]

Sorcha's judgement that not speaking about sex was 'really weird' reveals much about contemporary constructions of sexual normality. Foucault spoke of a prevailing 'incitement to discourse' taking hold in modernity; individuals are now constantly encouraged to 'speak sex' according to Foucault.[53] Many Catholic women now look back on the silences that defined their early sexual development as an anachronism, as something at odds with their present-day understanding of healthy sexual expression. However, it is important not to make assumptions about the moral evaluation Sorcha was making when she used the terms 'strange' and 'weird'. There was an ambivalence communicated with these expressions, even a sense of nostalgia. Later in the interview Sorcha was to explain that her youthful innocence was not something she resented, but a 'vital ingredient of a very happy period in her life'.[54] The mood and tone that accompanied the interviewees' recollections of their youthful innocence spoke of the way this life-cycle stage was remembered retrospectively but also experienced at the time. A telling case was Teresa, whom we met in the last chapter when discussing the difficulties she experienced with NFP. She spoke candidly about her own naivety:

> I was a real goody-goody, I was very law-abiding (chuckles).
> We used to have a Palais. Generally young people. Talk about innocents abroad, to say we were naive is an understatement (chuckles). It was all ... jiving – that was very adventurous! The boys were over there, the girls on the other side .... I mean we were very sheltered, very sheltered.[55]

When she spoke of meeting her eventual husband Michael at university, her testimony was peppered with giggles and laughter at the innocence of their early courtship. She spoke affectionately of them meeting at the Catholic chaplaincy and the rigid formalities of their early relationship.[56] Her laughter expressed the peculiarity of their sexual innocence, but also the warmth with which she viewed it now. There was a distinct break in the tone of Teresa's interview that can be pinned down to a particular question. Up to this point in the interview, she had responded to questions about her pre-marital life in a light, jovial manner:

> DG So we'll move on to talk about sex in your marriage. Can you talk about the experience of using NFP?

> Teresa [Sigh and long pause] Yes well, we've used it all our lives and I think it's just … [breaks into tears][57]

For the remainder of the interview, Teresa moved between sorrow, anger and remorse as she recalled her years of martial sexuality. Put simply, the subject of sex brought tears. The experience of using NFP had undoubtedly affected the way she evaluated her youthful innocence, but this should not be seen to undermine the value of her testimony. Teresa's mood when recalling her adolescence should not simply be dismissed as nostalgia, but viewed as an indicator of the way she and many other women of her generation experienced this life-cycle stage. Many of the interviewees communicated a sense of warmth, even longing for the sexual innocence of their upbringing. Their light and uninhibited tone when recalling this period was in direct contrast to the despondency present when discussing sex.

Brown's rendering of 'pious femininity' placed power in the hands of central authorities such as the Church and the state, casting individual women as inert victims of social control.[58] There has, though, been a move to challenge this reading of gendered power dynamics in the historiography of mid-twentieth-century England. The key contribution that Kate Fisher's oral history research made to the historiography of pre-1960s sexual politics was in reasserting the agency of working-class women in marital relations. Her interviewees viewed their passivity as an active choice rather than being imposed upon them by the various forces of patriarchy.[59] The participants in my oral history research did not always remember their youthful innocence as an active choice, but often worked to discredit the idea that it was imposed upon them:

> This idea that we were poor little girls being forced into our white dresses. As I said, I knew that girls at other schools were different, they would talk about sexy things and dress differently, but I didn't want that. It was not for me. And I was very happy waiting for things like that.[60]

Another interviewee spoke of the kind of man she wanted to marry as a teenage girl:

> Well to be honest, when I was a teenager girl I wanted the man I was with to want me to be … you know, wholesome. Someone who

valued that in a woman. That's the sort of man I wanted to marry ... and did![61]

Just as the interviewees were eager to stress the agency they exercised in contraceptive decisions during marriage, they equally presented their youthful 'innocence' as something that they played a role in constructing. Catholic women's early sexual development in the 1950s was shaped by 'pious' expectations, but this did not always amount to the form of subjugation that Brown described.[62]

The interviewees' memories of early sexual development revealed a complex interplay between ideological structures and their own sense of autonomy, as well as an acute awareness of how this interplay might be interpreted by 'others' in a contemporary setting. Questions of coercion and control were clearly at the forefront of their and my consciousness when discussing the sexual desire of young Catholic women. Following this line, the next section delves deeper into the way the interviewees' understandings and experiences of Catholicism in their early lives were affected by external interpretations of religious belief. In a post-war setting, the relationship between Catholicism and notions of immaturity was to receive unprecedented levels of attention from secular intellectual actors, reshaping the way early life was experienced and understood for many Catholics in England.

Religiosity and infantilism

In the decades after the Second World War, childhood became endowed with a new and augmented significance in popular and academic thinking about religion. As Michal Shapira and Matthew Thomson have shown, understandings of childhood in general underwent unprecedented changes in the middle of the century.[63] The emotional legacy of total war, coupled with the infiltration of psychoanalytical modes of understanding, worked to recalibrate perceptions of infantile selfhood. Erik Erikson extended Freud's 'developmental theory' in his work of 1950, *Childhood and Society*, identifying childhood as a determinative stage in the 'psychosocial development' of religious identities.[64] In the same year, Erich Fromm published *Psychoanalysis and Religion*, which argued that religion primarily constituted a childish desire to remain attached to protecting figures.[65] Together, these works of popular psychoanalysis, aimed at a wider, non-academic readership, encapsulated the tethering of religion and childhood. They informed and were informed by an ascendant understanding of religion that affected the way Catholic institutions and individuals thought of their own beliefs, identities and approaches to parenthood. This section examines how dominant constructions of infantilism and childhood intersected with personal Catholic religiosities. In this sense, it deals with early life more as a theme and social category than a lived life-cycle stage.

For ease of communication, the deterministic association between religious belief and childhood that has been sketched here will be referred to as the 'infantilism hypothesis'. It was, of course, a collection of diffuse, evolving and sometimes contradicting concepts rather than a unified theory, but at its centre was the idea that childhood played a determinative role in the construction of religious identities. The infantilism hypothesis took the form of two related indictments in the interviews. First, that early religious beliefs were merely the product of psychological indoctrination and therefore less 'legitimate' than beliefs held in adulthood. Second, that personal religiosity was itself a 'childish' phenomenon. The interviewees' memories of their early religious development worked within, around and against the infantilism hypothesis. It was an almost unavoidable discourse for the interviewees when making sense of their religious beliefs, particularly their beliefs on sexual morality, in the early stages of their lives. I am not interested in evaluating the intrinsic validity of the infantilism hypothesis. Instead, the intention here is to explore how it affected and continues to affect the religious identities of Catholic women in post-war England.

The idea that childhood theological beliefs were somehow less authentic than those held in adulthood was present in the testimony of Michaela, the interviewee who rejected her Catholic identity in her late teenage years. This was her response when I asked if she had ever truly believed in a Catholic God:

> That's the thing, I don't know if I can remember. I used to pray, there was a dialogue, but did I truly believe in a God? Thing is you don't know what you're doing as a child. I was just doing as I was told. It's difficult to separate that from what you actually thought yourself.[66]

As well as showing an awareness of the potential frailties of her own memory here, Michaela was grappling with the question of agency in childhood. At a number of points in the interview she asked whether she was a suitable participant for the research as she could not be sure whether she was ever a 'proper Catholic'.[67] A handful of other interviewees also questioned the authenticity of their Catholic beliefs at an early stage of their life. They spoke of 'following the rules' or 'being spoon-fed' their beliefs, a language that was rooted in the idea that children were particularly vulnerable to religious indoctrination.[68]

Some of the interviewees explicitly reflected on the connection between religious belief and childhood. Angela adopted elements of the infantilism hypothesis in the construction of her life story but ultimately showed an ambivalence towards it. She asserted that the 'childish mind is very receptive' when speaking of her own religious upbringing, and maintained that her beliefs had not had any 'sound philosophical basis' until she went to university:

> I found out that far from being a childish irrelevant distraction, it was a very serious matter. It had given rise to a lot of philosophy, art, history; it's all connected with religion.[69]

She downplayed the legitimacy of her early Catholic beliefs – it was not until she had gained the 'enlightenment' offered by the works of Rousseau, Kierkegaard and other philosophers that her Catholicism took on its 'full meaning'.[70] This way of interpreting religious belief was one that accorded with the basic tenets of the infantilism hypothesis. At the same time, Angela recognised the way this hypothesis had contributed to the denigration of religious faith:

> I learnt my religion as an adult, rather than having it spoon-fed to me as a child. Which is one of the main reasons I think people throw away their religion because they regard it as childish.[71]

Angela went beyond commenting on how childhood had been viewed as a determinative stage in religious development and detailed how in reciprocation, religious belief had become understood as 'childish' in nature. In this way, she connected the two indictments of the infantilism hypothesis, recognising its impact on collective devotion but still subscribing to its reading of early religiosity at a personal level.

Many of the interviewees expressly resisted the dual indictments of the infantilism hypothesis:

> I know there are people who will tell you that a child has no ability to decide for itself. I heard Christopher Hitchens, you know, good friend of Richard Dawkins, I heard him saying it should be illegal to teach someone about religion until the age of thirteen ... what he called the age of reason.[72]

Doreen's reference to the more militant form of secularism represented by public figures like Richard Dawkins and Christopher Hitchens underlined her awareness of the link between religious decline and the infantilism hypothesis. She went on to emphasise her own agency when describing her Catholic upbringing:

> Well I was questioning things from an early age – that was my father that really encouraged the questioning. My beliefs changed as I did, they weren't simply set in stone or forced on to me. Or they weren't any more than they might be right now![73]

Like Doreen, a number of the interviewees explicitly acknowledged the dominance of the infantilism hypothesis and worked to contradict it in the interview. Georgina observed that:

> There is this idea these days that Catholics must have been indoctrinated as children. Why is it when it comes to religion it is always indoctrination? Well my faith is no different from someone else's beliefs about right and wrong. It was made up of decisions then just as it is now. I chose to follow Catholic ways on sex, to wait until marriage, and I was very happy.[74]

The interviewees' ardour to respond to the indictments of the infantilism hypothesis may have been encouraged by my own presence – an academic researcher looking to analyse religious belief. This notwithstanding, the way they worked to stress their own youthful agency was a sign of its salience in contemporary Catholic consciousness.

Georgina made a point of emphasising that her beliefs on sexual morality in particular were active choices rather than products of childhood indoctrination. Her decision to focus on questions of sex when counteracting the infantilism hypothesis was replicated by many of interviewees. In Chapter 3 on later marriage, we saw how the orthodox interviewee Elizabeth critiqued the notion of 'female emancipation', maintaining that she had always 'felt free' to 'choose my boyfriends, husband, lived independently from age eighteen, treasured my virginity until marriage, never used contraception'.[75] The interviewees were conscious that their beliefs on sexual morality in particular were vulnerable to the pathological diagnoses of the infantilism hypothesis. In a post-liberationist culture, Catholic beliefs on the body were increasingly identified as the paragon of religion's psychological bankruptcy. Elizabeth's comments underlined the way that dominant constructions of 'sexual liberation' were often premised on psychoanalytical definitions of sex, childhood and individual autonomy.

Doreen was right that Hitchens had called for 'religious instruction' to be denied until a child had 'attained the age of reason'.[76] Positioning 'reason' as the counterpoint to religious belief characterises a form of 'enlightenment secularism' which can be traced back to the eighteenth century. Mapping this on to childhood, however, was a typically post-Freudian critique of religion. As Matthew Thomson has demonstrated, it was not until the middle of the twentieth century that psychoanalytical interpretations of childhood began to take hold in the popular domain.[77] With this, the concept of the immature mind was readily applied to religious belief, reshaping personal and prescriptive approaches to the religious development of the young.

What impact, then, did the infantilism hypothesis have on the interviewees' approach to parenting, specifically the sexual instruction they provided to their offspring? Moreover, what can this approach tell us about the way they conceptualised the future? Of the twenty-seven interviewees, nineteen said at least one of their children continued to identify as Catholic, but only eight had a child who attended Mass every week. Even fewer had grandchildren who regularly attended Mass, regardless of their age. Although this seems to loosely mirror the changing character of Catholic devotional practice that Hornsby-Smith described, the size of the sample means that reliable conclusions cannot be drawn from these figures.[78] I am more interested in the interviewees' personal interpretations of these generational discrepancies and what they can tell us about the shifting relationship between Catholic belief and childhood in the post-war years.

Some interviewees lamented their offspring's rejection of traditional forms of Catholic worship. Elizabeth thought it a 'great shame' that her daughter, who still 'strongly identified' as a Catholic, did not 'feel the importance of the Catholic Mass'.[79] Elizabeth said she regularly prayed for a turnaround on this front. She was eager to see her daughter and her family find a 'nice local church' when they moved house later in the year – she even encouraged her to move to a certain area because she knew the parish priest there.[80] Other interviewees were less concerned with their offspring's lack of church attendance. Angela described her grandchildren as 'solidly Catholic', but said almost all of them did not attend church every week. She did not have a problem with this, though:

> It's for the older generations to spend their times on their knees, the young have better things to do, they need to experience things.[81]

There is, then, some evidence of a generational break in the devotional practices of the interviewees and their offspring in terms of Mass attendance. However, the clearest distinction between the interviewees' generation and that of their offspring (both their children and their grandchildren) was in their beliefs and early instruction on contraceptive morality. Only two interviewees thought that their children had used NFP in their marriages, one of whom could not be sure as they had never discussed the issue. Every other interviewee felt certain that their children had practised artificial means of contraception during their marriages. This knowledge was sometimes gleaned from open discussions with their sons and daughters, but more often than not was assumed because of birth spacing.

The interviewees' attitudes towards their children's beliefs on contraception, both at the point of interview but also when bringing up their children, reveal much about the way sex and religion have been categorised since the 1960s. Perhaps unsurprisingly, the 'liberal' interviewees were happy to see their children disregarding the Church's teaching:

> Oh no, they don't have to go through any of the struggles that I went through. I wouldn't wish it on my worst enemy … and I think their faith will be all the better for that![82]

Some interviewees spoke of expressly teaching their children about artificial means, others 'left them to their own devices'. Either way, their children were brought up to see contraception as a matter of 'individual conscience'. The Church's teaching on the matter was either an irrelevance, or something to be actively warned against. The 'liberal' form of

Catholicism which they had worked to construct in the course of their lives, with its active compartmentalisation of questions relating to sex and contraception, was the starting point for the next generation's religious upbringing.

The orthodox interviewees' opinions of their children's contraceptive practice were less expected. Although Elizabeth bemoaned her daughter's disenchantment with traditional forms of Catholic devotion such as weekly Mass attendance (and worked hard to redress this situation), she accepted her disobedience in relation to the Church's teaching on contraception:

> Elizabeth Yes I find it in my own children [use of artificial means].
> DG Did you teach them about the Church's teaching on contraception when they grew up?
> Elizabeth No. I think they knew we didn't practise artificial contraception, but it was not our place to intervene in their bodies. It's up to them. There's one, the middle boy, who I think practises the faith.[83]

Elizabeth reaffirmed her belief that 'practising the faith' meant keeping to the Church's teaching on contraception, but unlike other matters of Catholic morality, did not instruct her children on the subject. Her attitude epitomised a popular emphasis on individual 'conscience' that had developed in Catholic thinking about contraception since the 1970s, as well as a continuing reticence to discuss sexual matters within the family. Indeed, Lesley Hall has shown that this reticence was a feature of wider familial relations throughout the twentieth century.[84] This notwithstanding, Elizabeth's and the other 'orthodox' interviewees' attitudes towards their children's contraceptive behaviour was indicative of the way questions of sex were increasingly seen to be removed from other aspects of Catholic belief.

Bridget, also an avowedly orthodox interviewee, went beyond an acceptance of her children's use of artificial means and openly applauded it. We have seen how in the course of our interview, Bridget reformed her position on birth control, acceding by the end that she would have been 'happy if *Humanae Vitae* had been different'.[85] She was also 'very happy' that her children, all still Catholic believers, had not adhered to the Church's teaching on birth control.[86] Bridget provided her children with clear moral instruction that accorded with the Catholic doctrine in all areas apart from questions of sex. Near the end of the interview, she reflected on the generational nature of 'sexual liberation':

> I think we who were born just before the outbreak of World War Two were quite a bit different to those born after World War Two. They had more choices, some of which were sexual liberation. The young people of my generation, we were expected to obey.
>
> We didn't know any different. Then we saw gradually the increased licence in every area ... those that had been through the war had been through privation and hardship, and knew what it was like to feel like you could die at any moment ... so it's a natural reaction to want to give your children not only greater material, but also greater freedom.[87]

In seeing the war as a point of generational partition, Bridget's testimony affirmed elements of Brown's model of sexual change. For Brown, it was the 'baby boom' generation who were to cast off the shackles of Christian prudishness that had tied down their parents.[88] However, we get here an idea of 'youth', and indeed 'sexual liberation', being a licensed thing – not simply a breaking away from traditional values but something that was tolerated and even encouraged by the parental generation. This is not to say that the interviewees' children's religious identities were determined by the parenting they received any more or less than any other generation, but that this parenting was itself a signifier of significant cultural changes in dominant understandings of sex and religion. The interviewees' memories in general suggested a more gradual transition in femininity than Brown's model of 'sudden and abrupt' revolution. While a generational shift is clearly discernible, the movement away from piousness was not viewed as a violent rebellion driven by the counter-cultural forces of sixties permissiveness, but a subtler reworking of the moral and existential values around the body.

Lynn Abrams' oral history study of mid-century Christian femininity suggests that a generational change in approaches to religious parenting was not limited to Catholicism. Her research showed that the 'mothers' of the post-war generation, who loosely correlated to the mothers of my interviewees, often deployed religious discourse to criticise the new form of femininity that their daughters were constructing. Sexual morality in particular was an area that the 'mothers' felt compelled to intervene in, with this generation offering perspectives and advice that drew on traditional Christian ideals of chastity and monogamy.[89] Abrams found that the post-war generation by contrast were far less likely to pass judgement or offer religious instruction in the area of sexual morality when bringing up their own children in the 1960s and beyond. The parental behaviour of this generation of 'daughters' chimes with that of Bridget and many of my interviewees. Their approach to childrearing reflected the ascendency of psychological values around 'personal autonomy' and 'individual conscience' when it came to matters of sex, as well as a growing belief that religious instruction represented a 'neurotic' obstacle to these principles. The ethics of the body was no longer considered a legitimate subject for religious inculcation.

Abrams interprets the retreat of 'Christian moral systems around the body' as amounting to an emancipation of the self:

> The post-war generation – the daughters – were beginning to develop a form of independent selfhood so characteristic of the modern West, which has been described as predicated on … time and space for oneself, and a sense of ownership of one's body, all of which conflicted with traditional Christian discourse on ideal womanhood.[90]

As such, her story of generational change accorded with her husband Callum Brown's narrative of individual liberation, as English women took control of their own bodily process and fashioned a 'modern', autonomous form of selfhood. When speaking of their approach to parenting, my interviewees confirmed elements of this discourse, but also highlighted a different set of forces at work. I pressed the orthodox interviewees as to why they worked hard to bring up their children within a firmly Catholic moral code, but were happy to let them take a different path when it came to sex. The way Lydia set out her rationale was particularly revealing:

> Well sex is just a different question these days. It's a concrete, natural … thing isn't it, you can't impose airy ideas on that, and that's what religion really is, isn't it, ideas.[91]

The disjuncture between the body as an object and religious belief as a concept was one that underpinned many of the interviewees' decisions to remove the topic of sex from their religious parenting. Brown's and

Abrams' tale of shifting power dynamics, of a movement from dogmatic coercion to individual autonomy, can be viewed on a different axis when the materiality of sex and religion are foregrounded in historical analysis.

The interviewees' approach to parenting clearly held little regard for the indictments of the infantilism hypothesis and its disapproval of religious instruction for the young, but adhered to this principle when it came to sex. At one level, this approach to parenting was a consequence of the Church's teaching on contraception not being deemed 'infallible', as well as the stigma that still surrounded sexual subjects in many family homes. However, it also represented a deeper schism that had emerged in the relationship between sex and religion. Catholic women's experience of married life in the post-war years had encouraged them to think of the body as distinctly 'this-worldly': an object that was somehow removed from other aspects of Catholic morality. It was this idea, above and beyond any other, that underpinned their approach to religious parenting.

The discrepancy between the interviewees' upbringing and that of their children and grandchildren was perhaps the most palpable indication of the break between sex and religion that this book has described. Growing up in the years immediately surrounding the war, the interviewees' early sexual development was closely regulated by religious codes and ideals. By the time the interviewees were bringing up their own children, few looked to Catholicism as a source of guidance on parenting when it came to matters of sex. Informed by the ascendancy of the infantilism hypothesis, many considered religious instruction to be an obstruction to young people's 'natural' sexual development. Just as had been the case in the rejection of the confessional, when it came to matters of sexual instruction Catholic women increasingly distrusted transcendental answers to what were understood to be material, earthly questions. It has been suggested that this generational divide amounted to the death of a traditional form of coercive Christianity, as the advent of 'post-modernity' shattered the concrete certainties on which religious authority had been based before the 1960s.[92] As we have seen, personal Catholic religiosities certainly changed shape in the decades after the war. But this break was as much about shifting categories of materiality as power relations. The close interconnection between understandings of faith and the human body which had been so central to the upbringing of Catholic women in the years either side of the war had been largely dissolved by the last decades of the century. Catholicism continued to be lived, practised and believed throughout the post-war period; its relationship with sex would never be the same.

Conclusion

The main conclusion of this chapter is a modest, even self-effacing, one. Early life was *not* the determinative life-cycle stage in Catholic women's sexual and religious development that certain intellectual authorities have thought it to be.[93] Their contraceptive decisions, sexual behaviour and religious identities were not rooted in the experiences of childhood or adolescence, but formed and reformed at different stages throughout their lives. At the same time, it is clear that childhood provided an important context for the interviewees' marital experiences. It was the point at which understandings of gender, desire and sexuality started to interact with their religious beliefs and identities. Treating early life as a constitutive rather than determinative stage allows us to see how Catholic women 'lived forwards', as Kierkegaard would have it, even if academic investigators often insist on understanding their lives backwards. The causal connection between religious beliefs and infantilism, popularised by psychoanalytical writers in the middle of the twentieth century, continues to affect intellectual and personal understandings of Catholic devotion. It represented an unavoidable presence for the interviewees when composing their life stories and also in their day-to-day living.

The question of autonomy has continually been applied to young Catholic girls. The interviewees' early sexual development was often shaped by codes of passivity and piety, but this was not always experienced or interpreted retrospectively as a form of subjugation. Many of the interviewees saw this feminine identity as an active choice, one that was increasingly denied to them in their married lives. Their testimony emphasised the agency that they exercised in forming and living out these identities. Similarly, the limited sex education the interviewees received from formal authorities encouraged them to seek out new and highly individual sources of sexual knowledge. In some ways, Catholic girls going through adolescence after the 1960s were to have their sex lives directed by external authorities to a greater extent than those of the generation before them. The values, ideals and language that made up this direction changed significantly, though, as emergent Catholic educators worked to engage with a liberationist construction of sexual well-being. Power continued to operate in the construction of young, Catholic sexualities, but operated in a new and essentially different way. Changes in Catholic understandings of pre-marital sexuality, like the ascendency of this liberationist ideology more generally, did not simply amount to an emancipation from sexual repression, but signified a deeper shift in the way sex and religion were materially categorised. Sex became understood as a 'natural' process that revealed humanity's essential animalism; the imposition of abstract religious ideas on the early development of this instinct was increasingly viewed with suspicion. Religion on the other hand was confined to the realm of the transcendent, removed from the earthly matter of the body and its processes. These two developments cannot be understood in isolation from one another, as historians of religion and sexuality have tended to do. They were one and the same thing; it was the *relationship* between sex and religion that was irreversibly changed in the post-war years.

Notes

1 For example, see B. Osgerby, *Youth in Britain since 1945* (Oxford, 1998).
2 This reading of religiosity has been taken to an extreme by Richard Dawkins, who provocatively described bringing up a child in a religion as 'child-abuse' in an open letter to the then Secretary of State, Estelle Morris. R. Dawkins, 'Children Must Choose Their Own Beliefs', *Guardian*, 30 December 2001.
3 For example, R. Dawkins, *The God Delusion* (London, 2007), p. 206.
4 L. King, 'Review of *Psychological Subjects*', *Reviews in History* (2014), accessed at www.history.ac.uk/reviews/review/1641.
5 The term 'infantilism' is defined and unpacked in more detail in the final section of the chapter.
6 Teresa, interviewed 04/04/2012; June, interviewed 20/02/2012.
7 C. Brown, *The Death of Christian Britain: Understanding Secularisation, 1800–2000* (Cambridge, 2000), p. 87.
8 L. Sauerteig and R. Davidson (eds), *Shaping Sexual Knowledge: A Cultural History of Sex Education in Twentieth-Century Europe* (New York, 2009).
9 W. Reich, *The Sexual Revolution: Towards a Self-Governing Character Structure* (London, 1969).

10 Mary, interviewed 02/10/2013.
11 Leonie, interviewed 10/12/2013.
12 Sorcha, interviewed 09/02/2014.
13 Penny, interviewed 28/07/2013.
14 This view was set out by the sociologist Christine Farrell in the 1970s and has been subsequently corroborated by Fisher and Szreter among others. C. Farrell, *My Mother Said ... The Way Young People Learn about Sex and Birth Control* (London, 1978); K. Fisher and S. Szreter, *Sex before the Sexual Revolution* (Cambridge, 2010), p. 74.
15 Teresa, interviewed 04/04/2012.
16 Patricia, interviewed 03/05/2013.
17 Fisher and Szreter, *Sex before the Sexual Revolution*, pp. 113–162.
18 Mary, interviewed 02/10/2013.
19 Angela, interviewed 07/01/2013.
20 Ibid.
21 Ibid.
22 Ibid.
23 C. Paglia, *Sexual Personae: Art and Decadence from Nefertiti to Emily Dickinson* (New Haven, CT, 1990).
24 C. Taylor, *A Secular Age* (Cambridge, MA, 2007), p. 706.
25 'Facts of Life' is a subheading that is used by Fisher and Szreter, but the term is not discussed in any depth: Fisher and Szreter, *Sex before the Sexual Revolution*, p. 63.
26 Q. de la Bedoyere and I. de la Bedoyere, *Choices in Sex* (London, 1964).
27 M. Richards and B. J. Elliot, 'Sex and Marriage in the 1960s and 1970s', in D. Clark (ed.), *Marriage, Domestic Life and Social Change* (London, 1991), p. 37.
28 *Choices in Sex* included numerous references to popular culture, citing the character Pussy Galore, for example, from the recently released John Bond film *Goldfinger*, to illustrate a point about the varying levels of sexual responsiveness in different women.
29 Q. de la Bedoyere, interviewed 20/06/2011.
30 *Catholic Herald*, 10 August 1973, p. 2.
31 H. McLeod, *The Religious Crisis of the 1960s* (Oxford, 2007), pp. 6–30.
32 Wendy, interviewed 15/12/2013.
33 For a more detailed discussion of what sex education in British schools involved, see L. Hall, 'In Ignorance and in Knowledge: Reflections on the History of Sex Education in Britain', in Sauerteig and Davidson, *Shaping Sexual Knowledge*, pp. 19–36.
34 Wendy, interviewed 15/12/2013.
35 J. Dominian, *The Church and the Sexual Revolution* (London, 1967), p. 23.

36 Brown, *Death of Christian Britain*, p. 87.
37 Ibid., p. 200.
38 Michaela, interviewed 07/04/2013.
39 Teresa, interviewed 04/04/2012.
40 Sorcha, interviewed 09/01/2014.
41 Patricia, interviewed 03/05/2013.
42 Penny, interviewed 28/07/2013.
43 Teresa, interviewed 04/04/2012.
44 Lynn, interviewed 12/04/2012.
45 M. Eaton, 'What Became of the Children of Mary?', in M. Hornsby-Smith (ed.), *Catholics in England 1950–2000: Historical and Sociological Perspectives* (London, 1999), p. 220. Also see A. Harris, *Faith in the Family: A Lived Religious History of English Catholicism, 1945–1982* (Manchester, 2013), pp. 130–201.
46 Anne, interviewed 24/03/2012.
47 Rosie, interviewed 11/09/2012.
48 Michaela, interviewed 07/04/2013.
49 K. Fisher, *Birth Control, Sex and Marriage in Britain, 1918–1960* (Oxford, 2006), pp. 26–75.
50 Sorcha, interviewed 09/01/2014.
51 Ibid.
52 Ibid.
53 M. Foucault, *The History of Sexuality*, vol. 1 (London, 1976), pp. 17–35.
54 Sorcha, interviewed 09/01/2014.
55 Teresa, interviewed 04/04/2012.
56 Ibid.
57 Ibid.
58 Brown, *Death of Christian Britain*, p. 87.
59 Fisher, *Birth Control, Sex and Marriage*, pp. 238–244.
60 Patricia, interviewed 03/05/2013.
61 Doreen, interviewed 11/08/2012.
62 Brown, *Death of Christian Britain*, p. 87.
63 Michal Shapira, *The War Inside: Psychoanalysis, Total War, and the Making of the Democratic Self in Postwar Britain* (Cambridge, 2013), pp. 170–197; M. Thomson, *Lost Freedom: The Landscape of the Child at the British Post-War Settlement* (Oxford, 2013), pp. 1–20.
64 E. Erikson, *Childhood and Society* (New York, 1950).
65 E. Fromm, *Psychoanalysis and Religion* (New York, 1950).
66 Michaela, interviewed 07/04/2013.
67 Ibid.
68 Angela, interviewed 07/01/2014; Rosie, interviewed 11/09/2014.
69 Angela, interviewed 07/01/2014.

70 Ibid
71 Ibid.
72 Doreen, interviewed 11/08/2012.
73 Ibid.
74 Georgina, interviewed 22/11/2012.
75 Elizabeth, interviewed 15/07/2013.
76 C. Hitchens, *God Is Not Great* (New York, 2007), pp. 217–228.
77 Thomson, *Lost Freedom*.
78 M. Hornsby-Smith, *Roman Catholic Beliefs in England: Customary Catholicism and Transformations of Religious Authority* (Cambridge, 2009), p. 60.
79 Elizabeth, interviewed 15/07/2013.
80 Ibid.
81 Angela, interviewed 07/01/2014.
82 Anne, interviewed 24/03/2012.
83 Elizabeth, interviewed 15/07/2013.
84 Hall, 'In Ignorance and in Knowledge', p. 22.
85 Bridget, interviewed 16/04/2013.
86 Ibid.
87 Ibid.
88 Brown, *Death of Christian Britain*, p. 183.
89 L. Abrams, 'Mother and Daughters: Negotiating the Discourse on the "Good Woman" in 1950s and 1960s Britain', in N. Christie and M. Gauvreau (eds), *The Sixties and Beyond: Dechristianization in North America and Western Europe, 1945–2000* (Toronto, 2013), pp. 60–83.
90 Ibid., p. 69.
91 Lydia, interviewed 20/03/2013.
92 Brown, *Death of Christian Britain*, p. 244.
93 For example Erikson, *Childhood and Society*; Hitchens, *God Is Not Great*, pp. 217–228.

Conclusion

In concluding this book, I would like to invoke an admittedly lengthy musing from David Lodge, included in the afterword to the 1981 edition of his book *The British Museum is Falling Down* (first published in 1965). The size of the quotation is justified by its profoundly poetic capacity to crystallise both the theological quagmire faced by many post-war Catholics, and the overarching argument that has been made here:

> In *How Far Can You Go?* a number of the characters, gathered in a pub, ask themselves why they 'persevered for so many years with that frustrating, inconvenient, ineffective, anxiety-and-tension creating regime' [NFP], and come up with a variety of answers: it was conditioning, it was the repressive power of the clergy, it was guilt about sex, it was the fear of Hell. Let me put forward another reason here, which was perhaps not given its due in *How Far Can You Go?* Any intelligent, educated Catholic of that generation who had remained a practising Catholic through adolescence and early adulthood had made a kind of existential contract: in return for the reassurance and stability afforded by the Catholic metaphysical system, one accepted the moral imperatives that went with it, even if they were in practice sometimes inhumanly difficult and demanding. It was precisely the strength of the system that it was total, comprehensive and uncompromising, and it seemed to those brought up in the system that to question one part of it was to question all of it, and that to pick and choose among its moral imperatives, flouting those which were inconveniently difficult, was simply hypocritical.[1]

Lodge, both observer and participant of Catholic marriage in the post-war years, was not convinced by 'repressive' explanations of why Catholics persisted with NFP, or indeed their faith in general. Neither were Catholic women themselves. Catholic sexualities were certainly shaped by the governing structures of the clergy, doctrine and guilt, but not determined by them. Despite the wryly pessimistic tone, Lodge shows how Catholic men and women exerted a sense of agency in constructing their religious belief systems, even when these systems seemed to challenge their bodily instincts.

The 'existential contract' he proposes reminds us of Margaret's reflections on the condition of post-Vatican II Catholicism that this book opened with.[2] Margaret staunchly defended her form of 'pick and mix' Catholicism from accusations of hypocrisy, celebrating it as the liberation of her autonomous self. At the same time, she found herself confronting new questions and uncertainties as she approached the end of her life. For liberal Catholic women, the 'existential contract' was broken: in Margaret's words 'the cork was let out of the bottle and it could never be put back'. Lodge's contract and Margaret's corkless bottle analogies were both undergirded by a conceptual recategorisation of the religious and sexual. Lodge's use of the terms 'metaphysical system' to describe Catholic religiosity and 'in practice' to frame sexual behaviour reveals much about the nature of these categories. They were not simply about power relations, but also materiality.

There was, then, something of a rupture in the relationship between sex and Christianity in the post-war decades, as Brown maintained. However, the nature and timing of this rupture did not amount to the story of sixties 'cultural revolution' which he described.[3] Rather than being simply about an emancipation from the confines of 'traditional' religious subjugation, the memories of Catholic women suggest that a deeper, conceptual separation between the religious and the sexual opened up in the decades after the war. It was a separation which was rooted in the social and intellectual developments of the preceding decades, notably the emotional and existential fallout from the Second World War and the ascendency of psychoanalytical modes of understanding. It was also a separation that worked along fundamentally material lines, driven by everyday, embodied experiences rather than liberating discursive formulations. The way Brown and many other historians have defined Christian belief has coloured their narratives of religious decline. Indeed, this 'discursive' approach was itself a product of the very times and processes they were attempting to describe.[4] The relegation of the religious to the realm of numinous abstraction is perhaps one of the most underappreciated legacies of a 'sixties' ideology.

In a number of ways, the active categorisation of sexual and religious experiences provided something of a lifeline for many of the interviewees' Catholic faith. It was a mechanism that developed in the later stages of their marriages to deal with the conflicts, tensions and frustrations they encountered in early marriage. Just as Catholic women pursued creative, physical tactics to negotiate spiritual and sexual impulses while practising NFP, their decisions to reject Catholic teachings on contraceptive morality allowed them to balance and maintain both their marriages and religious identities. The rationale behind this break was as much metaphysical as it was emancipatory. Matters of faith were increasingly believed to be numinous, theological abstractions, while sex was defined as an intuitive, biological 'fact of life'. It was through this compartmentalisation that 'liberal' Catholic women made sense of their peculiarly post-war Catholic identity. In some ways, then, the rupture between sex and religion amounted to the very opposite of a 'death' of Christian Britain. It was the lived process and the discursive tool that ensured the continued survival, albeit in a different form, of Christian beliefs and identities in a hostile, late-modern setting.

At the same time, the separation of the religious and the sexual had damaging consequences for Catholic devotion at both a personal and an institutional level. Catholic beliefs on sexual morality, which had been so central to Catholic culture in the immediate post-war years, were increasingly dismissed as irrelevant and antiquated by the end of the century. This unprecedented cleaving between personal Catholic religiosities and the processes of the body represented a significant contraction in the ethical territory occupied by Catholic beliefs. The Catholic Church made its bed in the 1960s – of those who continue to lie in this bed, few chose to have sex in it.

Certain historians have been eager to dismiss any conclusions that faintly hint at the 'secularisation thesis', but changes in post-war Catholicism did amount to, perhaps not the death, but certainly the deterioration of a certain kind of religious devotion. The paradox at the heart of post-war, 'liberal' Catholicism, according to Lodge and Hornsby-Smith, was that the rejection of absolute doctrinal codes on sexual morality allowed many Catholics to uphold their faith, while at the same time opening up uncomfortable questions about the basis of religious authority per se.[5] Indeed, this can be seen to feed into a larger paradox that has been applied to the post-war condition, with existentialist philosophers and historians like Avner Offer arguing that expanded choices and liberties had the propensity to undermine rather than augment individual well-being.[6] However, Catholic women grappled with a tension that went beyond this epistemological matter of conscience and autonomy. The theological belief system through which they made sense of the world and their own position in it was increasingly seen to be at odds with the embodied rules and processes of human sexuality. Their faith was severed from the symbolic and corporeal arena of the body. It was this problematic, above and beyond any other, which defined the late-modern Catholic experience.

The conceptual separation between sex and religion has held significant implications for public discussions about and within the Catholic Church throughout the second half of the twentieth century. The Catholic birth-control debate of the 1960s existed in a climate in which this separation was at its zenith in academic discourses. It informed the Pope's eventual rejection of the 'liberal' case for change, but was equally present in the way this case was constructed by progressive members of the Papal Commission for Birth Control. Sexual experiences were evaluated in a way that neglected their potentially transcendent dimensions, while religious sensibilities were seen to bear little relation to the materiality of the body. These oversights coloured the notion of the 'personal' which ran throughout the Catholic birth-control debate. An alternative means of gauging the personal has been advanced here, one in which spoken word and memory have been afforded a privileged position. The intention has been to shine a light on the intimate and emotional aspects of both sexual and spiritual sensibilities which have hitherto been overlooked by Catholic commentators. Retrospection, often derided for its adjudged inaccuracy, can illuminate the meanings that are attached to these highly personal aspects of experience, thereby offering an alternative window into the way Catholic moralities are constructed and lived out.

What emerged from this approach to the 'personal' was the centrality of life-cycle stage to the sexual development of Catholic women. The interviewees described a clear break in their marriages, as the relationship between their religious beliefs and sexual behaviour was irreversibly disrupted in later marriage. The 'liberal' Catholic identity that was adopted at this stage was understood to represent a new form of selfhood, or more precisely the realisation of a more authentic form of self that had previously been obscured. A sense of individual agency was therefore central to the way these changes in personal identity were remembered and experienced. The interviewees worked to present themselves as authors of their own stories, conscious of the pervasive perception of religious individuals as passive victims of psychological indoctrination. Reading their stories backwards allows us to nullify the indictments of the 'infantilism hypothesis' and recognise how Catholic women's lives were made up of transitory moments of experience. The Catholic Church now needs to recognise these moments of experience. Pope Francis' tactfully engineered strategy of moving on from issues around sex and gender has ensured that Catholic women's voices continue to fall on deaf ears. We can only hope that the voices contained in this book find some reception within the walls of the Vatican.

The focus here has been on sex within marriage, notably birth control, but other aspects of the Church's approach to sexuality have been making the headlines in recent years. The revelations of clerical child abuse shook the world.[7] The Oscar-winning film *Spotlight* (2016) offered a chilling insight into the extent of the crimes that were committed, while also illustrating the central role of the media in uncovering and then constructing a popular knowledge of the abuse. Cultural and journalistic representations of the scandals have often been predicated on the notion that Catholicism's approach to human sexuality is not just circumstantially abusive to individual victims, but also socially destructive by its very nature.[8] This reading of the abuse has even gained some accreditation from leading Church representatives; the report *Time for Action*, written by a committee of leading clerics from across the Christian churches, concluded that the Church as an institution, but also Christianity as a religion, has encouraged a 'culture of shame' which 'feeds abuse'.[9] The theologian Paul Dokecki casts clerical child abuse in the context of what he calls the Church's longstanding violations of 'professional ethics', wielding an authority which is both 'uncaring' and at odds with 'life experience'.[10] Taking up Dokecki's critique, Mary Gail Frawley-O'Dea writes that:

> Pope Paul VI, John Paul II and now Benedict XVI refused to enter empathically into the life experiences of Catholics to discern the wisdom, ethical care, and grace woven through the approaches of these men and women to sexuality and love. Instead, the official Church, through these popes, spurned the life experiences of millions of men and women in order to preserve a moribund

theology of sexuality that the vast majority of their people respond to as uncaring and of little value in helping them to grow as individuals, partners, or Christians.[11]

The scandals have therefore been placed in a continuum with *Humanae Vitae*, positioned as the archetypal expression of the Church's antiquated, unmodern and pathologically unhealthy understanding of sex.

What has proved particularly unsettling is the growing body of evidence which shows how the Church actively covered up and supressed the allegations. It is apparent that the abuse, to some extent, was made possible by a culture of silence surrounding sexual matters that permeated the Church at all levels. *Humanae Vitae* has been viewed as a consequence of similar failures. It is commonly considered to be the product of the Church's closeted approach to sex, its refusal to engage with the cultural, technological and intellectual advances of modernity.[12] The evidence sourced here suggests that this reading of the encyclical's intellectual basis needs some revision. *Humanae Vitae* was not produced by a refusal to engage with the outside world or an ignorance of secular thinking. In some ways, the commission's case for change was undermined by its zealous adherence to contemporary secular understandings of sex. The Church's approach to sexuality was and is made up of different strands, rooted in varying and sometimes conflicting theological, doctrinal and institutional sources. Acknowledging these distinctions, rather than tarring them with the same explanatory brush, will allow for a more incisive and fruitful interrogation of the problems that are present within its pastoral structures.

Humanae Vitae was, however, the consequence of a deep-seated conceptual divide between sexual and religious domains of knowledge. The central hierarchy, as well as both liberal and conservative members of the lay community, defined sexuality as the earthly, biological counterpoint to the divinity of Catholic theology. The operation of this divide in the child abuse scandals, in terms of the mentalities of those committing the crimes, those who orchestrated their cover-up and those who reported on the phenomenon, is a subject which urgently demands historical attention. The perceived materiality of sexuality has been central to secular commentators' diagnoses of celibate repression; priests' inability to relate to the material, bodily experience of sex has been viewed as the root cause of their perversion. Equally, the 'transcendence' of the religious has been a disconcerting presence in the rationale and practical operation of the clerical hierarchy's cover-up of the scandals. As Marie Kennan has illustrated, the justification behind not submitting priests to legal authorities was often based on the idea that the clergy existed in a state above and beyond the earthly domain.[13]

Celibacy has been identified by many in the media as the cause of both the Church's position on contraceptive morality and of child sex abuse.[14] Indeed, leading clerical representatives within the Vatican have publicly affirmed this explanation of the relative preponderance of paedophiles within the clergy.[15] For a number of the interviewees, though, celibacy was part and parcel of a larger problem with the clergy and its position with regards to sex. As Marian eloquently articulated:

> The main thing is because they rejected the earthly experience, they grew up in theory. You don't live in theory, theoretically you don't live in theory, and practically you don't.[16]

The line that Marian drew between the theory and earthly experience characterised a distinctly late-modern way of thinking about Catholicism's relationship with sexuality. This *way of thinking* was not merely a discursive pattern limited to the realm of the cerebral, but a division that had momentous, sometimes destructive, consequences for the everyday lives of many Catholic individuals.

The break between sex and religion that has been described here was both specific to the Catholic experience and also reflective of broader trends in English society. As was stated in the Introduction, my intention has been to draw out commonalities in the conceptions of religion advanced by Brown, his 'liberated', secular subjects and those who continued to identify as Christian. There is now a need to take this further and explore how a material framework, demanded by the lens of Catholicism, related to the experiences of those who rejected their Christian identities. The Catholic experience was both peculiar to and also a composite part of mainstream, historical processes. The firm boundaries that Brown and McLeod draw around 'internal' and 'external' causes of Christian change, between 'religious' and 'secular' groupings are misleading.[17] Equally, attempts to entirely downplay the specificity of Catholic life run against the very particular experiences that were recalled by the interviewees. Recognising the 'same-but-different' nature of Catholicism in the post-war is a vital imperative for historians and theologians alike.

The development of app technologies which monitor fertility cycles has seen NFP, traditionally regarded as the 'Catholic method', became popularised amongst non-Catholic couples in the twenty-first century. The Swedish company Natural Cycles advertise their app as offering a 'digital contraceptive', a more accurate, simple means of measuring basal temperature than the graph- and thermometer-laden procedure which haunted Catholic women's early marriages. Targeted social media campaigns market the app as 'natural, hormone-free and non-invasive', a message which has resonated with the growing number of women unhappy with the side-effects of the pill.[18] NFP is beginning to shake off its association with both the 'Vatican' and 'roulette'. Natural Cycles is sold as a means of 'getting to know yourself' – the CMAC used this very phrase to encourage its clients to take up NFP in the 1960s and 1970s. This is an interesting reversal of the 'self-liberation' narrative which commonly accompanies assessments of the pill. Writing in the *Guardian* in 2018, Dawn Foster points out that the popularity of fertility apps can be explained by the fact that they are not mediated by the medical profession, a profession which 'too often dismisses and fails women, and has ignored the concerns of many women disenchanted with the side-effects of hormonal contraception'.[19] NFP advocates now claim to offer women a greater sense of autonomy – control over their own bodies without the intervention of chemical or medical agents. The shifting status of NFP epitomises the interplay between secular and Catholic ideas around sex and gender which took place in late-modern England. The way Catholic authorities respond to innovations such as this, and there seems to be little or no response to date, may be crucial to the Church's continued currency in questions of sexual morality in the future.

The extent to which Catholic communities in other British territories, notably Ireland and Scotland, underwent similar changes would make for a valuable avenue of further research. Moreover, extending the study beyond these boundaries to consider the Catholic experience in continental Europe and North America would mirror the larger geographical platforms with which advocates of a 'sexual revolution' thesis, such as Brown and Marwick, have engaged.[20] Nevertheless, it must be reiterated that the changes outlined here can claim to be to representative only of an English Catholic experience. Furthermore, it was a particular Catholic experience. Lodge's allusion to an 'existential contract', cloaked in the jargon of French philosophers and literary critics, was appended with the qualification 'Any intelligent, educated Catholic ...'. Quite who intelligent, educated Catholics were is left unclear, but, like Lodge's fictionalisations, this project has also paid more attention to certain demographic groups than others. The working-class and immigrant Catholic communities, generally concentrated in industrial towns in the north of England, have been slightly under-represented within the sample. Integrating a fuller analysis of these perspectives would be a welcome addition to the field, and one that could open up a discussion of how racial identities intersected with sexual practices and moralities.

It is, of course, possible to locate counter-discourses that ran against the pattern sketched here, notably those produced by actors and agencies working beyond mainstream organised Christianity. The expansion of New Religious Movements in the 1960s has been well documented by the likes of Arthur Marwick and Gerald Parsons.[21] Many of these groups propounded spiritualties which were closely tied to bodily, in many instances sexual, sensations. Equally, free-love initiatives were to espouse the ecstatic, 'out-of-body' potential of sexual pleasure. Crucially though, both these movements were explicitly forged *against* the dominant culture.[22] They served as conscious protests against not only mainstream Christian thought, but also the norms and mores of a wider climate. In this sense, subaltern attempts to emphasise the materiality of spirituality (notably different from religiosity, as Linda Woodhead and Paul Heelas have discussed) and the transcendence of sexuality indicated the extent of the ascendency of the recategorisation outlined here.[23] It was a trend which shaped individuals, institutions and ideas in ways which remained largely unrecognised throughout the post-war era.

'Who thinks of the Pope when surrendering to the pleasures of love?' asked Emmanuelle Arsan, the author of a collection of commercially successful erotic novels, in an open letter to Pope Paul VI following the publication of *Humanae Vitae*.[24] It turns out that many Catholics did. In bedrooms, below crucifixes, moments after nightly prayers, Catholic couples grappled with the Pope's dictate on how sexual love should and should not be expressed. Emmanuelle Arsan's novels, and the eponymous soft-core pornographic films which were based on them, typified a version of liberationist sexuality which was to become synonymous with the cultural shifts of a 'sexual revolution'. The Pope's condemnation of birth control established the Catholic Church as the counterpoint to this understanding of sex, and by extension, claimant to progressive modernity. Catholic women who married in the postwar years found themselves at the frontier of a contest between competing moral and existential ideologies, but this was not always the way they experienced everyday intimacy. Their life stories remind us to keep questioning our approach to history, to appreciate the messy and complex relationship between sex and religion, and to listen to women when they make sense of their worlds.

Notes

1. D. Lodge, *The British Museum Is Falling Down* (London, 2011, first pub. 1965), p. 168.
2. Margaret, interviewed 29/09/2013.
3. C. Brown, *The Death of Christian Britain: Understanding Secularisation, 1800–2000* (Cambridge, 2000), p. 115.
4. Ibid., pp. 9–17
5. Lodge concluded his book by saying 'On the whole, the disappearance of Hell was a great relief, though it brought new problems', D. Lodge, *How Far Can You Go?* (London, 1980), p. 113. M. Hornsby-Smith, *Roman Catholic Beliefs in England: Customary Catholicism and Transformations of Religious Authority* (Cambridge, 2009).
6. A. Offer, *The Challenge of Affluence: Self-Control and Wellbeing in the United States and Britain since 1950* (Oxford, 2006), p. 1.
7. The analysis presented here is concerned with marital sexuality and so does not attempt to provide an explanation of the crimes committed. The setting within which the incidents occurred, in terms of time and space, is, though, irrefutably linked to this study's subject matter.
8. While the ESRC Urgency Grant-funded project 'Historical Child Sex Abuse' represents the first major attempt to document the recent spate of revelations in the UK, historians continue to overlook the Catholic example or treat it as an undifferentiated part of a broader problem.
9. H. Freeman, 'Church Culture of Shame "Feeds Abuse"', *Guardian*, 4 December 2002, p. 9.
10. P. Dokecki, *The Clergy Sexual Abuse Crisis: Reform and Renewal in the Catholic Community* (Washington, DC, 2004), p. 145.
11. M. Frawley-O'Dea, *Perversion of Power: Sexual Abuse in the Catholic Church* (Nashville, TN, 2007), p. 84.

12 For example, Robert Nowell's assertion that the encyclical was 'no more than the private views of the Bishop of Rome' has found much consensus with both Catholic and secular commentators. R. Nowell, 'Sex and Marriage', in P. Harris (ed.), *On Human Life* (London, 1968), pp. 45–71. A recently published study suggests that four out of five Vatican priests are gay, and goes on to claim that this 'closeted culture' created the conditions which allowed child abuse to go unchecked. F. Martel, *In the Closet of the Vatican: Power, Homosexuality, Hypocrisy* (London, 2019).
13 M. Keenan, *Child Sexual Abuse and the Catholic Church: Gender, Power and Organizational Culture* (Oxford, 2012), pp. 24–53, 154–229.
14 For example, this indictment was at the heart of Diarmaid McCulloch's three-part BBC documentary *Sex and the Church*. He concluded the series with this comment on the Catholic Church's problems with both child abuse and women: 'The problem is an institutional one peculiar to the Western Church and its Catholic successor: compulsory celibacy for the clergy, which Protestants rejected 500 years ago. Celibacy puts the Catholic clergy on a spiritual pedestal. It's very easy to move from that to thinking you're exempt from the ordinary rules of everyday society.' *Sex and the Church*, part 3: 'Christianity v. the West', BBC, first aired 24 April 2015.
15 C. Wahlquist, 'Celibacy Rule May Have Contributed to Child Sex Abuse, Says Catholic Church', *Guardian*, 11 December 2014, accessed at: www.theguardian.com/world/2014/dec/12/celibacy-rule-may-have-contributed-to-childsex-abuse-says-catholic-church.
16 Marian, interviewed 26/09/2013.
17 C. Brown, *Religion and Society in Twentieth-Century Britain* (London, 2006), pp. 240–253; H. McLeod, *The Religious Crisis of the 1960s* (Oxford, 2007), p. 4.
18 The efficacy of Natural Cycles has been questioned following the revelation that thirty-seven women seeking an abortion in one hospital in Sweden were using the app. As Olivia Sudjic has shown, there has been a backlash against these apps in response to these stories: O. Sudjic, '"I Felt Colossally Naive": The Backlash against the Birth Control App', *Guardian*, 21 July 2018, accessed at www.theguardian.com/society/2018/jul/21/colossally-naive-backlash-birth-control-app. On 28 August 2018, the UK Advertising Standards Agency found that Natural Cycles' claim to offer a 'highly accurate contraceptive' was misleading. The relevant advertisements and marketing videos were ordered to be removed. N. Davies, 'Natural Cycles App: "Highly Accurate Contraceptive" Claim Misled Consumers', *Guardian*, 29 August 2018,

accessed at www.theguardian.com/technology/2018/aug/29/natural-cycles-app-highly-accurate-contraceptive-claim-misled-consumers.
19　D. Foster, 'Women Are Turning to Birth Control Smartphone Apps for a Reason', *Guardian*, 24 July 2018, accessed at www.theguardian.com/commentisfree/2018/jul/24/women-birth-control-smartphone-apps-contraception-technology.
20　C. Brown, *Religion and the Demographic Revolution: Women and Secularisation in Canada, Ireland, UK and USA since the 1960s* (Woodbridge, 2012); A. Marwick, *The Sixties: Cultural Revolution in Britain, France, Italy, and the United States, c. 1958–c. 1974* (Oxford, 1998), p. 36
21　Marwick, *The Sixties*, pp. 288–358; G. Parsons, *The Growth of Religious Diversity*, vol. 1 (New York, 2012), pp. 275–304.
22　The relationship between new religious movements and the counter culture in the 1960s is developing a growing historiography. For an introduction to this area, see McLeod, *The Religious Crisis*, pp. 141–160.
23　P. Heelas and L. Woodhead, *The Spiritual Revolution: Why Religion is Giving Way to Spirituality* (Oxford, 2005).
24　Referenced in T. P. Marquez, 'The Politics of Catholic Medicine: "The Pill" and *Humanae Vitae* in Portugal', in A. Harris (ed.), *The Schism of '68: Catholicism, Contraception and Humanae Vitae in Europe, 1945–1975* (Oxford, 2018), pp. 161–186.

Appendices

Appendix A: Project description used in advertisements

An oral history project is underway at the University of Sussex that explores the sexual and religious experiences of Catholic women in post-war England. Funded by the Arts and Humanities Research Council, the research provides Catholic individuals with an opportunity to speak about their memories of the period for the first time in historical analysis. It examines the way married Catholic women negotiated spiritual and sexual demands on a day-to-day basis – including topics such as contraceptive decisions, religious practice and family life. The project is currently looking for participants – complete anonymity is guaranteed for all interviewees and a questionnaire is submitted in advance. If you would like more information about the project, please email David Geiringer at dg202@sussex.ac.uk

Appendix B: Biographies of interviewees

1. Penny: born 1927, four children
2. Veronica: born 1927, six children (email correspondence)
3. Anne: born 1928, eight children
4. Elizabeth: born 1929, four children
5. Doreen: born 1930, two children
6. Margaret: born 1930, six children
7. Rosie: born 1931, three children
8. Angela: born 1931, four children
9. Marian: born 1932, four children
10. Mary: born 1934, three children
11. Lucy: born 1934, four children
12. June: born 1934, four children

13. Katherine: born 1934, eight children (two adopted)
14. Frank: born 1935, five children
15. Gregory: born 1935, four children
16. Lynn: born 1936, four children
17. Bridget: born 1938, four children.
18. Sarah: born 1938, five children.
19. Lydia: born 1939, three children
20. Georgina: born 1940, six children
21. Leonie: born 1945, two children
22. Sorcha: born 1946, one child
23. Teresa: born 1947, two children
24. Joan: born 1949, five children
25. Patricia: born 1951, three children
26. Wendy: born 1954, three children
27. Michaela: born 1956, two children

Select bibliography

Articles

Alexander, H., 'Reflections on Benjamin Button', *Philosophy and Literature*, 33 (2009), pp. 1–17.

Brewitt-Taylor, S., 'Christianity and the Invention of the Sexual Revolution in Britain, 1963–1967', *Historical Journal*, 60 (2017), pp. 519–546.

Brown, C., 'What was the Religious Crisis?', *Journal of Religious History*, 34 (2010), pp. 468–479.

—— 'Sex, Religion, and the Single Woman c.1950–75: The Importance of a "Short" Sexual Revolution to the English Religious Crisis of the Sixties', *Journal of Social History*, 22 (2011), pp. 189–215.

Chester, R., 'Shaping the Future: From Marriage Movement to Service Agency', *Marriage Guidance*, Autumn (1985), pp. 5–15.

Cocks, H., 'The History of Sexuality Meets Evolutionary Biology', *Contemporary British History*, 24 (2010), pp. 109–129.

Cook, H., 'Emotions, Bodies, Sexuality and Sex Education in Edwardian England', *Historical Journal*, 55 (2012), pp. 475–495.

Daly, G., 'Catholicism and Modernity', *Journal of the American Academy of Religion*, 53 (1985), pp. 773–796.

Finke, R., and Stark, R., 'Catholic Religious Vocations: Decline and Revival', *Review of Religious Research*, 42 (2000), pp. 125–145.

—— and Wittberg, P., 'Organizational Revival from Within: Explaining Revivalism and Reform in the Roman Catholic Church', *Journal for the Scientific Study of Religion*, 39 (2000), pp. 154–170.

Greeley, A., 'The Sexual Revolution in the Catholic Clergy', *Review of Religious Research*, 14 (1973), pp. 91–100.

—— 'Protestant and Catholic: Is the analogical Imagination Extinct'? *American Sociological Review*, 54 (1989), pp. 485–502.

Green, A., 'Individual and "Collective" Memory: Theoretical Presuppositions and the Contemporary Debates', *Oral History*, 32 (2004), pp. 35–44.

Halperin, D., 'Is There a History of Sexuality?', *History and Theory*, 23 (1989), pp. 257–274.

Hamilton, C., 'On Being a "Good" Interviewer: Empathy, Ethics and the Politics of Oral History', *Oral History*, 36 (2009), pp. 35–43.

Houlbrook, M., 'Sexing the History of Sexuality', *History Workshop Journal*, 60 (2005), pp. 216–222.

—— ' "A Pin to see the Peepshow": Culture, Fiction and Selfhood in Edith Thompson's Letters, 1921–1922', *Past and Present*, 207 (2010), pp. 215–249.

Irwin, R., ' "To Try and Find Out What is Being Done to Whom, by Whom and with What Results": The Creation of Psychosexual Counselling Policy in England, 1972–1979', *Twentieth Century British History*, 20:2 (2009), pp. 173–197.

Kane, P., ' "She Offered Herself Up": The Victim Soul and Victim Spirituality in Catholicism', *Church History*, 71 (2002), pp. 80–119.

Layman, L., 'Reticence in Oral History Interviews', *Oral History Review*, 36 (2009), pp. 207–230.

Lynch, M., 'Against Reflexivity as an Academic Virtue and Source of Privileged Knowledge', *Theory, Culture & Society*, 17 (2000), pp. 26–54.

Manning, C. J., 'Women in a Divided Church: Liberal and Conservative Catholic Women Negotiate Changing Gender Roles' *Sociology of Religion*, 58 (1997), pp. 375–390.

Nash, D., 'Reconnecting Religion with Social and Cultural History: Secularization's Failure as a Master Narrative', *Cultural and Social History*, 1 (2004), pp. 302–325.

Norris, C., 'The Papal Commission on Birth Control – Revisited', *Linacre Quarterly*, 80 (2013), pp. 8–16.

Pollen, A., 'Research Methodology in Mass Observation Past and Present: "Scientifically, About as Valuable as a Chimpanzee's Tea Party at the Zoo"?', *History Workshop Journal*, 75 (2013), pp. 213–235.

Portelli, A., 'A Dialogical Relationship. An Approach to Oral History', online article, accessed at www.swaraj.org/shikshantar/expressions_portelli.pdf.

Ramsay, L., 'The Ambiguities of Christian Sexual Discourse in Post-War Britain: The British Council of Churches and Its Early Moral Welfare Work', *Journal of Religious History*, 40:1 (2016), pp. 82–103.

Robinson, E,. Schofield, C., Sutcliffe Braithwaite, F., and Thomlinson. N., ' Telling Stories about Post-War Britain: Popular Individualism and the "Crisis" of the 1970s', *Twentieth Century British History*, 28:2 (2017), pp. 268–304.

Scheper-Hughes, J., 'A Materialist Theory of Religion: The Latin American Frame', *Method and Theory in the Study of Religion*, 24 (2012), pp. 430–444.

Seidman, S., 'Power of Desire and the Danger of Pleasure, Victorian Sexuality Reconsidered', *Journal of Social History*, 24 (1990), pp. 46–67.

Sitzia, L., 'A Shared Authority: An Impossible Goal?', *Oral History Review*, 30 (2003), pp. 87–101.

Summerfield, P., 'Culture and Composure: Creating Narratives of the Gendered Self in Oral History Interviews', *Cultural and Social History*, 1 (2004), pp. 65–93.

Thomson, A., 'Four Paradigm Transformations in Oral History', *Oral History Review*, 34 (2007), pp. 49–70.

Todd, S., 'Class, Experience and Britain's Twentieth Century', *Social History*, 39 (2014), pp. 489–508.

Wallace, R. A. 'Catholic Women and the Creation of a New Social Reality', *Gender and Society*, 2 (1988), pp. 24–38.

Williams, S., 'The Problem of Belief: The Place of Oral History in the Study of Popular Religion', *Oral History*, 24 (1996), pp. 27–34.

Woodhead, L., 'Gendering Secularization Theory', *Social Compass*, 55 (2008), pp. 187–199.

Books

Aquinas, T., *Summa Theologiae, Questions on God*, ed. B. Davies and B. Leftow (Cambridge, 2006).

Atkinson, R., *The Life Story Interview* (Thousand Oaks, CA, 1998).

Augustine, *City of God*, trans. R. W Dyson. (Cambridge, 1998).

Aune, K., Vincent, G., and Sharma, S. (eds), *Women and Religion in the West: Challenging Secularisation* (Abingdon, 2008).

Berger, P., *The Sacred Canopy: Elements of a Sociological Theory of Religion* (New York, 1967).

Blauvelt, A. (ed.), *Strangely Familiar: Design and Everyday Life* (London, 2003).

Bordo, S., *Unbearable Weight: Feminism, Western Culture and the Body* (Berkeley, CA, 2003).

Bourdieu, P., *The Weight of the World: Social Suffering in Contemporary Society* (Cambridge, 2006).

Brewitt-Taylor, S., *Christian Radicalism in the Church of England and the Invention of the British Sixties, 1957–1970* (Oxford, 2018).

Brooke, S., *Sexual Politics: Sexuality, Family Planning and the British Left from the 1880s to the Present Day* (Oxford, 2012).

Brown, C., *Religion and Society in Scotland since 1707* (Edinburgh, 1997).

—— *The Death of Christian Britain: Understanding Secularisation, 1800–2000* (Cambridge, 2000).

—— *Religion and Society in Twentieth-Century Britain* (London, 2006).

—— *Religion and the Demographic Revolution: Women and Secularisation in Canada, Ireland, UK and USA since the 1960s* (Woodbridge, 2012).
Brown, C., and Snape, M., *Secularisation in the Christian World* (London, 2010).
Bruce, S. (ed.), *Religion and Modernization: Sociologists and Historians Debate the Secularisation Thesis* (Oxford, 1992).
Bullivant, S., *Mass Exodus: Catholic Disaffiliation in Britain and America since Vatican II* (Oxford, 2019).
Carrette, J. (ed.), *Religion and Culture: Michel Foucault* (New York, 1999).
Castelli, E. A., and Rodman, R. C. (eds), *Women, Gender, Religion: A Reader* (New York, 2001).
Christie, N., and Gauvreau, M. (eds), *The Sixties and Beyond: Dechristianization in North America and Western Europe, 1945–2000* (Toronto, 2013).
Clack, B., *Sex and Death: A Reappraisal of Human Mortality* (Cambridge, 2002).
Clark, D. (ed.), *Marriage, Domestic Life and Social Change* (London, 1991).
Coleman, J. A. (ed.), *One Hundred Years of Catholic Social Thought: Celebration and Challenge* (New York, 1991).
Collins, M., *Modern Love* (Great Britain, 2003).
Cook, H., *The Long Sexual Revolution: English Women, Sex and Contraception 1800–1975* (Oxford, 2004).
Cook, M., *London and the Culture of Homosexuality 1885–1914* (Cambridge, 2003).
Cornwell, J., *The Black Box: A Secret History of Confession* (London, 2014).
Cozzens, D., *The Changing Face of the Priesthood: A Reflection on the Priest's Crisis of Soul* (Collegeville, MN, 2000).
Davie, G., *Religion in Britain since 1945: Believing without Belonging* (Oxford, 1994).
de Certeau, M., *The Practice of Everyday Life*, trans. Steven Rendell (Berkeley, CA, 1984).
de la Bedoyere, Q., *Autonomy and Obedience in the Catholic Church* (London, 2002).
Delap, L., and Morgan, S. (eds), *Men, Masculinities and Religious Change in Twentieth-Century Britain* (Basingstoke, 2013).
Dokecki, P., *The Clergy Sexual Abuse Crisis: Reform and Renewal in the Catholic Community* (Washington, DC, 2004).
Donnelly, M., *Sixties Britain* (London, 2004).
Durkheim, É. *The Elementary Forms of the Religious Life*, trans. Carol Cosman (Oxford, 2001).

Dyhouse, C., *Girl Trouble Panic and Progress in the History of Young Women* (London, 2013).
Eichenbaum, A., *The Cognitive Neuroscience of Memory* (Oxford, 2002).
Fisher, K., *Birth Control, Sex and Marriage in Britain, 1918–1960* (Oxford, 2006).
Fisher, K., and Szreter, S., *Sex before the Sexual Revolution* (Cambridge, 2010).
Fitzgerald, T., *The Ideology of Religious Studies* (New York, 2000).
Foucault, M., *The History of Sexuality*, vol. 1 (London, 1976).
Frawley-O'Dea, M., *Perversion of Power: Sexual Abuse in the Catholic Church* (Nashville, TN, 2007).
Frisch, M., *A Shared Authority: Essays on the Craft and Meaning of Oral and Public History* (Albany, NY, 1990).
Gluck, S. B., and Patai, D. (eds), *Women's Words: The Feminist Practice of Oral History* (London, 1991).
Green, J., *All Dressed Up: The Sixties and the Counterculture* (London, 2000).
Hacking, I., *Historical Ontology* (Cambridge, MA, 2004).
Hanson, E., *Decadence and Catholicism* (Cambridge, MA, 1997).
Harris, A., *Faith in the Family: A Lived Religious History of English Catholicism, 1945–1982* (Manchester, 2013).
Harris, A. (ed.), *The Schism of '68: Catholicism, Contraception and Humanae Vitae in Europe, 1945–1975* (Oxford, 2018).
Harris, A., and West, T. (eds), *Love and Romance in Britain, 1918–1970* (New York, 2015).
Harris, P. (ed.) *On Human Life* (London, 1968).
Hatch, J., and Wisniewski, R. (eds), *Life History and Narrative* (London, 1995).
Heelas, P., *Religion, Modernity and Postmodernity* (Oxford, 1998).
Heelas P., and Woodhead, L., *The Spiritual Revolution: Why Religion is Giving Way to Spirituality* (Oxford, 2005).
Hinton, J., *Nine Wartime Lives* (Oxford, 2012).
Hitchens, C., *God Is Not Great* (New York, 2007).
Hornsby-Smith, M., *Roman Catholics in England* (Cambridge, 1987).
—— *The Changing Parish: A Study of Parishes, Priests and Parishioners after Vatican II* (London, 1989).
—— *An Introduction to Catholic Social Thought* (Cambridge, 2006).
Hornsby-Smith, M. (ed.), *Catholics in England 1950–2000: Historical and Sociological Perspectives* (London, 1999).
Houlbrook, M., *Queer London: Perils and Pleasures in the Sexual Metropolis, 1918–1957* (Chicago, 2005).
Houlbrook, M., and Cocks, H. G. (eds), *Palgrave Advances in the Modern History of Sexuality* (London, 2006).

Irigaray, L., *An Ethics of Sexual Difference*, trans. C. Burke and G. C. Gill (Ithaca, NY, 1993).
Jantzen, G., *Becoming Divine: Towards a Feminist Philosophy of Religion* (Manchester, 1998).
Jeffreys, S., *Anticlimax: A Feminist Perspective on the Sexual Revolution* (London, 1990).
Jones, B., *The Working Class in Mid-Twentieth-Century England* (Manchester, 2012).
Jones, T. W., and Matthews-Jones, L. (eds), *Material Religion in Modern Britain: The Spirit of Things* (London, 2015).
Kaiser, R., *The Encyclical That Never Was* (London, 1989).
Keenan, M., *Child Sexual Abuse and the Catholic Church: Gender, Power and Organizational Culture* (Oxford, 2012).
Kelly, G., *The Battle for the American Church* (New York, 1981).
Kimmel, M. (ed.), *The Sexual Self: The Construction of Sexual Scripts* (Nashville, TN, 2007).
Koopman, C., *Genealogy as Critique: Foucault and the Problems of Modernity* (Bloomington, IN, 2013).
Kung, H., *The Catholic Church* (New York, 2001).
Langhamer, C., *Women's Leisure in England* (Manchester, 2000).
—— *The English in Love: The Intimate Story of an Emotional Revolution* (Oxford, 2013).
Laqueur, T., *Solitary Sex: A Cultural History of Masturbation* (New York, 2003).
Lewis, J., Clark, D., and Morgan, D. (eds), *Whom God Hath Joined Together: The Work of Marriage Guidance* (London, 1992).
Lodge, D., *The British Museum Is Falling Down* (London, 2011, first pub. 1965).
Lyotard J., *The Post-Modern Condition: A Report on Knowledge* (Minneapolis, MN, 1984).
McLaughlin, L., *The Pill, John Rock, and the Church* (Boston, 1982).
McLeod, H., *European Religion in the Age of the Great Cities* (London, 1995).
—— *Religion and Society in England 1850–1914* (Basingstoke, 1995).
McLeod, H. *Secularisation in Western Europe, 1848–1914* (London, 2000).
McLeod, H., *The Religious Crisis of the 1960s* (Oxford, 2007).
Marks, L., *Sexual Chemistry: A History of the Contraceptive Pill* (London, 2001).
Marshall, J., *Love One Another: Psychological Aspects of Natural Family Planning* (London, 1995).
—— *Fifty Years of Marriage Care* (London, 1996).
Martel, F., *In the Closet of the Vatican: Power, Homosexuality, Hypocrisy* (London, 2019).

Martin, D., *On Secularisation* (Aldershot, 2005).
Marwick, A., *The Sixties: Cultural Revolution in Britain, France, Italy, and the United States, c. 1958–c. 1974* (Oxford, 1998).
Morgan, S., and de Vries, J. (eds), *Women, Gender and Religious Cultures in Britain, 1800–1940* (Abingdon, 2010).
Nash, D., *Christian Ideals in British Culture: Stories of Belief in the Twentieth Century* (Oxford, 2013).
Offer, A., *The Challenge of Affluence: Self-Control and Wellbeing in the United States and Britain since 1950* (Oxford, 2006).
Osgerby, B., *Youth in Britain since 1945* (Oxford, 1998).
Paglia, C., *Sexual Personae: Art and Decadence from Nefertiti to Emily Dickinson* (New Haven, CT, 1990).
Parker, S., *Faith on the Home Front: Aspects of Church Life and Popular Religion in Birmingham 1939–1945* (Bern, 2005).
Parsons, G., *The Death of Christian Britain: Exploring a Thesis* (Milton Keynes, 2005).
—— *The Growth of Religious Diversity*, vol. 1 (New York, 2012).
Perks, R., and Thomson, A. (eds), *The Oral History Reader*, 2nd edn (London, 2006).
Plamper, J., *The History of Emotions: An Introduction* (Oxford, 2015).
Plummer, K., *Telling Sexual Stories: Power, Change and Social Worlds* (London, 1995).
Portelli, A., *The Death of Luigi Trastulli and Other Stories: Form and Meaning in Oral History* (New York, 1991).
Pyle, L. (ed.), *Pope and Pill* (London, 1968).
Ritchie, D. (ed.), *The Oxford Handbook of Oral History* (Oxford, 2012).
Rock, J., *The Time Has Come: A Catholic Doctor's Proposals to End the Battle over Birth Control* (New York, 1963).
Rose, N., *Governing the Soul: The Shaping of the Private Self* (New York, 1989).
Sauerteig, L., and Davidson, R., *Shaping Sexual Knowledge: A Cultural History of Sex Education in Twentieth-Century Europe* (New York, 2009).
Schofield, M., *The Sexual Behaviour of Young People* (London, 1965).
Smart, N., *The Science of Religion and the Sociology of Knowledge* (Princeton, NJ, 1973).
Stoller, S. (ed.), *Simone de Beauvoir's Philosophy of Age: Gender, Ethics, and Time* (Berlin, 2014).
Stourton, E., *Absolute Truth: The Struggle for Meaning in Today's Catholic Church* (London, 1999).
Strawser, M., *Both/And: Reading Kierkegaard: From Irony to Edification* (New York, 1997).
Summerfield, P., *Reconstructing Women's Wartime Lives: Discourse and Subjectivity in Oral Histories of the Second World War* (Manchester, 1998).

Taylor, C., *A Secular Age* (Cambridge, MA, 2007).
—— *The Culture of Confession from Augustine to Foucault* (New York, 2009).
Thane, P., and Bothelo, L., *Women and Ageing in British Society since 1500* (Oxford, 2001).
Thompson, P., *The Voice of the Past: Oral History* (Oxford, 2000).
Thomson, M., *Psychological Subjects: Identity, Health and Culture in Twentieth-Century Britain* (Oxford, 2006).
—— *Lost Freedom: The Landscape of the Child at the British Post-War Settlement* (Oxford, 2013).
Tosh, J., *The Pursuit of History* (Great Britain, 2006).
Toulanlan, S., and Fisher, K. (eds), *The Routledge History of Sex and the Body: 1500 to the Present* (Abingdon, 2013).
Vasquez, M., *More Than Belief: A Materialist Theory of Religion* (Oxford, 2010).
Weeks, J., *Sex, Politics and Society: The Regulations of Sexuality since 1800*, 4th edn (Oxford, 2014).
West, C., *Good News about Sex and Marriage: Answers to Your Honest Questions about Catholic Teaching* (New York, 2000).
Wolffe, J., *God and Greater Britain: Religion and National Life in Britain and Ireland 1843–1945* (London, 1994).
Wolffe, J. (ed.), *Religion in History: Conflict, Conversion and Coexistence* (Manchester, 2004).
Woodhead, L., and Catto, R. (eds), *Religion and Change in Modern Britain* (New York, 2012).
Woodhead, L., and Heelas, P., *Religion in Modern Times: An Interpretive Anthology* (Oxford, 2000).

Chapters in edited collections

Bourdillon, M., 'Anthropological Approaches to the Study of African Religion', in J. Platvoet, J. Cox and J. Olupona (eds), *The Study of Religions in Africa: Past, Present and Prospects* (Cambridge, 1996).
Elia, A., 'Vatican', in D. Leeming, K. Madden and S. Marlan (eds), *Encyclopaedia of Psychology and Religion: L–Z* (New York, 2009).
Hufford, D., 'The Scholarly Voice and the Personal Voice: Reflexivity in Belief Studies', in R. McCutcheon (ed.), *The Insider/Outsider Problem in the Study of Religion* (London, 1999).
Orsi, R., 'Everyday Religion and the Contemporary World: The Un-Modern, or What was Supposed to Have Disappeared but Did Not', in S. Schielke and L. Debevec (eds), *Ordinary Lives and Grand Schemes: An Anthropology of Everyday Religion* (Oxford, 2012).

Penelhum, T., 'Personal Identity', in *Encyclopedia of Philosophy*, vol. 6 (New York, 1972).

Segal, R., 'Contributions from the Social Sciences', in P. Clayton and Z. Simpson (eds), *The Oxford Handbook of Religion and Science* (Oxford, 2006).

Theses

Robinson, L., 'Gay Men and the Revolutionary Left since 1957', PhD thesis (University of Sussex, 2003).

Woolfson, S., 'The Experience of Lithuanian Jews', PhD thesis (University of Sussex, 2013).

Index

abstinence 124–143
abortion 28, 32, 36, 43 n.8, 196 n.18
abuse 132–133
  see also violence
academic gaze 40, 73
adolescence 149
adultery 74–75, 95, 108
affluence 3, 72–73
afterlife *see* heaven; hell
agency 4–5, 20, 30–33, 79, 171, 189
aggiornamento 8
agnosticism 34
anal sex 139
Anglicanism 10, 75
  see also Protestantism
animal instinct 76, 156–157
annulment 74–75
Arsan, E. 1, 194
authenticity 35, 70, 172–173, 189
authority 16, 57–60
  clerical authority 97–101
  papal authority 13–14, 130

basal temperature method 37, 93, 127–128, 193
  see also natural family planning
Beatles, The 168
bed 91
bedroom 67, 91–92
Berger, P. 12, 16, 85
birth control
  condoms 10
  debate 32–33, 42, 59–60, 189
  decisions 6, 12, 66–69, 76, 82–97

pill (contraceptive)
  experience 2, 125, 129
  introduction of 2, 7, 82–83
  morality 81
  see also natural family planning
black Catholic experiences 27
Broome, V. 1
Brown, C. 3, 13–15, 27, 60, 70, 85, 94, 151, 163, 170, 180, 187
Bolton 27, 132
Bullivant, S. 9–10
Burns, T. 48

Cambell, A. 33
Casti Connubii 10
Catechism of the Catholic Church 31
Catholic Church, the 3, 46
Catholic Herald 46 n.38
Catholic Marriage Advisory Council 37, 109–124
Catholic population 6
Catholic Priests Association 136, 158
Catholic school 155
Catholic Truth Society 92
causation 97
celibacy 100, 192
chastity *see* pious femininity; virginity
child abuse 40–41, 190–191
childhood 149, 173
Children of Mary 166
Choices in Sex, (1964) 136, *158–159*
church hall 8
class 28, 72, 86, 132

clitoris 118
coitus interruptus *see under* withdrawal
cold war 12
confession 79, 86, 98–100, 141–143
Congregation for the Doctrine of Faith 57
conjugal love 132
contraception *see* birth control
conversion 75
courting 164–170
crucifix 93
cunnilingus 138

Darwinism 157
daughters 177–179
Dawkins, R. 174
Davis, C (Rev) 49
De Certeau, M. 133–134
De La Bedoyere, Q. and I. 13–14, 115, 117, 158–160
De Locht, P. 46
De Riedmatten, H. 47, 49, 57–58
discursive Christianity 3, 13–14
doctors 12, 60, 87, 108–109, 113, 127
Dominian, J. 87–88, 135, 162
Durkheim, E. 13, 85

Economist, The 49
ecumenism 8
emotions 129–132, 151
  see also love
empiricism 34, 48–52, 59, 119–125, 157
encyclicals *see Casti Connubii; Humanae Vitae*
Erikson, E. 171
Europe 193
evenings 91–95
everyday life 133–134
evolutionary psychology 157
experience 3–4, 6, 15, 18, 31–33, 48, 69, 85, 90–91, 100–101, 192

facts of life 157
family life 8, 79–80, 94–95, 110, 143
female sexuality 8, 49–56, 117–121
  sexual desire 52, 134–136, 163–166
  sexual pleasure 52–56, 114–115, 138
  see also orgasm
fellatio *see under* oral sex
feminism 30–31, 72
First World War 119
Fitzgerald, F.S. 21
Ford, J. 58
foreplay 118
Foster, D. 193
Foucault, M. 16–17, 21, 34, 55, 70, 77, 89–90, 112, 123, 169
Freudian theory *see* psychoanalysis
friends 150–169
Fromm, E. 171

Gagnon, J. and Simon, W. 59, 71
gender 3, 27, 35–39, 55, 98, 121–123, 137, 163–171
genealogy 21
generational change 175–178
ghetto 9
grandchildren 80, 175
Grisez, G. 58

Häring, B. 46, 57
Harris, A. 9–10, 56, 79, 123
heaven 14, 140
Heenan, J. (Cardinal) 50
hell 140, 166–167
Hitchens, C. 174–175
Holy Spirit 58
holy water 93
home 26, 95–96, 153, 168
homosexuality 89
  see also lesbianism
Humanae Vitae
  basis of 46, 48, 56–60, 191–192

content of 76, 101
responses to 1, 8, 194
humour 116, 139–140, 158
husbands 27, 42, 125, 127, 129, 132, 137, 142, 131–133

ignorance 39, 108–109, 118, 120, 150–155, 167
clerical ignorance 100
immanence 16, 35
impotence 126–127
indoctrination 1
infallibility, papal 14, 36, 130, 180
infantilism 4, 20, 150, 171–181
innocence 150–151, 155, 169–170
insider/outsider debate 36–37
interviewees sample 11, 23 n.13, 26–33
Irish Catholics 23 n.23, 27, 193

Jesuits 150

Kaiser, R.B. 62 n.2
Kierkegaard, S. 21, 173, 181
Kinsey, A. 50

laity 14, 48, 101, 112
Lambeth Conference 10
Laqueur, T. 76
Latin 58
leisure 93
lesbianism 22
'liberal' Catholicism 2, 6, 10–11, 28–30, 37, 67–68, 78, 176, 187
life cycle 19–20, 66, 189
Life of Pi, (2001) 34, 44 n.25
lions 156–157
Liverpool 27, 132
Lodge, D. 11–12, 84, 140–141, 186–187
love 114, 122–123, 132
see also emotions
lubrication 127, 122–123

make-up 93
Manchester 27
marriage 19–20, 131–132
sanctity of marriage 164
marriage guidance *see* Catholic Marriage Advisory Council
Marshall, J. 18, 37–38, 124–125
Martel, Y. 34, 44 n.25
marxism 70
Mary Mother of God 166
masculinity 27, 42, 126–127, 142
Mass 8, 72, 100, 165
missing 72, 154, 175–177
Latin 8
mass media 77
Mass Observation 43 n.5, 85, 86
Masters, W. and Johnson, V. 49–50, 121–122
masturbation 4, 137–138, 149
mutual masturbation 135–136
materiality
material religion 4, 15–16, 69, 91–92, 96–97
recategorisation of 5–6, 16–18, 48, 56–61, 81–82, 142–144, 180–182, 194
memory 20–22, 26–27, 30–33, 151, 189
menopause 66
menstruation 108
methodological agnosticism 33–34
migration 6, 27–28, 136, 194
motherhood 66–68, 108–110
interviewees' mothers 77, 80–81, 153

Natural Cycles 193
natural family planning
app technologies 193
endorsement 11
experiences 2, 11–13, 86, 97–98, 108–112, 124–143, 193
Papal Commission analysis 37, 51–56, 162

nature 49, 152, 157
New Religious Movements 194
New Statesman 1
Non-Catholic friends 150
North of England 132–133
Northern Ireland 23 n.13
Nowell, R. 56

obedience 19, 117
O'Leary, M. 116
oral history
    methodology 4–5, 30–33
        interviewer–interviewee
            relationship 38–39
        value of 96, 32
    methods 15, 19
        interviewee recruitment 27–30
        sample composition 26–27
oral sex 138–139
ordination of women 11, 55
orgasm 2, 77, 83–84, 86, 114–115, 117–121, 126, 138, 158
    see also female sexuality
'orthodox' Catholicism 6, 10–11, 28–30, 66–67, 71–72, 176
Ottaviani, A. (Cardinal) 57
overpopulation 46
ovulation 11, 61, 134, 135

paedophilia 40–41, 192
Paglia, C. 157
Papal Commission on Birth Control 189
    establishment of 7, 46–48
    Majority Report 7, 49
    Minority Report 57–58
paradox of choice 3, 73
parenthood 175–181
parish priest 98–100
Paul, L. 50–51
periods 153
permissiveness 61
personal, the 33–41, 61, 189
Peyton, P. (Fr.) 79

pill (contraceptive) *see* birth control
pious femininity 151, 163–164
Pope Benedict XVI 190
Pope Francis 32, 190
Pope John XXIII 7, 8, 37, 42
Pope John Paul II 192
Pope Paul VI 52, 56–60
    see also Humanae Vitae
Pope Pius XI 10
pornography 1, 194
post-modernism 15, 31, 180
post-secular 22 n.10, 32
prayer 78–82, 86–93, 141–143
    Glory be to the Father 80
    Hail Mary 80
    Our Father 80
    Prayer Before Making Love 92
premature ejaculation 126
pre-conciliar Catholicism 9, 72
promiscuity 76
Protestantism 7, 23 n.13, 60, 75
    see also Anglicanism
psychoanalysis 20, 53–56, 59, 71, 117–118, 150, 171–173, 187

race 27
radio 2, 117
reflexivity *see* personal, the
Reich, W. 152
rhythm *see* natural family planning
Rock, J. 60–61
romance *see* love
Rome 46, 56
rosary 79–80
Rosary Crusade 79
Rose, N. 71
rural 156
Ryan, J. 110

safe period 124–143
    tactics for dealing with the safe period 133–143
    see also natural family planning
school 92, 153–155, 161

science 48–56, 59–61, 162, 114–124
Scottish Catholics 23 n.13, 193
Second Vatican Council 2, 8, 58, 72, 80, 187
Second World War 66, 171, 178, 187
secularisation theory 5, 13–16, 168
selfhood 2, 53–56, 67, 71, 75–77, 80, 89–90, 189–190
self-abuse *see under* masturbation
seventies 19, 55, 59, 66, 68, 74, 92, 99, 103 n.8
sex manuals 109, 158–159, 166
sexology 5, 119
sexual awakenings 41, 74–75, 78, 95, 168
sexual education 151–162
sexual liberation 5, 67–71, 176
sexual revolution 2, 3, 7, 9, 49, 82–83, 194
sexual science 119–121
sin 53, 76, 98, 140–142, 154, 166–167
single women 50
sixties 1, 3, 9–10, 61, 178, 187
Smart, N. 33
Spotlight (film) 190
sociology 50–56
sodomy *see* anal sex
spatial theory 96
sperm 108
spontaneity 127
stallion 156
St. Francis Xavier 150

Stopes, M. 119
Sundays 94

Tablet, The 48, 53
Taylor, C. 16, 35, 78
teddy bears 139–140
television 100
telling case 85–86
theology 37, 46–47, 56, 87–89, 135, 150, 191
Time for Action 190
Time magazine 53
transcendence 1, 6, 16, 35, 48, 58, 59, 99, 112, 114, 180, 182, 189, 191, 194

United Nations 46
United States of America 9, 193
university 168

Vaseline 93, 127
Vatican (clerical hierarchy) 100–101
Vatican II *see* Second Vatican Council
violence 132–133, 156–157
virginity 71, 108, 164, 166

Walsingham conference 79
withdrawal 135
work 66, 72, 92
World War Two *see* Second World War

youth 149

EU authorised representative for GPSR:
Easy Access System Europe, Mustamäe tee 50,
10621 Tallinn, Estonia
gpsr.requests@easproject.com

www.ingramcontent.com/pod-product-compliance
Lightning Source LLC
Chambersburg PA
CBHW070238240426
43673CB00044B/1837